Liberty
After
Freedom

Celebrating
30 Years of Publishing
in India

'What makes Alva's book special is its attempt to answer the question that has puzzled both legal experts and students of law, as to why the drafters of the Constitution gave up the "due process" guarantee in the context of exceptions to be made to the right to personal liberty, and their decision to opt for the much more supine phrase, "except according to procedure established by law".'

—*The Week*

'The book demonstrates how a simply written sentence in intelligible English becomes a site of ideological contestation and a strong framework of rights in India. The book is also about the beauty of the argumentative Indian mind and a peek into the thinking of our founding fathers. It must be read by anyone interested in the making of the idea of India.'

—*Hindustan Times*

'Alva has collated diverse materials, in what must have been an arduous task, and presented views on both sides. Alva's well-put-together book gives us the genesis of Article 21, which needs to be known by judge, lawyer, law-maker and layperson alike, in order to appreciate not only the past, but the present as well.'

—*Business Standard*

'Rohan J. Alva's *Liberty After Freedom* enquires into the fascinating history of one such instance of changed meaning: the fate of "due process" in Article 21 of the Constitution. Alva's presentation of the proceedings of the Assembly allows us a rare glimpse into the full arc of a single provision's evolution. Alva's investigation reveals the limits of speculating on the motivations of the drafters and the understanding of the members of the Assembly regarding the implications of the drafting choices they voted on.'

—*The Telegraph*

'Rohan J. Alva's debut work is an eye-opener regarding the migration of the present Article 21 from the "due process of law" to the "procedure established by law." *Liberty After Freedom* is an important addition to the existing academic writing on Indian Constitutional history. To lawyers, law students and legal academics, the familiar phraseology of the right to life and personal liberty clause is almost taken for granted, finding mention in so many judgments of the constitutional courts. Alva has brought to bear an impressive grasp of legal history to shine light, however, on the arduous journey that Article 21 undertook to reach its present form. Through meticulous research, Alva shows how fragile the Article was at its inception, and how important it is for citizens to continue to ensure that this most important of rights remains protected, so that it, too, may in turn protect us in the future as it has done in all the years gone past.'

—**K.K. Venugopal, Attorney General for India**

'*Liberty After Freedom* is an ambitious and fascinating account of how India's post-World War II Constitution, consciously drafted to resist American-style judicial hostility towards Progressive-era economic regulation, was nonetheless later interpreted to protect substantive liberty interests, such as privacy. Alva sheds interesting historical and comparative light on the well-nigh irresolvable conflict between a society's commitment to protecting the fundamental rights of individuals and constraining the power of unrepresentative and politically less-accountable judges.'

—**Michael Klarman, The Charles Warren Professor,**
Harvard Law School

'The extraordinary story of due process in India must be told, and there is no one better to tell it than Rohan J. Alva. This monumental book is simultaneously a rich legal history excavated from the annals of India's Constituent Assembly, a careful doctrinal analysis of the domestic law of due process, a global escapade through the great constitutional democracies of the world and a manifesto for an evermore just reading of the Indian Constitution. *Liberty After Freedom* places Alva in the pantheon of the most thoughtful contemporary scholars of India's democratic constitution.'

—**Richard Albert, Professor of World Constitutions and Director of Constitutional Studies, The University of Texas at Austin**

Liberty
After
Freedom

A History of Article 21, Due Process
and the Constitution of India

ROHAN J. ALVA

HarperCollins *Publishers* India

First published in hardback in India by HarperCollins *Publishers* 2022
4th Floor, Tower A, Building No. 10, Phase II, DLF Cyber City,
Gurugram, Haryana – 122002
www.harpercollins.co.in

This edition published by HarperCollins *Publishers* 2023

2 4 6 8 10 9 7 5 3 1

P-ISBN: 978-93-5699-027-2
E-ISBN: 978-93-5489-313-1

Typeset in 11/14 Minion Pro at
Manipal Technologies Limited, Manipal

Printed and bound at
Thomson Press (India) Ltd

For
Nina, Zarina, and Cyrus

Contents

Prologue: Life, Liberty and Due Process: The Future's Past   xi

1   Due Process at Its Zenith   1

2   Due Process: The Middle-Path Solution of BN Rau   49

3   Slings and Arrows: From 'Due Process' to 'Procedure Established by Law'   94

4   The Ignominious Retreat: Due Process on the Floor of the Constituent Assembly   135

5   Due Process: Abandonment and Atonement   187

6   The Winter of (Dis)Content   207

7   The Dissonant Constitution   226

8   Article 21 and the Chimera of Original Intent   244

Epilogue: Life, Liberty and Due Process: The Pasts' Future   265
Acknowledgements   279
Index   283

Article 21

No person shall be deprived of his life or personal liberty except according to procedure established by law.

Prologue

Life, Liberty and Due Process: The Future's Past

———◆———

SOARING HIGH INTO THE NEW DELHI SKYLINE IS THE GRAND DOME OF the Supreme Court of India, which in popular culture has come to be recognized as the defining image of the highest court of the land. Beneath it lies Court Room No. 1, an expansive and tastefully decorated court room which by tradition is occupied by the Chief Justice of India.

On a warm summer day on 19 July 2017, nine justices led by the Chief Justice of India assembled in Court Room No. 1 to hear a case which would forever reshape the landscape of fundamental rights in India. The question the justices were invited to answer was whether the Constitution of India guaranteed to the people a fundamental right to privacy.

For the Constitution Bench, by no means did this case present any easy answers or self-evident truths.[1] After a marathon hearing which lasted for nearly two weeks, on 24 August 2017, the Supreme Court spoke.[2] The decision spans over 600 pages, since six of the nine justices wrote their judgments,[3] but all the justices were united in declaring that the Constitution did in fact guarantee to the people a fundamental right to privacy. For the Supreme Court, this right was firmly rooted in the fundamental right to life and personal liberty in addition to being guaranteed by the other rights contained in the Constitution. This was despite the fact that the right to privacy was not expressly mentioned in the text of the Constitution.[4]

This decision broke new ground in constitutionalism and served as a high-water mark in the wholesome realization of fundamental rights. It rested on the idea that Article 21 recognizes due process, which allows for individuals to exercise a range of rights to protect their life and liberty. In the process of achieving that constitutional vision, the Supreme Court has over the last fifty years read into Article 21 such rights which are necessary for living a decent life even though they might not be present as categorical rights in the Constitution.[5]

It is well known that within the language of Article 21, the Supreme Court has found a home for over thirty fundamental rights, applying to various sections of the population—from those who live behind prison walls to those who toil to earn a living in the most trying circumstances.[6] After all, the Indian Constitution says nothing about the fundamental right to privacy, but because these rights are considered absolutely essential for individuals to realize their full worth, they have been read into Article 21.

With the Supreme Court deciding that the fundamental right to life and personal liberty guarantees to all persons a right to privacy, Article 21 of the Constitution was catapulted into public consciousness as one of the most important fundamental rights which the Indian Constitution guarantees.[7]

The fact that the recognition of the fundamental right to privacy was of prime importance and would have an enormous impact on the future of constitutional rights in India was something that the Supreme Court had acknowledged.[8] For too long the fundamental right to privacy had eluded Indians and its emphatic recognition, at long last, by the Supreme Court was widely celebrated in the public sphere,[9] and welcomed internationally as well.[10]

Nearly a year after announcing that the Indian Constitution protected privacy rights, the Supreme Court turned its attention to another equally important and pressing issue. In July 2018, a Constitution Bench of five justices, led by the Chief Justice of India, decided to comprehensively resolve whether the Indian Constitution recognized the rights of those in same-sex relations.[11] Here the Supreme Court was faced with a law of colonial vintage used to criminalize homosexuality: Section 377 of the Indian Penal Code (IPC).[12]

The resolution of this question posed some difficulties, given that not too long ago, the Supreme Court had ruled that Section 377 was perfectly constitutional.[13] But that changed on 6 September 2018, when the Supreme Court announced its verdict and emphatically declared that Section 377 was unconstitutional and could not be used as a weapon to criminalize people on the basis of their sexual orientation.[14]

Invoking the high value of the fundamental right to life and personal liberty, dignity, human rights as well as the newly recognized fundamental right to privacy, the Supreme Court ruled that it is the function of the Constitution to protect and preserve the zone of intimate relations which individuals seek to enter with another. What animated the decision was the central idea that all persons, regardless of their gender and sexual orientation, are equal members of society and entitled to the same set of rights. No law could permit the relegation of persons to the margins based on their sexual identity. In declaring so, the Supreme Court overruled its past precedent, which had validated Section 377, and because of Article 21 and due process, it was able to probe more rigorously and declare the constitutional invalidity of laws such as Section 377, which grated against all notions of constitutional morality. Article 21 had prevailed yet again. The decision to decriminalize homosexuality was path-breaking and welcomed with much public joy and jubilation.[15]

To say today that Article 21 is one of the most precious fundamental rights and that due process rights are guaranteed to the people of India would be to state a truism.[16] In fact, the overarching and far-reaching importance of Article 21 was recognized by the Supreme Court when in 2018, it termed Article 21 as the 'Ark of the Covenant so far as the Fundamental Rights Chapter of the Constitution is concerned.'[17]

In a Constitution which prides itself as being one of the longest in the world, Article 21 is one of its shortest articles. Nonetheless, what it lacks in length, it has more than made up for it in terms of constitutional impact. Given that due process is now a central feature in any discourse on rights in India, it is critical to take stock of its genesis and to remind ourselves of how fractured and divisive the origins of Article 21 truly were. Despite being an extraordinarily powerful right today, it was not always meant to be this way and its pithy wording betrays its fraught history.

The Importance of Due Process

The Constitution of India came to life on 26 January 1950. The nation's founding document was multi-layered and minutely detailed, for it had to provide free India a new form of government, apportion powers between the Centre and the states and provide details for the working of matters which a country as varied and as large as India needed.

The supreme responsibility of giving India her Constitution was vested in the Constituent Assembly, which began its deliberations in December 1946. When the constitution making process was in its formative stage, the Assembly had decided that the new Constitution must dedicate itself to enumerating a charter of fundamental rights for free India. This vision translated itself into Part III of the Constitution which contains numerous fundamental rights, creating for individuals a zone of freedom, free from governmental intrusion. In Part III, the fundamental right to life and personal liberty would be enumerated in Article 21.

The due process guarantee essentially secures for the people an entitlement to a range of rights which ideally ought not to be taken away by law. And if at all there is a compelling reason for doing so, then the restriction must be the most minimal.[18] During the Constituent Assembly's deliberations, many members believed that the nation's future constitution must incorporate a fundamental right which guarantees the preservation of life, liberty and property and shields it from forms of deprivation which are inconsistent with the principles of due process. There were several reasons which animated this demand.

For some, the due process guarantee, which found mention in the American Constitution, was worthy of emulation since it was necessary to ward off governmental overreach which invaded a person's freedom without justification and in the most disproportionate manner.[19] For others, the due process guarantee was a necessary fundamental right since it had been accepted the world over, albeit in varying forms. Many also viewed the due process guarantee as representing a new age of judicial review in which state action and particularly the law-making power of the state would not go unquestioned, and that in free India, through the medium of the due process guarantee, any person could interrogate the correctness of state action. To hold the government accountable was a major reason which animated the demand for a due process guarantee in the Indian Constitution.

Nevertheless, regardless of the ideology which motivated the incorporation of the due process guarantee, what offered itself as a common ground was the extraordinary trauma inflicted by British rule on India. That had been a regime which distinguished itself by its gruesome efforts in attempting to crush the Indian nationalist movement, and those fighting for India's freedom.[20] Indeed, the memory of the wanton manner in which the rule of law was disregarded and discarded by the colonial powers haunts our collective consciousness even today.[21]

In the Constituent Assembly, members offered first-hand accounts of the brutality they had faced and deemed it absolutely essential that the Constitution see to it that such horrors would never be repeated in India. For this important reason, it was considered necessary if not paramount for the new Constitution to enumerate a justiciable due process guarantee which would respect the inviolable rule that those who come into contact with the justice system, particularly the criminal justice system, are not denuded of their rights. Rights such as having a counsel of choice, being informed of the charge being levelled, the right to examine witnesses and the right to be heard before judgment was passed were the sort of basic guarantees which the Constitution ought to protect. The need for an enforceable due process guarantee as a fundamental right was thus born out of historical necessity.

The Twists and Turns of Due Process: History Undone through a Footnote

This is a book about the history of Article 21. Between 1946 and 1950, the Constituent Assembly struggled with giving shape to due process in the Indian Constitution. By setting out and exploring the events in the life of Article 21, this book provides some answers to that one fundamental question: how exactly did the Constituent Assembly come to disavow making any reference to 'due process' in the Constitution? Without it, Article 21 travelled to the other end of the spectrum: rather than operating as a bulwark against the state, it opened the gates for life and personal liberty to suffer all forms of deprivation so long as the method of deprivation enjoyed legal backing.

The phrase 'except according to procedure established by law', which the Constituent Assembly ultimately chose for Article 21 over 'due process', meant that no matter how unconscionable the procedure and how odious the ends it hoped to attain, the fact that a law had been enacted conferred complete immunity on the state. Questions of whether the law was necessary, proportional or justified were rendered irrelevant. Indeed, at the time at which the Constitution was founded, Article 21 was widely considered even unworthy of being labelled a fundamental right.

The story of how Article 21 came to be approved by the Constituent Assembly for inclusion in the Constitution is deeply layered and it is this story which this book explores.

In the summer of 1947, the Constituent Assembly voted overwhelmingly to accept the due process guarantee as a fundamental right. The vote on due process marked one of the greatest triumphs for the cause of fundamental rights.

Shortly thereafter, in October 1947 the due process guarantee was retained but its scope of operation was attenuated in the Draft Constitution put together by the Constitutional Advisor, Sir BN Rau.

Then between 1947 and 1948, the Drafting Committee under the chairmanship of Dr BR Ambedkar, which was the apex committee in charge of preparing a Draft Constitution for the Constituent Assembly, abandoned due process altogether in favour of a right to life and personal liberty which we find in the present-day Article 21.[22]

The Constituent Assembly would have none of this flip-flop and in the winter of 1948 it witnessed one of the most intense debates over due process. These debates had been, as one scholar observed, on 'one of the most controversial subjects of the Constitution.'[23] But the right to life and personal liberty, without a due process guarantee, managed to sail through.

However, its inclusion in the Constitution only precipitated discontent. The public was unhappy with it, and some members of the Drafting Committee did not hide their disappointment with the language used in it.

Faced with this, the Drafting Committee could not in good conscience shrug off the barrage of criticism it received for unceremoniously abandoning the due process guarantee. And so, the Drafting Committee proposed a brand new fundamental right which afforded a semblance of due process protection, but only to situations relating to imprisonment and preventive detention. This would be Article 22.[24] However, a broader due process guarantee, which applied to all aspects of human life was conspicuous by its absence.

Although some members of the Drafting Committee congratulated themselves for this act of magnanimity, for many in the Constituent Assembly, Article 22 was not a triumph. Coupled with Article 21, these two articles were viewed as performing the greatest act of disservice to the cause of a person's liberty. In exploring the history of due process and Article 21, this book will also unpack the major arguments which opponents of due process raised at various points in time, as the inclusion of the due process guarantee in the Constitution was debated. It will also contend with theories and speculative accounts which attempt to piece together the puzzle of how due process came to be deleted from Article 21. As we shall see, these accounts tend to overlook the sequence of events leading up to the preparation of the Draft Constitution and even otherwise overstate the role that BN Rau played in the crafting of Article 21.

The making of Article 21 is not entirely clear, and in some sense is shrouded in an inscrutably mysterious air. To this day it remains an enigma as to how the Drafting Committee came to reject due process. There are neither exact records which reproduce the discussions of the members of the Drafting Committee, nor are there any minutes of meetings which detail the thought process at play in the decision to reject due process. This is of some import since for other fundamental rights as well as for many other aspects of the Constitution, the Drafting Committee was deeply engaged for days with crafting their language and scope with the discussions recorded in detail. All that we have in concrete terms then are a set of brief reasons which were appended as a footnote to the right to life and personal liberty in the Draft Constitution which the Drafting Committee presented in February 1948 to Dr Rajendra Prasad, the Chairman and President of the Constituent Assembly.

As the book will demonstrate, the reasons presented by the Drafting Committee justifying the rejection of due process not only strained logic to its breaking point, but were also internally contradictory as well as inconsistent with the basic aim which the Drafting Committee sought to apparently achieve by removing due process. Above all, none of these stated reasons had ever been the basis to reject due process in the past. These new reasons for discarding due process in the 1948 Draft Constitution demonstrated the hollowness of the justification which the Drafting Committee sought to offer as its witness statement, against the charge of unfairly rejecting due process.

History was undone through a footnote.

Due Process and the Originalism Paradox

In Indian constitutional thought, an idea that holds enormous sway is that a historical reading of Article 21 suggests that we must not treat the fundamental right to life and personal liberty as encompassing due process rights. The logic underlying this idea is that since the Drafting Committee had recommended that the phrase 'due process' should not find mention in Article 21, we must remain respectful of that decision.

The foundation of this idea lies in what can be termed an 'originalist reading' of Article 21. According to this viewpoint, it is the observations and opinions of the Drafting Committee alone which must control the meaning and development of Article 21. This book engages with this proposition and examines whether it provides a sufficiently strong basis to conclude that the original intention and original meaning of Article 21 was to exclude due process.

Early on and in fact from its very first decision on Article 21, the Supreme Court assiduously rejected invitations for reading the due process guarantee into Article 21. This book will show that Article 21 could not possibly reflect the views of the entire Drafting Committee because for a whole host of reasons, it did not function as a cohesive whole, but often in a fragmented and unstructured manner.

In reality, the Drafting Committee's decision to delete due process from Article 21 was not a moment of statesmanship but an act which negated the express will of the Constituent Assembly to include a fundamental right on due process in the Constitution. Since the circumstances of its creation are so seriously questionable, Article 21 can have no original intent and no original meaning.

Towards the end, this book offers a glimpse into how the Supreme Court came to respect due process in the latter half of the 1970s and onwards, leading to the reanimation of Article 21. The process of reform occurred with the Supreme Court engaging with due process rights in Article 21. Key decisions on due process are examined to highlight how Article 21 came to be treated as an open-textured fundamental right whose meaning was not limited by its plain text or the historical circumstances of its founding.

As we shall see, the development of Article 21 and due process went along a trajectory which perhaps none of its opponents foresaw. But above all, the recognition of due process in Article 21 resulted in more wholesome protection being provided to those who get entangled in the criminal law process.[25] Many such rights, which the founders of the Constitution had placed a premium on when tirelessly defending the need for a due process guarantee, have in large measure been attained in modern India because of due process.

Much of what we hold precious and dear today in terms of rights is because of Article 21 and a result of not being chained to the past. Article 21 has now become the prime basis for persons to become equal members in society and to enable them to fulfil their individual worth. The fundamental right to life and personal liberty is not an arcane right: it was a site of political contest, ideological dispute and above all a struggle to realize a strong framework of rights for India.

This book presents that history.

Endnotes

1   According to Article 145(3) of the Constitution, any case in the Supreme Court which raises important questions of law pertaining to the interpretation of the Constitution must be decided by a bench of not less than five justices. Benches of such strength are referred to as a Constitution Bench.

2   *KS Puttaswamy v. Union of India*, (2017) 10 SCC 1 [hereinafter *Puttaswamy*]. The justices who heard this case were Chief Justice JS Khehar, Justice J Chelameshwar, Justice SA Bobde, Justice RK Agrawal, Justice RF Nariman, Justice AM Sapre, Justice Dr DY Chandrachud, Justice SK Kaul, and Justice SA Nazeer.

3   In *Puttaswamy*, only Chief Justice Khehar, and Justices Agrawal and Nazeer did not write their own judgment. They joined the opinion of Justice Dr Chandrachud.

4   Since six of the nine justices authored their own judgments, the Supreme Court in *Puttaswamy* issued an 'Order of the Court' which was signed by all nine justices. In para 652.3 of the decision, the Order declared: 'The right to privacy is protected as an intrinsic part of the right to life and personal liberty under Article 21 and as a part of the freedoms guaranteed by Part III of the Constitution.'

5   Samaraditya Pal, *India's Constitution: Origins and Evolution*, vol. 2 (New Delhi: Lexis Nexis, 2015), p. 460.

6   See, *Puttaswamy*, para 501, note 378 (per RF Nariman, J.) exhaustively enumerating the over thirty rights which are protected by Article 21.

7   Krishandas Rajagopal, 'Right to privacy is "intrinsic to life and liberty" rules SC', *The Hindu*, 24 August 2017 (available at https://www.thehindu.com/news/national/privacy-is-a-fundamental-right-under-article-21-rules-supreme-court/article19551224.ece).

8   *Puttaswamy*, para 429 (per RF Nariman, J.). ('The importance of the present matter is such that whichever way it is decided, it will have

huge repercussions for the democratic republic that we call "Bharat" i.e. India. A Bench of nine Judges has been constituted to look into questions relating to basic human rights.')

9   Express News Service, 'Right to Privacy: Citizens welcome SC judgment, hope court will now give relief in Aadhaar', *The Indian Express*, 25 August 2017 (available at https://indianexpress.com/ article/india/citizens-welcome-sc-judgment-hope-court-will-now-give-relief-on-aadhaar-right-to-privacy-4812219/).

10 HT Correspondent, 'Justice Rohinton F Nariman recognized as "hero" for privacy judgment', *Hindustan Times*, 10 October 2017 (available at https://www.hindustantimes.com/india-news/justice-rohinton-f-nariman-recognised-as-hero-for-privacy-judgment/story-HF63FI2hyRy9eeBg5NqueI.html).

11 The five justices were Chief Justice Dipak Misra, Justice RF Nariman, Justice AM Khanwilkar, Justice Dr DY Chandrachud and Justice Indu Malhotra.

12 Section 377: Whoever voluntarily has carnal intercourse against the order of nature with any man, woman or animal shall be punished with imprisonment for life, or with imprisonment for either description for a term which may extend to ten years, and shall also be liable to fine.

13 *Suresh Kumar Koushal v. Naz Foundation*, (2014) 1 SCC 1.

14 *Navtej Singh Johar v. Union of India*, (2018) 10 SCC 1.

15 FP Staff, 'Supreme Court's verdict on Section 377: LGBTQ community members, activists celebrate landmark judgment', *Firstpost*, 14 February 2019 (available at https://www.firstpost.com/india/supreme-courts-verdict-on-section-377-lgbtq-community-members-activists-celebrate-landmark-judgment-5129631.html).

16 See *Mohd Arif v. Supreme Court of India*, (2014) 9 SCC 737, para 28 (per RF Nariman, J.). ('The wheel has turned full circle. Substantive due process is now to be applied to the fundamental right to life and liberty.') [hereinafter *Mohd Arif*]. Due process, however, still has its fair share of critics. See BN Srikrishna, *Skinning a Cat*, (2005) 8 SCC-J 3.

17 *Nikesh Tarachand Shah v. Union of India*, (2018) 11 SCC 1, para 24 (per RF Nariman, J.)

18 The concept of due process is discussed in more detail in Chapter 1.

19 At the time at which the Constituent Assembly conducted its deliberations, the American Constitution seemed to have presented the best model of how a nation's founding document could weave together fundamental rights with judicial enforcement. See PK Tripathi, 'Perspectives on the American Constitutional Influence on

the Constitution of India', in *Constitutionalism in Asia: Asian Views of The American Influence*, ed. Lawrence W Beer (California: University of California, 1979), pp. 59–60, 76 [hereinafter Tripathi, 'Perspectives'].

20   See Bipin Chandra, 'The Split in the Congress and the Rise of Revolutionary Terrorism', in *India's Struggle for Independence*, ed. Bipin Chandra, Mridula Mukherjee, Aditya Mukherjee, KN Pannikar and Sucheta Mahajan (India: Penguin Books, 1989), pp. 135–145.

21   See *Sushila Aggarwal v. State (NCT of Delhi)*, (2020) 5 SCC 1, para 87 (per Ravindra S Bhat, J.). ('The history of our Republic—and indeed, the Freedom Movement has shown how the likelihood of arbitrary arrest and indefinite detention and the lack of safeguards played an important role in rallying the people to demand Independence. Witness the Rowlatt Act, the nationwide protests against it, the Jallianwala Bagh Massacre and several other incidents, where the general public were exercising their right to protest but were brutally suppressed and eventually jailed for long.') Also see, Shashi Tharoor, *An Era of Darkness* (New Delhi: Aleph Book Co., 2016), pp. 105–112.

22   In the Drafting Committee's Draft Constitution of 1948, the right to life and personal liberty was enumerated in draft Article 15. In the Constitution which came into force on 26 January 1950, draft Article 15 was renumbered as Article 21. This is discussed in more detail in Chapters 3 and 4.

23   Charles Henry Alexandrowicz, *Constitutional Developments in India* (Bombay: Oxford University Press, 1957), p. 22 [hereinafter Alexandrowicz, *Constitutional Developments*].

24   Article 22 was originally draft Article 15-A, which is how it was known when it was introduced for the first time by Dr Ambedkar in the Constituent Assembly on 15 September 1949. This is discussed in more detail in Chapter 5.

25   See Upendra Baxi, 'Taking Suffering Seriously: Social Action Litigation in the Supreme Court of India', *Third World Legal Studies*, vol. 4, Article 6 (1985): 107 at pp. 115–116 (1985) [hereinafter Baxi, 'Social Action Litigation'].

1

Due Process at Its Zenith

———•———

ON 9 DECEMBER 1946, THE NEWLY ELECTED MEMBERS OF THE Constituent Assembly met for the first time in the Constitution Hall, New Delhi.[1] Two days later, the Assembly unanimously elected Dr Rajendra Prasad as its Chairman and President.[2] With Dr Prasad at the helm, the Assembly was now ready to discuss and debate the form which the Indian Constitution must take. The first step in that direction was taken on 13 December 1946, when Dr Prasad invited Jawaharlal Nehru to present the Objectives Resolution to the Assembly.[3]

The introduction of the Resolution was a momentous occasion since it would provide the Constituent Assembly a framework within which it would operate and lay down the essential principles which the Constitution must provide for an independent India. It constituted the first charter which the Assembly would consider as a guide to its functioning.

The Resolution contained high ideals and ends which the Assembly must achieve. These included constituting India

1

into an independent republic, uniting the different states into a Union, and determining the status of such states in terms of the Constitution. For Nehru, the new nation would derive its authority not from the British, but directly from the people of India—something that the Resolution emphatically announced.

In terms of rights, paragraph 5 of the Resolution envisaged a range of rights which were to be guaranteed to the people of India. The three pillars of rights were to be justice (social, economic and political), equality (of status, of opportunity and before the law) and freedom (of thought, expression, belief, faith, worship, vocation, association and action).[4] In his speech introducing the Resolution, Nehru said:

> It is a Resolution, and yet, it is something much more than a resolution. It is a Declaration. It is a firm resolve. It is a pledge and an undertaking and it is for all of us I hope a dedication. And I wish this House, if I may say so respectfully, should consider this Resolution not in a spirit of narrow legal wording, but rather to look at the spirit behind the Resolution. Words are magic things often enough, but even the magic of words sometimes cannot convey the magic of the human spirit and of a Nation's passion. And so, I cannot say that this Resolution at all conveys the passion that lies in the hearts and the minds of the Indian people today. It seeks very feebly to tell the world of what we have thought or dreamt of so long, and what we now hope to achieve in the near future.[5]

Before the Resolution could be debated on the floor of the Assembly, Dr MR Jayakar, a member from Bombay who was also a member of the Privy Council, moved an amendment motion which would have permanently deferred the Resolution's consideration.

On 16 December 1946, Dr Jayakar moved an amendment which sought postponement of the Resolution till the time the Indian states and the Muslim League participated in the proceedings of the Constituent Assembly.[6] This was a dangerous proposition because towards the end of 1946, the Muslim League had made it abundantly clear that they would not participate in the Constituent Assembly.[7] If this amendment motion were to succeed, then the functioning of the Assembly would have come to a grinding halt.[8]

Although, Dr Jayakar was supported by some members such as Frank Anthony,[9] most others spoke eloquently in favour of the Resolution. For Syama Prasad Mookherjee,[10] Gopalaswami Ayyangar,[11] Alladi Krishnaswami Ayyar,[12] DP Khaitan[13] and S Radhakrishnan,[14] the Resolution presented a golden opportunity for India to constitute herself into a constitutional republic and that process ought to continue unhindered. That the Resolution was a matter of moment is best represented by the fact that members across ideological lines, wholeheartedly supported it. At any rate by the beginning of 1947, it was evident that the Muslim League would be permanently staying away from the Constituent Assembly.[15] Perhaps realizing the futility of it all, on 21 January 1947, Dr Jayakar announced that he would no longer press for his amendment.[16]

It was in the debates that ensued after the Resolution was introduced, that the importance of a constitution incorporating a due process guarantee was first highlighted. On 17 December 1946, Dr Prasad called on Dr BR Ambedkar to address the Constituent Assembly. Interestingly, on that day, Dr Ambedkar had assumed he would not be called upon to speak since over twenty speakers were yet to speak before him.[17]

In the course of his address, Dr Ambedkar raised several concerns regarding the Resolution. Chief amongst them was that the Resolution did not envisage any remedies for enforcing the rights it spoke of. What also concerned Dr Ambedkar was that although the Resolution spoke about rights that must be guaranteed to the people, it surprisingly did not contain any reference to due process rights for protecting a person's life, liberty and property:

> The Resolution suffers from certain other lacuna. I find that this part of the Resolution, although it enunciates certain rights, does not speak of remedies. All of us are aware of the fact that rights are nothing unless remedies are provided whereby people can seek to obtain redress when rights are invaded. I find a complete absence of remedies. *Even the usual formula, that no man's life, liberty and property shall be taken without the due process of law, finds no place in the Resolution.*[18]

Dr Ambedkar went on to add:

> These fundamentals set out are made subject to law and morality. Obviously what is law, what is morality will be determined by the Executive of the day and when the Executive may take one view another Executive may take another view and we do not know what exactly would be the position with regard to fundamental rights, if this matter is left to the Executive of the day.[19]

Dr Ambedkar had voiced a critical concern. In order to ensure that rights are truly meaningful, it was important for them to be justiciable (in the sense of being enforceable by having recourse to the judicial system). To properly ensure that rights are not easily violated, the incorporation of a due process guarantee protecting life, liberty and property ought to be a paramount consideration. It is one of the first instances of the Constituent Assembly being put on notice that rights must be protected through the means of a due process guarantee.

Dr Ambedkar's speech shows that his conception of rights included ensuring a rigorous layer of security around them. He was of the view that the Constituent Assembly must be tentative in conferring on the State unrestrained powers to diminish the full scope of rights. It is also interesting to note that for Dr Ambedkar, the inclusion of a due process guarantee was a minimum requirement, a fundamental right that the Constitution must naturally include, and that its inclusion would otherwise be uncontroversial.

The Function of Due Process

As a principle of the rule of law, the general concept of due process is of ancient vintage. As the constitutional scholar, DD Basu, tells us in his multi-volume *Commentary on the Constitution of India*, under English law, the idea of due process really meant that action could not be taken against a person without the backing of a law. Thus, the *Magna Carta* in 1215 proclaimed that no one could be subject to the process of criminal law except by the 'law of the land.' Thereafter in the Petition of Grievances of 1610, it was proclaimed that people could not be punished except when 'ordained by the common laws of the land, or the statutes made ... in parliament' which was carried forward into the Petition of Rights of 1628. But the specific words 'due process' were used in a fourteenth century statute of Edward III, and it is from there that the concept of due process travelled to America.[20]

The constitutional avatar of due process traces its origins to the 5th Amendment[21] and to Section 1 of the 14th Amendment to the US Constitution.[22] The 5th Amendment became a part of the US Constitution in 1791 when the Bill of Rights was approved. The 14th Amendment was added to the US Constitution, after the end of the US Civil War, in 1868.[23] Unlike the 5th Amendment, Section 1 of the 14th Amendment enumerates the due process guarantee and the equality guarantee.[24] Additionally, it also enumerates citizenship rights and declares that all citizens are entitled to privileges and immunities which cannot be taken away by a state.

From a constitutional standpoint, due process has two parts to it and is categorized as procedural due process and substantive due process.

Procedural due process focuses on the nature and correctness of the procedure adopted in any measure which results in a person being deprived of their life, liberty or property. Procedural due process demands, as a matter of right, fairness in the treatment of any individual. Steps taken to deprive a person of their rights must conform to specific standards of fairness and natural justice.[25] Fundamentally, in procedural due process the focus lies on examining whether the deprivation of rights attempted by the law in question presents a constitutionally appropriate procedure.[26]

Substantive due process permits a more expansive form of judicial review.[27] In terms of the power of review available against laws and measures affecting a person's life, liberty, or property, substantive due process allows courts to review a law's proffered merits, justification, rationale, feasibility, purpose, appropriateness and also the motive for making it. In substantive due process, a law affecting a person's rights cannot be sustained unless it is demonstrated that it is motivated by a sufficiently compelling justification.[28] This form of review implies that courts are not confined to only examining the form of the law and judging whether its enactment is consistent with the constitutional procedure for law-making.

Furthermore, substantive due process is an important tool used by the judicial branch to locate in the due process guarantee, rights which are essential for a person's life and liberty to be truly meaningful, even if such rights have not been mentioned in the Constitution. Its distinctive value lies in presenting it as a constitutional scheme, so that certain rights cannot be taken away even by the best of legal procedures.[29]

The recognition of new and unenumerated rights ranging across a spectrum is a hallmark of substantive due process.[30] From the 1970s, in America, the due process guarantee became the prime basis for recognizing and extending constitutional protection for abortion rights and marriage rights.[31] The central principle for recognizing such new rights under the due process guarantee is the belief that a definitive catalogue of what liberty means can never be drawn up. Which is why the American Constitution and especially the 14th Amendment 'entrusted to future generations a charter protecting the right of all persons to enjoy liberty as we learn its meaning.'[32]

Due Process and the American Constitution: A Brief History

In propounding the importance of due process, Dr Ambedkar invoked the language of the due process guarantee found in the US Constitution. Before moving on to see how the Constituent

Assembly dealt with due process, we must take stock of the development of due process rights in American constitutional law in the first half of the twentieth century, with a focus on the development of substantive due process.[33] This is to provide a background framework to contextualize how the Assembly and the various committees constituted by it, perceived and interpreted due process.

Starting from 1905, the US Supreme Court embarked on a system of interpretation where under the rubric of substantive due process, it came to be held that the 'liberty' right in the 14th Amendment included the 'liberty to contract', even though such a right was not specifically enumerated. This allowed courts to review the very substance of laws which either directly or incidentally affected this liberty right.[34] The rise of the substantive due process doctrine and the recognition of the liberty to contract, was heralded by the decision of the US Supreme Court in *Lochner v. State of New York*.[35]

In 1895, New York enacted the Bakeshop Act, which stipulated the maximum hours workers could be made to work in bakeries.[36] In *Lochner*,[37] this law came under challenge. Writing for the majority, Justice Rufus Peckham declared that both the baker as well as the workers enjoyed the full freedom of contract as a constitutional right under the due process clause of the 14th Amendment.[38] Moreover, courts were entitled to substantively review laws to adjudge their fairness, appropriateness and reasonableness. For that reason, laws made in exercise of a state's police powers must be viewed rigorously given that the liberty to contract cannot be lightly interfered with.[39]

Justice John Marshall Harlan authored a dissenting judgment speaking for himself and on behalf of Justices Edward White and William Day. The point of dissent was that the state's police powers allow for the regulation of contracts, and a court only needs to see whether the law has been enacted in a constitutionally sanctioned manner.[40] Justice Oliver Wendell Holmes Jr, too, dissented. For him, by no means did the 14th Amendment 'enact Herbert Spencer's Social Statics.' Since the Constitution did not 'embody a particular economic theory' courts should be slow to interfere with laws particularly since the Constitution was 'made for people of fundamentally differing views.'[41]

This case inaugurated the *Lochner* era and with it the stage was set for recognizing that the 'due process clause in the fifth and the fourteenth amendments protect liberty of contract and private property against putatively unwarranted government interference.'[42]

However, close on the heels of *Lochner*, a law capping the duration for which women could work in certain establishments was upheld,[43] for the liberty to contract under the 14th Amendment was subject to restrictions imposed by a state.[44] And for good measure, it was noted that the law was being upheld despite the decision in *Lochner*.[45] But then in a pair of cases decided in 1908[46] and 1915,[47] laws imposing restrictions on the freedom of employers' to set terms of employment, such as requiring employees not to participate in labour unions and organizations were declared unconstitutional.[48]

In 1917,[49] a law regulating payment of overtime wages was upheld[50] because the measure in question was not viewed as controlling work hours.[51] But in 1923[52] a Congressional law was struck down for it stipulated procedures for payment of minimum wages (for children and women). It was treated as a 'price fixing law'[53] which unfairly restricted the liberty to negotiate the 'price for which one shall render service.'[54] Four years later,[55] a law which capped the resale price of tickets to theatres and other establishments was declared unconstitutional for it was viewed as a measure of state interference in the 'free competition among buyers and sellers.'[56]

On 29 October 1929, the New York Stock Exchange crashed, plunging America into the Great Depression, resulting in widespread unemployment and a collapse in levels of production with businesses suffering irreparable harm.[57] In 1933, Franklin D Roosevelt was elected President and he embarked on a project to revive the American economy. His programme would be called the New Deal.[58] During the New Deal era, the US Supreme Court handed down decisions on several laws which were aimed at alleviating the harms of the Great Depression.

In 1934[59] a law providing relief to mortgagees effected during the Great Depression[60] was upheld, since it was made for the 'protection of a basic interest of society.'[61] Shortly thereafter, a law authorizing regulation of milk prices was upheld.[62] The liberty right could be interfered with in reasonable circumstances[63] and states could adopt an 'economic policy' which promotes 'public welfare'[64] to regulate activities which 'inflict injury upon the public at large.'[65] But, then between 1935 and 1936,[66] a series of cases saw the invalidation of laws which were important for the implementation of the New Deal.[67] The last of these decisions came in *Morehead*,[68] in which a New York law which sought to establish payment of minimum wages was found to have violated the 14th Amendment.[69]

With the *Morehead* decision, matters reached a tipping point.[70] After being re-elected President overwhelmingly in 1937, Roosevelt unveiled an audacious plan to ensure that the New Deal could be implemented, unhampered by judicial intervention. Roosevelt's plan was called the 'Court Packing Plan.'[71]

Since 1869, the US Supreme Court has had a strength of nine justices, except when Justice Stephen Field was appointed in 1863 by Abraham Lincoln, as the tenth justice. But in 1937, that 'magic' number of nine would come under siege.

On 5 February 1937, Roosevelt proposed that for every justice in the US Supreme Court who was older than seventy and who chose to continue as a judge, an additional justice would be appointed. Six of the justices were above the age of seventy, which meant that six new justices would be added.[72] Although Roosevelt's proposal did not materialize,[73] from 1937 laws aimed at achieving public welfare were upheld with Justice Owen Roberts now consistently siding with the majority.[74]

It is widely believed that to save the US Supreme Court from being packed with additional justices who would probably help tip the scales in favour of the New Deal, Justice Roberts effected a change in his voting pattern. The switch of Justice Roberts would forever be remembered with the epithet: 'Switch in Time That Saved Nine.'[75]

Thus in 1937 itself[76] a minimum wage law was upheld under the 14th Amendment, since it aimed to neutralize the inequality of bargaining power of employees.[77] In so holding, the 1923 decision declaring minimum wage laws unconstitutionally affected liberty was overruled.[78] In the same year,[79] the National Labour Relations Act enacted by Congress to safeguard the interest of labour and regulate labour relations was upheld.[80] Justice Roberts sided with the majority in both these cases. In 1941,[81] a unanimous Court upheld the Fair Labour Standard Act, a Congressional law, which barred the sale of goods between states, if the producer of the goods had failed to comply with the labour regulations of the Act.[82]

This trend would continue in several later decisions, where the due process guarantee would be used to uphold laws motivated by economic welfare and public good aim.[83]

As we shall see, on almost all of the occasions when due process was discussed in the Constituent Assembly and its various committees and sub-committees, the American jurisprudential formulation of due process, and particularly of substantive due process in the years leading up to the deliberations in the Constituent Assembly, was often a point of serious debate and contestation. The first occasion when due process would come under the spotlight would be in the Advisory Committee.

Constitution of the Advisory Committee

After a marathon debate on the Objectives Resolution which carried on for several weeks after it was introduced in the Constituent Assembly, the President on 22 January 1947 put the Resolution to vote. Recognizing the gravity of the moment and the 'solemnity of the occasion and the greatness of the pledge and the promise which the Resolution contains,'[84] Dr Prasad invited the members to stand and vote. On that day, the Objectives Resolution was adopted in the form as it was when first moved in the Assembly.[85]

Almost immediately, on 24 January 1947, Govind Ballabh Pant moved a resolution in the Constituent Assembly seeking the 'Election of the Advisory Committee.'[86] This resolution was moved because in pre-independent India, the Constituent Assembly functioned under the aegis of the Cabinet Mission Statement of 16 May 1946.[87]

The Cabinet Mission, sent to India by Britain's Prime Minister Clement Atlee, had in paragraph 16 of their Statement recommended that it was time 'to set in motion the machinery whereby a constitution can be settled by Indians for Indians.'[88] Since Britain would not in any way participate in the constitution making process, paragraph 20 of the Cabinet Mission Statement stipulated that the Constituent Assembly elected to draft the Constitution, must constitute an Advisory Committee.

The task of the Advisory Committee was, amongst others, to recommend to the Constituent Assembly 'a list of fundamental rights' and to make recommendations on other matters such as measures for safeguarding minorities. Further, the Advisory Committee was to have broad-based representation so that competing interests and viewpoints could be considered by the Committee.[89]

After a brief debate, Pant's resolution was approved. The Constituent Assembly settled on electing fifty members to the Advisory Committee, with the President being given the power to nominate an additional twenty-two members. Importantly, the Advisory Committee could constitute sub-committees to aid the Advisory Committee's efforts in preparing its report.[90]

Nearly a month after it was constituted, the Advisory Committee met for the first time on 27 February 1947, during which Sardar Vallabhbhai Patel was elected as its Chairman.[91] On that day, the Advisory Committee set up five different sub-committees, including a Fundamental Rights Sub-Committee comprising of ten members.[92]

Fundamental Rights Sub-Committee Deliberates on Due Process

In March 1947, two members of the Fundamental Rights Sub-Committee, Alladi Krishnaswami Ayyar and KM Munshi submitted their Notes for the Sub–Committee's consideration. Ayyar, a member of the Constituent Assembly from Madras was one of India's most distinguished lawyers, having served as the Advocate General of Madras from 1929–1944. Munshi, a member from Bombay, was a renowned lawyer from the Bombay High Court and had served as the Home Minister for Bombay in the 1930s.

In 'A Note on Fundamental Rights' of 14 March 1947,[93] Ayyar set out his concerns over a due process clause. He argued that since the US Constitution only generally defined rights, it had fallen to the US Supreme Court to determine both the content as well as the limits of such rights. This had especially been the case with the 14th Amendment. However, some of the other constitutions which came later in time took a different approach. Rather than simply copying the American Constitution, these later constitutions structured fundamental rights after closely studying how the American Bill of Rights had been judicially interpreted.

Ayyar thus observed that in thinking of how to structure the language of rights, the Constituent Assembly had to choose between two models. Either follow the model of the American Constitution and generally define rights, as was the case of the 14th Amendment, or follow the model set out in certain later constitutions, which incorporated as fundamental rights the dicta from various US Supreme Court decisions.[94]

Moreover, he observed that many rights such as those enumerated in the first eight amendments to the US Constitution (which apply only against the Federal Government) such as the freedom of speech guaranteed by the 1st Amendment, had been incorporated into the due process clause of the 14th Amendment (which applies only against the states). Ayyar thus framed the choice that lay before the Constituent Assembly in the following way:

> The later constitutions framed on the model of the U.S. have tried to expand the working in the U.S. Constitution by compendiously seeking to incorporate the effects of the

American decisions. The question before the Constituent Assembly of India is whether to follow the model of the United States or the later constitutions.[95]

Munshi's 'Note and Draft Articles on Fundamental Rights' of 17 March 1947, was exhaustive both in terms of detail as well as the manner in which he presented a draft of fundamental rights.[96] In his vision, the two important ways in which fundamental rights could be strengthened was by making them justiciable and permitting restrictions on rights only by law which was made by the Union.[97]

In the 'Draft Articles' which Munshi drew up, several fundamental rights were enumerated in great detail.[98] The draft fundamental rights contained a series of civil rights pertaining to the Right to Equality (Article III), the Right to Freedom (Article V), and the Right to Religious and Cultural Freedom (Article VI). Apart from this, Munshi's draft articles also dealt in considerable detail with social and economic rights such as the Right of Workers (Article VII); the Right to Education (Article VIII), and the Right to Freedom of Family Relations (Article XI). The clause on due process was contained in Article V(4), and read:

No person shall be deprived of his life, liberty or property without due process of law.[99]

In some measure, the inclusion of a due process clause in Munshi's draft reflected his commitment to civil liberties and personal freedom which were essential requirements for people to truly enjoy fundamental rights. Munshi's focus, lay in ensuring a system of rights which were justiciable, for in the absence of enforcement, rights would be meaningless. In paragraph 6 of his Note, Munshi presented a four-point model to make rights effective:

The essential conditions for the effective guarantee of fundamental rights are:

(a) Enforceability must be the essence of any instrument defining fundamental rights and duties;

(b) A person or a State under an obligation cannot claim the right to determine whether he would comply with the obligation and if so to what extent;

(c) The observance of fundamental rights and duties must be determined by a procedure and a machinery common to the Union as a whole;

(d) Limitations to such law whenever necessary must only be imposed by the law of the Union.[100]

For this reason, the Right to Constitutional Remedies was provided in Article XIII of the draft fundamental rights. Here Munshi enumerated a rigorous process for making fundamental rights justiciable and enforceable in courts of law by invoking the court's writ jurisdiction.[101] By Article XII(3), the writ courts would be vested with the powers to declare legislation as '*ultra vires* the Constitution'[102] (which means that it is unconstitutional and therefore ought to be struck down). In Munshi's vision, the dual requirements for rights were that they be enumerated and that they be justiciable in constitutional courts. Justiciability of rights was a *sine qua non* for the effective working of fundamental rights.

Ayyar and Munshi's vision on the need to have a due process clause in the Constitution was in fact anticipated by another member of the Sub-Committee, KT Shah. In 'A Note on Fundamental Rights' of 23 December 1946,[103] Shah drew up 'Draft Clauses' on fundamental rights, and in particular, in Clause 52, stipulated for a due process clause to be part of the Constitution:

No one shall be deprived of life, limb or property except
under due process of law.[104]

What was stated by Ayyar, Munshi and Shah in their respective
notes and draft fundamental rights regarding the incorporation of
a due process clause, was emphatically reiterated by Dr Ambedkar.

On 24 March 1947, Dr Ambedkar submitted his famous
'Memorandum and Draft Articles on the Rights of States and
Minorities.'[105] The Memorandum provided in considerable detail
not only a charter of fundamental rights (Article II–Section
I) and detailed procedures for remedies against the invasion of
fundamental rights (Article II–Section II), but also a series of
clauses for the protection of minorities (Article II–Section-III)
and for the protection of scheduled castes (Article II–Section
IV). In the draft articles, in Clause 2 of Article II–Section I, Dr
Ambedkar provided for a detailed due process clause as part
of fundamental rights, mirroring the Bill of Rights of the US
Constitution.[106] The due process clause read:

No State shall make or enforce any law or custom which
shall abridge the privileges or immunities of citizens; nor
shall any State deprive any person of life, liberty or property
without due process of law; nor deny to any person within
its jurisdiction equal protection of the laws.[107]

It is important to note that so far as Ayyar, Munshi, Shah and Dr
Ambedkar were concerned, each had their own vision of how the
Constitution must deal with fundamental rights.[108] But they all
converged on the idea that the inclusion of a due process guarantee
as a fundamental right in the Constitution was paramount—each
of them had a core commitment to the protection and promotion
of civil liberties. It is also interesting to note that four out of ten

members of the Fundamental Rights Sub-Committee had laid out
in considerable detail their vision for the Constitution to include
a due process clause.

The Fundamental Rights Sub-Committee had met for the first
time on 27 February 1947, and by 31 March 1947, it concluded its
deliberations.[109] The Sub-Committee had decided that it would
use Munshi's draft fundamental rights as a template version
alongside the other drafts that had been submitted to the Sub-
Committee.[110] The eventual draft of the Sub-Committee largely
reflected Munshi's draft on fundamental rights.[111]

On 26 March 1947, the Sub-Committee took up for discussion,
amongst other articles, Article V(4) from KM Munshi's draft,
which dealt with the due process clause.[112] On that day, only
Maulana Abul Kalam Azad did not attend the meeting.

The Sub-Committee considered the fact that with due
process, and particularly substantive due process becoming
a right, land reform laws transferring rights to the tenant
without properly compensating the landlord, might be rendered
constitutionally suspect. But this concern did not worry the
Sub–Committee for too long, and by a majority of five to two,[113]
the text of Article V(4) from Munshi's draft was adopted.[114] This
is important because as we shall see, conferring due process
protection on property rights would become a serious point
of contestation in the Advisory Committee. On 3 April 1947,
the Sub-Committee submitted the 'Draft Report of the Sub-
Committee' to the Chairman of the Advisory Committee along
with the draft clauses on 'Fundamental Rights.'[115] The Draft
Report had separate chapters for justiciable and enforceable
fundamental rights (Chapter I) which were from Clauses
1–34 and judicially unenforceable principles akin to Directive

Principles (Chapter II), which were from Clauses 35–46. Clause 11 contained the due process clause, which read:

> No person shall be deprived of his life, liberty or property without due process of law.[116]

These and other fundamental rights enumerated in Chapter I were made justiciable, since Clause 32 empowered the people to move the Supreme Court to enforce their fundamental rights, which it would enforce by issuing a variety of writs.[117]

After submitting its Draft Report, the Sub-Committee met again on 14 and 15 April 1947.[118] Some members had dissented on certain clauses, but the Draft Report that had been submitted did not reflect whether the members had signed it subject to their dissent. It was then decided to submit the Report yet again, with this caveat in place.[119] On 14 April 1947, the Sub-Committee began its clause-wise deliberation of the draft clauses contained in its Draft Report of 3 April 1947. In this second reading of the Report, the clause on due process underwent a dramatic transformation.

In the meeting of 14 April 1947, the Sub-Committee agreed to accept Clause 11 from its earlier Draft Report.[120] The next day, however, the Sub-Committee drastically altered its language.[121] When the Sub-Committee came to Clause 11, a decision was taken to redraft it. In doing so, the Sub-Committee was now going to substantially replicate the latter part of the 14th Amendment to the US Constitution. On 15 April 1947, the new Clause 11 read:

> No person shall be deprived of his life, liberty or property without due process of law nor shall any person be denied the equal treatment of the laws within the territories of the Union provided that nothing herein contained shall

prevent the Union Legislature from legislating in respect of foreigners.[122]

The new Clause 11 would now contain two fundamental rights. The first part pertained to the due process guarantee protecting a person's life, liberty and property against unconstitutional deprivation. The second part contained the equality guarantee: all persons would receive equal treatment of the laws. This redrafted Clause 11 suggests that in some measure, the Sub-Committee decided to adopt the model of enumerating a generally defined due process guarantee, which would be the model of the US Constitution, rather than detailing the various rights thought to be a part of the 14th Amendment.

On 16 April 1947, the Chairman of the Sub-Committee, JB Kripalani, submitted the 'Report of the Sub-Committee on Fundamental Rights' to the Chairman of the Advisory Committee for the second time, along with the draft clauses on 'Fundamental Rights' as well as the minutes of dissents which had been filed,[123] In the new draft clauses, the due process clause, now renumbered as Clause 12, read:

No person shall be deprived of his life, liberty or property without due process of law nor shall any person be denied the equal treatment of the laws within the territories of the Union: Provided that nothing herein contained shall prevent the Union Legislature from legislating in respect of foreigners.[124]

Due Process and the Advisory Committee

In consonance with the scheme set out by the Constituent Assembly in its Resolution of 24 January 1947, the Advisory Committee took up the Report of the Sub-Committee on Fundamental Rights and determined the language of each of the rights. The Advisory Committee, under the chairmanship of Sardar Vallabhbhai Patel met on 21–22 April 1947, to discuss the Report as well as the Interim Report of the Minorities Sub-Committee.[125] On 21 April 1947, the Advisory Committee discussed the feasibility of the due process clause recommended by the Fundamental Rights Sub-Committee.

During the deliberations in the Advisory Committee, Alladi Krishnaswami Ayyar presented a strong defence of the due process guarantee.[126] At the outset and before delving into the history of due process in America, which proved to be a controversial point of debate in itself, Ayyar proclaimed that the Sub-Committee made its decision to recommend the due process guarantee 'after knowing where we stand.'[127] This statement was made perhaps to remove any misgivings that the Sub-Committee's recommendation on due process was made without careful consideration.

Ayyar noted that in American constitutional law, due process was traditionally understood as providing procedural guarantees of fairness. But over time, due process had come to acquire a substantive meaning and thus would also apply to substantive guarantees. He then pointed out that in America itself on the question of substantive due process, the law seemed to be in a state of flux. For instance, in the New Deal Era, the US Supreme Court had at different points of time used substantive due process to both invalidate as well as uphold social welfare legislations.[128]

It was with this knowledge and 'after understanding the full implications' Ayyar told the Advisory Committee, that the phrase due process was settled on by the Sub-Committee. Putting the point as persuasively as he could, Ayyar declared, 'Personally I am for the retention of the clause. I am not against the clause. I am willing to take that chance, but there is that danger.'[129]

In the Advisory Committee, Ayyar had been at pains to highlight just how methodical the Sub-Committee had been when deciding to recommend the due process guarantee. It had carefully surveyed the entire body of American constitutional law on due process including the 'frequent oscillations and adjustments' in them.[130] Only after ascertaining all the viewpoints on due process, did the Sub-Committee recommend the due process clause. This was a decision that had been taken advisedly and after appreciating all the implications that would arise.[131]

The 'danger' of which Ayyar spoke had to do with the fact that in America, due process was under constant change. Despite that he was emphatic that the new constitution must incorporate a due process guarantee, and must do so with the full knowledge of the possible risks that would arise with its incorporation. Being risk averse on due process was inadvisable, for the due process guarantee held great promise.[132] Ayyar had thrown his full support behind the due process guarantee, which is why he let the Advisory Committee once again know: 'I am for the retention of the clause.'[133]

During Ayyar's address, Govind Ballabh Pant expressed concern that due process must relate only to procedure. Ayyar's answer was that in the ultimate analysis, incorporation of a clause on due process would mean 'limitation upon legislative power by a constitutional guarantee.'[134] This suggestion by Ayyar caused some disquiet.

C Rajagopalachari pointed out that if due process were to operate as a fetter on legislative powers, it would be impossible to make laws affecting property rights.[135] Sardar Vallabhbhai Patel expressed the view that 'certain old type of judges may

misinterpret this "due process of law.'"[136] Pant shared this view—
he felt that a general guarantee on due process would mean that
the nation's destiny would be determined by the 'fiats of those
elevated to the judiciary.'[137] Pant suggested that it may be better to
avoid due process altogether in favour of a right on which 'every
judge may be expected to give the same sort of ruling.'[138] For his
part, Ayyar was not able to say with certainty that the due process
guarantee would be interpreted and understood in one particular
manner.[139]

Due Process and Prolonged Detention

It had become clear to the Advisory Committee that the due
process clause recommended by the Sub-Committee really had
two parts which had to be examined separately. The first part
related to protection of persons against unwarranted detention
and the second part pertained to property rights enjoying
due process protection. This delineation was made by Sardar
Vallabhbhai Patel.[140]

Early on Pant had raised a flurry of queries as to whether the
due process guarantee would allow for the preventive detention
of a person for half a year (C Rajagopalachari and Ayyar's answer
was that it would not), and whether property could be acquired
by the State for far lower than its actual value (Ayyar thought
it unlikely).[141] After some discussion, Sardar Vallabhbhai Patel
asked the Advisory Committee to first consider the question of
'whether a man can be detained without trial.'[142]

At this point, Dr Ambedkar intervened to caution the Advisory
Committee that it was unconscionable to imprison anyone for
long periods without due process. But he felt that in respect of
property rights, the Advisory Committee could devise a suitable

amendment which would obviate the fears that property reform would be stalled.[143] To this point, Pant inquired whether the State should have the power to preventively detain those causing widespread disruption in several provinces.[144]

Dr Ambedkar in reply to Pant's concerns suggested that a due process guarantee would not allow perpetrators of violence to run amok with impunity. In times of crisis such as a declared emergency, a provision may be made to ensure the operation of fundamental rights could be halted. This would mean that the due process guarantee would be unenforceable during such times.[145]

Seeking to allay some of the fears about due process entirely stultifying the legislature's functioning, KM Munshi pointed out that the due process guarantee applied not only to cases of detention but to all matters, and that even in America an overwhelming majority of laws which were challenged, passed muster under the due process guarantee. In his definition, due process meant:

> Due process of law only comes to this; that the legislation which is brought forward is a *proper and necessary legislation to secure the end in view and that it is not extravagant with respect to each particular situation.* ... The American Supreme Court has every time applied these canons whether the legislation is a proper one. It has allowed socialistic legislation; it has allowed detention to some extent... In most cases it has upheld drastic legislation. It is not correct to say that judges will put themselves in the place of the legislature.[146]

Munshi, however, was unable to fully allay the fears over due process. For instance, C Rajagopalachari was certain that if legislation was passed authorizing the detention of persons for half a year in times of crisis, such legislation would probably be invalidated under the due process clause by the Supreme Court.[147]

Dr Ambedkar remained steadfast in his belief that there was no proper justification for 'giving a *carte blanche* to the government to arrest any person' or for that matter enacting a 'facile provision' which authorized the government to arrest people without adherence to due process, at all times.[148] To ensure that in times of a 'grave emergency' alone, the due process guarantee would remain in abeyance, Dr Ambedkar's suggestion remained that of introducing a provision which would clarify this point.[149]

For Dr Ambedkar, this was the preferred formula since nothing could persuade any rational person to allow for the suspension of fundamental rights during times of peace and empower governments to detain any person for whatever duration, without due process.[150] Other members such as C Rajagopalachari, KM Pannikar and Dr Bakshi Tek Chand also accepted this formula and were agreed that an appropriate amendment to reflect this position could be made.[151]

Delinking Property from Due Process

The Advisory Committee then turned to the question of property rights. What had perturbed members such as Sardar Vallabhbhai Patel and C Rajagopalachari was that with the reference to 'property' in the clause on due process, substantive due process would possibly endanger laws which affected property rights.[152] It was Govind Ballabh Pant, however, who staunchly opposed any reference to due process in the fundamental rights.

In Pant's view, legislation enacted for agrarian reform and land reform would be haunted by the spectre of being invalidated on account of being inconsistent with the due process right. Fearing that a clause on due process would empower courts to constantly question legislative wisdom and bring legislation aimed at ensuring property redistribution to a grinding halt, Pant argued that a clause on due process should be clearly worded to rule out any possibility of changing interpretations of due process.[153]

To bolster his argument, Pant listed the example of his own province, the United Provinces,[154] which intended to abolish the *zamindari* system of land tenure. That the entire enterprise of achieving land reform would be set at naught if courts used the clause on due process to halt such measures.[155] As he put it:

> If you say that *zamindaries* should not be abolished, that private rights should not be touched, I can understand that. But to put a law which can be interpreted by different people in different ways is to stop all social progress. [156]

Pant went on to add:

> To allow the court to sit in judgment over the legislature or to control the legislature itself and to say that a law will not be valid unless it is declared to be so by a single individual sitting in the Supreme Court is extremely risky and I cannot subscribe to that proposition.[157]

The controversy which the Advisory Committee had to now resolve was to incorporate a clause on due process but ensure that legislation meant to achieve social welfare and land reform would not be threatened. At this point, KM Pannikar offered a three-part solution to the conundrum that the Advisory Committee faced: provide that the due process guarantee safeguards life and liberty; in order to strike a balance, enumerate provisions which allows for the 'maintenance of public order and tranquillity'; and enumerate property rights in such manner that they are subject to legislative will.[158]

With Pannikar's solution paving the way out of the due process thicket, Sardar Vallabhbhai Patel became insistent that this issue must now be settled, for the Advisory Committee 'could not continue arguing about it.'[159] To settle the controversy finally, C Rajagopalachari, taking a cue from Pannikar, offered a 'compromise amendment' on due process which would appeal to both sides. He presented a modified version of the clause on due process by deleting property from it, but retaining due process protection for life and liberty.[160]

This compromise clause seemed to be an acceptable solution for resolving the controversy over due process protecting property rights. Even KM Munshi and Dr Ambedkar agreed that excluding property from the clause on due process, and dealing with property as a separate subject was eminently acceptable.[161] The Advisory Committee also accepted C Rajagopalachari's amended version of the proviso to the clause on due process. Pant was still dissatisfied and made it clearly known that he disagreed with even the new version of the right on due process, but he did not take the matter further.[162]

However, before the Advisory Committee finally agreed that 'property' was to be removed from the due process guarantee, Dr Ambedkar sensed that with the deletion of 'property', perhaps the due process guarantee could possibly be truncated even further. To avoid such an eventuality, Dr Ambedkar made an impassioned plea before the Advisory Committee that under no circumstances should 'life' be removed from the clause on due process.

With regard to 'liberty', Dr Ambedkar argued that it ought to be retained but the Advisory Committee could consider how its meaning is to be modulated.[163] He felt that stipulating that in times of an emergency the due process guarantee could not be pressed into service was a sufficient limitation on the right, especially since he was certain in the belief that when an emergency is declared, the Supreme Court would never judicially review the correctness of such a declaration.[164] For Dr Ambedkar, the path of prudence dictated that the 'legislature or the executive should not be placed in absolute power to dispose of people's life or liberty.'[165]

The minutes of the meeting of 21 April 1947 record that the Advisory Committee voted to accept the clause on due process as revised during the proceedings. And consistent with the Advisory Committee's decision, the due process clause made no reference to property.[166]

On 23 April 1947, Sardar Vallabhbhai Patel submitted to the President of the Constituent Assembly, the 'Interim Report on the Subject of Fundamental Rights' along with the draft of 'Justiciable Fundamental Rights' (Interim Report).[167] In the Interim Report, Patel pointed out that the Fundamental Rights Sub-Committee had recommended that one report must pertain to enforceable fundamental rights, and a separate report be prepared on Directive Principles of State Policy, which although unenforceable are critical for governance.

Thus, the Interim Report of 23 April 1947, dealt only with justiciable fundamental rights and the recommendations were made on the basis of reports submitted by the Fundamental Rights Sub-Committee as well as the Minorities Sub-Committee.[168] With respect to the Directive Principles of State Policy, the Advisory Committee would on 25 August 1947, submit to the President of the Constituent Assembly, the 'Supplementary Report of the

Advisory Committee on the Subject of Fundamental Rights.' This report contained twelve clauses dealing with directive principles.[169]

The Interim Report was keen to highlight that an admirable feature of its recommendations was that fundamental rights were being made enforceable and the Constituent Assembly would have to consider defining the jurisdiction of the Supreme Court, when it came to the enforcement of rights. It was also pointed out that the fundamental rights recommended by the Advisory Committee were inspired by the American Constitution, which provided a worthy model of rights to protect the people. In paragraph 3 of the Interim Report, this unique aspect was highlighted:

> We attach great importance to the Constitution making these rights justiciable. The right of the citizen to be protected in certain matters is a special feature of the American Constitution and the more recent democratic constitution. In the portion of the Constitution Act, dealing with the powers and jurisdiction of the Supreme Court, suitable and adequate provisions will have to be made to define the scope of the remedies for the enforcement of these fundamental rights.[170]

The Interim Report had an annexure which contained the Justiciable Fundamental Rights.[171] In it, under the heading 'Rights of Freedom' the due process clause was enumerated in Clause 9, and read:

> No person shall be deprived of his life, or liberty, without due process of law, nor shall any person be denied the equal treatment of the laws within the territories of the Union: Provided that nothing herein contained shall

detract from the powers of the Union Legislature in respect of foreigners.[172]

An interesting aspect is that the Interim Report enumerated the right to equality in Clause 9 along with the due process clause. This is curious since the Interim Report contained a separate heading for 'Rights to Equality' (Clauses 4–7) but it did not contain any general provision on equality.[173]

On 29 April 1947, Sardar Vallabhbhai Patel, introduced a resolution in the Constituent Assembly, placing the Advisory Committee's Interim Report for debate. In his speech,[174] Patel laid out the general vision for Fundamental Rights. He emphasized that although the Assembly would debate the question of which rights must be part of the Constitution and their precise wording, the Assembly must accept the principles contained in each of the rights which were part of the Interim Report.

One of the most important facets of the Interim Report was that in addition to enumerating rights, it had recommended that fundamental rights be justiciable and enforceable. The enormity of this stride was something that Patel himself recognized:

> The report is a draft report ... What I would submit to the House to do today is generally to accept the principles of each of the clauses that have been suggested for consideration, so that we may not have to devote more time in considering technical legal details of the phraseology to be adopted. We have now suggested for the consideration of this House those rights which are justiciable.[175]

It is worth pointing out that the Interim Report separately recommended 'Rights to Constitutional Remedies' In Clause

22.[176] The Interim Report was extraordinarily far-sighted since it had determined that the new Constitution must not only contain a detailed charter of fundamental rights including a clause on due process, but that the people must have the right to move the Supreme Court—that was to be created—for enforcing their fundamental rights.

To that end, Clause 22(1) made it a fundamental right for the people to move the Supreme Court to seek enforcement of their fundamental rights, with the Supreme Court empowered, under Clause 22(2), to issue a variety of writs for the purposes of enforcement. Further, perhaps to give effect to the Advisory Committee's decision that in times of crisis, the due process guarantee apart from other fundamental rights must remain in abeyance, Clause 22(3) provided that the right to move the Supreme Court could be suspended only 'in cases of rebellion or invasion or other grave emergency', and additionally, only on a showing by the government that 'public safety may require it.'[177]

Thus, the Interim Report envisaged three layers of protection around fundamental rights: by enumerating specific and enforceable fundamental rights; by allowing the people to move the Supreme Court for enforcement of their fundamental rights and making that a fundamental right in itself; and, finally, by empowering the Supreme Court to issue any direction necessary for the enforcement of fundamental rights.

On 29 April 1947, after Patel's motion to consider the recommendations made in the Interim Report was adopted,[178] the Constituent Assembly commenced the clause wise discussion of the fundamental rights.[179] The next day, Clause 9 came up for discussion.

When the President called for Clause 9 to be taken up, KM Munshi moved two amendments. The first amendment sought that in Clause 9 the words 'equality before the law' must replace the phrase 'the equal treatment of the laws.' The second amendment sought the deletion of the proviso to Clause 9. Both the amendments were adopted without much debate and the amended Clause 9 was approved by the Constituent Assembly.[180] Thus, on 30 April 1947, the final version of the due process guarantee, and indeed the final version of Clause 9 read:

> No person shall be deprived of their life or liberty without
> due process of law, nor shall any person be denied equality
> before the law within the territories of the Union.[181]

The Enduring Teachings from 1946–1947

The entire process of the evolution and acceptance of the due process guarantee between 1946 and 1947 as a fundamental right, is rich with important teachings of the way in which the Advisory Committee and the Constituent Assembly dealt with this important right.

To begin with, after careful deliberation, the Constituent Assembly adopted the due process guarantee in Clause 9. It affirmed the idea that the State would need to cross a very high threshold before they could deprive a person of their life or liberty. In this respect, due process had three main functions. It was to protect persons from forms of detention which were arbitrary and lacking reasonable justification. It conferred a range of rights which could be exercised by persons when they came into contact with the criminal process. And, in its substantive aspect, the due process clause would be used to engage in subject-matter review of legislation. This meant that laws could be invalidated on the ground that the subject matter of the law was constitutionally unsustainable, even though such laws are passed by the Legislature in compliance with the applicable procedures for enacting such laws. The Constituent Assembly's assent for incorporating due process essentially meant that the people were now empowered to question the very wisdom of laws.

Moreover, the members of the Fundamental Rights Sub-Committee were well aware of the discursive trajectory of the jurisprudential development of due process in American constitutional law. They were also aware that a due process right may potentially endanger laws aimed at achieving public good and social welfare.

Fully cognisant of the risks that such a clause brought with it, the Sub-Committee was sure that the benefits of incorporating a guarantee on due process far outweighed its possible drawbacks. The discursive trajectory of the decisions of the American Supreme Court on the meaning of due process was not treated, at least at this stage, as a cautionary tale against the incorporation of a due process guarantee. This is what Ayyar had alluded to when defending the recommendation of the due process guarantee as a fundamental right, in the Advisory Committee on 21 April 1947.[182]

It is due to this reason that during the second reading of the Sub-Committee's report on 15 April 1947, it was decided to not only accept the due process guarantee but to entirely recast it. This resulted in the addition of a second fundamental right—the right to equality. In doing so, the Sub-Committee mirrored the 14th Amendment to the US Constitution. The recasting of the due process clause by the Fundamental Rights Sub-Committee on that day was an affirmation of the idea that robust fundamental rights were to be a hallmark of the new Constitution.

Furthermore, when the Advisory Committee took up the Report of the Sub-Committee on Fundamental Rights of 16 April 1947 for discussion, there was a sharp division of opinion on whether the due process guarantee was appropriate given the unique conditions of India as well as the land reform project which was to be embarked upon. But the Advisory Committee did not disavow its support for due process. However, keeping in mind the overarching importance of land reform, the decision was taken to only delete the word 'property' in the due process clause. This once again demonstrates that the Advisory Committee was cognisant of the fact that the due process guarantee, which empowers the people to check state action affecting their life or liberty, was a minimum requirement which ought to be fulfilled by fundamental rights.

When the Constituent Assembly took up the due process guarantee for discussion on 30 April 1947, neither did it raise much controversy nor did it attract sharp debate. This may have been perhaps because it did not relate to the protection of property rights. Here too, in voting to amend, approve and adopt the due process guarantee the essence of the protection for 'life' and 'liberty' were retained and the Constituent Assembly did not use any words to qualify either of them.[183]

To be sure, the Constituent Assembly, in adopting the clause on due process, also accepted that substantive due process would be a part of constitutional guarantees. But since property was no longer part of the clause on due process, the potential of the massive land reform project being unsettled would no longer arise. The vote on the due process guarantee did not occur, as if the Assembly did not know the true import of their decision.

The Constituent Assembly's vote, indicates an unbroken continuity in the general vision of incorporating in the Constitution a due process guarantee, an idea that was first voiced by Dr Ambedkar in 1946. For the Assembly, the due process guarantee was in fact the bare minimum which the Constitution must seek to provide for the newly freed people of India.

What must also be remembered is that the Interim Report also displayed how the different visions of the members of the Sub-Committee coalesced and were reflected in its Report. The Interim Report reflected the shared vision of KT Shah, KM Munshi, Dr Ambedkar and Alladi Krishnaswami Ayyar: any charter on fundamental rights must incorporate a due process guarantee. Further, the Interim Report in providing for a layer of security around fundamental rights by making them justiciable in the Supreme Court, and making the right to move the Supreme Court itself a fundamental right clearly signalled the important role that due process and judicial review were to play when it came to the development of fundamental rights. The Interim Report's recommendations demonstrated that in protecting life and liberty, the nature of the protection accorded must be of the highest possible order, which is what was achieved by incorporating a guarantee on due process and making it expressly justiciable.

Importantly, the incorporation of a general clause on due process, which was along the lines of the 14th Amendment to the US Constitution, also demonstrated that the Constituent Assembly did not want to stall the development of due process in India. In choosing to structure the due process guarantee at a broad level of generality rather than only enumerating those specific rights which form part of due process, the Constituent Assembly knowingly adopted the path of letting due process develop organically, at its own pace in India rather than in fits and starts or being imposed in a top-down fashion.

Interestingly, the recommendation of a clause on due process also showed the Advisory Committee's desire to balance

competing claims over fundamental rights and arrive at a solution
which was both acceptable as well as workable.

When Sardar Vallabhbhai Patel and C Rajagopalachari
expressed their fears over due process as a fundamental right,
and Govind Ballabh Pant strongly denounced the due process
clause and was adamant that fundamental rights must not make
a reference to due process at all, there were two paths open to
the Advisory Committee. Either to accept the denouncement
and abandon due process altogether, or to adopt the due process
guarantee with modifications which would make it acceptable
and at the same time preserve the strength of the guarantee.

The Advisory Committee in adopting the latter option and
deleting 'property' from the clause, but retaining 'life' and 'liberty',
presented a compromise which was accepted by all, with the
exception of Pant. The compromise solution on the language of
due process further enhanced its appeal. In its modified form
it found easy acceptance—the Constituent Assembly voted to
accept and adopt Clause 9 on 30 April 1947.

The fact that the Advisory Committee as well as the Constituent
Assembly agreed that fundamental rights can be enjoyed only
when they are enforceable demonstrates that the incorporation
of a clause on due process was intended to be a strong check on
governmental action through the medium of judicial intervention.
The importance of combining fundamental rights with judicial
review is most succinctly brought out in Sardar Vallabhbhai Patel's
speech of 2 May 1947 when Clause 22 was debated. According
to Patel:

> This is a clause which provides a judicial remedy. If we
> provide for fundamental rights, it is necessary that we
> must provide also for a remedy.[184]

In this matrix, the position of the courts was a superior one and strong judicial review was in fact, a condition precedent for ensuring that fundamental rights were enforceable. Nothing made this clearer than the fact that in Clause 22, the fundamental right to move the Supreme Court was formidably secured by the word 'guaranteed.'[185]

We can now begin to appreciate the far-sightedness of the both the Advisory Committee and the Constituent Assembly in 1946–1947 in respect of the fundamental right of due process protection for life and liberty.

For the Constituent Assembly, India was to emerge as a free nation and shed the shackles of its colonial past. In this new India, protecting a person's life and liberty would be an important goal to achieve. In large measure, this was sought to be achieved by adopting Clause 9 as a fundamental right, and by Clause 22 which would strengthen the individual's hand in moving the Supreme Court when their fundamental rights were under threat.

However, as we shall see in what follows, the great heights which the due process guarantee reached in 1946–1947, would soon be reduced to but a memory of a not so distant past.

Endnotes

1   Constituent Assembly Debates (New Delhi: Lok Sabha Secretariat, Sixth Reprint, 2014) [hereinafter CAD], vol. I, p. 1. By the mid 1930s, the nationalist movement had begun articulating its demand for a Constituent Assembly. See Gurmukh Singh Nihal, 'The Idea of an Indian Constituent Assembly', *The Indian Journal of Political Science*, vol. 2 (1941): p. 258.

2   CAD, vol. I, pp. 35–36.

3   Id., pp. 57–65. The Resolution was formally called 'Resolution Re: Aims and Objects.'

     'I beg to move:

'(1) This Constituent Assembly declares its firm and solemn resolve to proclaim India as an Independent Sovereign Republic and to draw up for her future governance a Constitution;

(2) WHEREIN the territories that now comprise British India, the territories that now form the Indian States, and such other parts of India as are outside British India and the States as well as such other territories as are willing to be constituted into the Independent Sovereign India, shall be a Union of them all; and

(3) WHEREIN the said territories, whether with their present boundaries or with such others as may be determined by the Constituent Assembly and thereafter according to the Law of the Constitution, shall possess and retain the status of autonomous Units, together with residuary powers, and exercise all powers and functions of government and administration, save and except such powers and functions as are vested in or assigned to the Union, or as are inherent or implied in the Union or resulting therefrom; and

(4) WHEREIN all power and authority of the Sovereign Independent India, its constituent parts and organs of government, are derived from the people; and

(5) WHEREIN shall be guaranteed and secured to all the people of India justice, social, economic and political; equality of status, of opportunity, and before the law; freedom of thought, expression, belief, faith, worship, vocation, association and action, subject to law and public morality; and

(6) WHEREIN adequate safeguards shall be provided for minorities, backward and tribal areas, and depressed and other backward classes; and

(7) WHEREBY shall be maintained the integrity of the territory of the Republic and its sovereign rights on land, sea, and air according to Justice and the law of civilised nations, and

(8) this ancient land attains its rightful and honoured place in the world and make its full and willing contribution to the promotion of world peace and the welfare of mankind.' Id., p. 59.

4   Ibid.

5   Id., pp. 59–60.

6   Id., pp. 71–74.

7   Granville Austin, *The Indian Constitution: Cornerstone of a Nation* (New Delhi: Oxford University Press, 32nd edition, 2018), p. 78 [hereinafter Austin, *The Indian Constitution*].

8   See speech of Dr Sir Hari Singh Gour. CAD, vol. I, p. 81.

9   Id., pp. 94–95.

10   Id., pp. 95–99.

11   Id., pp. 125–130.

12   Id., pp. 140–143.

13   Id., pp. 146–147.

14   CAD, vol. II, pp. 269–274.

15   Austin, *The Indian Constitution*, pp. 6–9.

16   Id., p. 308.

17   CAD, vol. I, p. 99.

18   Id., p. 100. (Emphasis added.)

19   Ibid.

20   DD Basu, *Commentary on the Constitution of India*, vol. 3 (New Delhi: LexisNexis, 8th edition, 2008), pp. 3078–3079 [hereinafter Basu, *Commentary on the Constitution of India*].

21   US Constitution, Amendment V: No person shall be held to answer for a capital, or otherwise infamous crime, unless on a presentment or indictment of a grand jury, except in cases arising in the land or naval forces, or in the militia, when in actual service in time of war or public danger; nor shall any person be subject for the same offense to be twice put in jeopardy of life or limb; nor shall be compelled in any criminal case to be a witness against himself, nor be deprived of life, liberty, or property, without due process of law; nor shall private property be taken for public use, without just compensation.

22   US Constitution, Amendment XIV, Section 1: All persons born or naturalized in the United States, and subject to the jurisdiction thereof, are citizens of the United States and of the state wherein they reside. No state shall make or enforce any law which shall abridge the privileges or immunities of citizens of the United States; nor shall any state deprive any person of life, liberty, or property, without due process of law; nor deny to any person within its jurisdiction the equal protection of the laws.

23   George Anastaplo, *The Amendments to the Constitution: A Commentary* (Baltimore: Johns Hopkins University Press, 1995), pp. 173–185.

24   Throughout the book, Section 1 of the 14th Amendment to the US Constitution will be referred to simply as 'the 14th Amendment.'

25   See Basu, *Commentary on the Constitution of India*, pp. 3084–3092. Also see, Henry J Friendly, '"Some Kind of Hearing"', *University of Pennsylvania Law Review*, vol. 123 (1975): 1267.

26   Erwin Chemerinsky, 'Substantive Due Process', *Touro Law Review*, vol. 15 (1999): 1501 [hereinafter Chemerinsky, 'Substantive Due Process'].

27   Substantive due process has been likened to a 'contradiction in terms—
     sort of like "green pastel redness."' See John Hart Ely, *Democracy and
     Distrust: A Theory of Judicial Review* (Cambridge, Massachusetts:
     Harvard University Press, 1980), p. 18.

28   See Chemerinsky, 'Substantive Due Process', pp. 1501–1502, 1509.
     ('Substantive due process asks the question of whether the government's
     deprivation of a person's life, liberty or property is justified by a
     sufficient purpose. Procedural due process, by contrast, asks whether
     the government has followed the proper procedure when it takes away
     life, liberty or property. Substantive due process looks to whether there
     is sufficient substantive justification, a good enough reason for such
     deprivation.') Id., p. 1501; Jamal Greene, 'The Meming of Substantive
     Due Process', *Constitutional Commentary*, vol. 31 (2016): p. 262.
     ('The distinction between substantive and procedural due process
     is intelligible, even if there is significant ambiguity on the margins. A
     due process violation requires that the asserted life, liberty, or property
     interest pass some threshold of importance and that it be deprived
     without crossing some other threshold of regularity or consistency with
     the way in which meaningfully similar rights are deprived. Substantive
     due process claims focus on the first of these thresholds while procedural
     claims focus on the second, and in both cases it is typically assumed that
     the other threshold has been crossed.') In modern times, substantive
     due process review has come to assume enormous importance and is
     considered a 'bedrock component of modern [American] constitutional
     law'. See Peter J Rubin, 'Square Pegs and Round Holes: Substantive Due
     Process, Procedural Due Process, and the Bill of Rights', *Columbia Law
     Review*, vol. 103 (2003): p. 835.

29   See Basu, *Commentary on the Constitution of India*, pp. 3092–3100;
     Daniel O Conkle, 'Three Theories on Substantive Due Process', *North
     Carolina Law Review*, vol. 85 (2006): p. 69. ('Instead, the Court has
     infused the Due Process Clause with substantive content. Focusing
     especially on the word 'liberty', it has declared for itself the power to
     define otherwise unenumerated constitutional rights, rights that are
     protected from governmental deprivation, no matter the procedure.')
     (internal citation omitted) [hereinafter Conkle, 'Three Theories'].

30   Chemerinsky, 'Substantive Due Process', pp. 1509–1510.

31   James E Fleming and Linda C McClain, 'Liberty', in *The Oxford
     Handbook of the U.S. Constitution*, ed. Mark Tushnet, Mark A Graber
     and Sanford Levinson (New York: Oxford University Press, 2015), pp.
     488–489.

32   *Obergefell v. Hodges*, 576 US 644 (2015).
33   Much as I would like to, an exhaustive examination of the law on due process is beyond the scope of this book. And although the account that follows may be a familiar one to those interested in constitutional law, it is intended on presenting a general outline of events which led to the growth and development of the substantive due process doctrine in America, in the years leading up to the deliberations in the Constituent Assembly.
34   See Conkle, 'Three Theories', p. 70.
35   Chemerinsky, 'Substantive Due Process', pp. 1502–1503.
36   See Melvin I Urofsky, 'Lochner v. New York', *Encyclopaedia Britannica*, 10 April 2018 (https://www.britannica.com/event/Lochner-v-New-York).
37   198 US 45 (1905) (SCC Online version).
38   Id., para 2.
39   Id., paras 2–4, 8, 10, 11, 13, 20–21. The US Supreme Court consists of nine justices including the Chief Justice and the all of the cases are decided *en banc*.
40   Id., paras 32, 34, 35, 44.
41   Id., para 48. Justice Holmes' dissent would go on to acquire canonical status with scholars praising it as a model of rectitude and judicial restraint. See Gerald Leonard, 'Holmes on the Lochner Court', *Boston University Law Review*, vol. 85: 1001 (2005).
42   Geoffrey R Stone, Louis Michael Seidman, Cass R Sunstein, Mark V Tushnet and Pamela S Karlan, *Constitutional Law* (New York: Aspen Publishers, 6th edition, 2009), pp. 735–736 [hereinafter Stone et al., *Constitutional Law*]. *Lochner* has since its time received an outpouring of scholarly attention. Some consider *Lochner* to be a case which is wrong on all counts. See Victoria F Nourse, 'A Tale of Two Lochners: The Untold History of Substantive Due Process and the Idea of Fundamental Rights', *California Law Review*, vol. 97 (2009): 751; Thomas B Colby and Peter J Smith, 'The Return of Lochner', *Cornell Law Review*, vol. 100 (2015): 527. On the other hand, some believe that *Lochner* has been criticized unfairly. See David E Bernstein, 'Lochner v. New York: A Centennial Retrospective', *Washington University Law Review*, vol. 83 (2005): 1474.
43   *Muller v. Oregon*, 208 US 412 (1908) (SCC Online version), para 2.
44   Id., para 11.
45   Id., para. 15. The US Supreme Court acknowledged the brief filed by Louis D Brandeis, a future justice of the US Supreme Court, which

contained empirical data on laws enacted by different states, which regulated the work hours for women, as well as data on such laws from other nations. Id., paras 9, 11. The art of filing briefs containing empirical data in constitutional cases would acquire the moniker 'Brandeis Brief.' For a scholarly analysis of the Brandeis Brief, see 'The Consideration of Facts in "Due Process" Cases', *Columbia Law Review*, vol. 30 (1930): 360; Mary E Becker, 'From Muller v. Oregon to Fetal Vulnerability', *University of Chicago Law Review*, vol. 53 (1986): 1219; David E Bernstein, 'Brandeis Brief Myths', *Green Bag 15* (2011): 9.

46   *Adair v. United States*, 208 US 161 (1908) (SCC Online version).
47   *Coppage v. Kansas*, 236 US 1 (1915) (SCC Online version).
48   See *Adair*, paras 14, 16, 18; *Coppage*, paras 2, 16, 18, 20–21, 29.
49   *Bunting v. Oregon*, 243 US 426 (1917) (SCC Online version).
50   Id., para 17.
51   Id., para 20.
52   *Adkins v. Children's Hospital of the District of Columbia*, 261 US 523 (1923) (SCC Online version).
53   Id., para 38. In this part of the analysis, the US Supreme Court was speaking in relation to adult women only.
54   Ibid.
55   *Tyson v. Banton*, 272 US 418 (1927) (SCC Online version).
56   Id., para 58.
57   Eric Hobsbawm, *The Age of Extremes: A History of the World, 1914–1991* (New York: Vintage Books, 1996), pp. 91–108; Howard Zinn, *A People's History of the United States: 1492–present* (New York: Harper Collins Perennial Classics, 2003), pp. 386–406.
58   David M Kennedy, 'What the New Deal Did', *Political Science Quarterly*, vol. 124 (2009): 251.
59   *Home Building & Loan Ass'n v. Blaisdell*, 290 US 398 (1934) (SCC Online version).
60   Id., para 2.
61   Id., para 32.
62   *Nebbia v. New York*, 291 US 502 (1934) (SCC Online version) (Justice Owen Roberts authored the judgment for the majority).
63   Id., para 35.
64   Id., para 36.
65   Id., para 37.
66   *Railroad Retirement Board v. Alton*, 295 US 330 (1935) (SCC Online version); *ALA Schechter Poultry Corporation v. United States*, 295 US 495 (1935) (SCC Online version); *United States v. Butler*, 297 US 1

(1936) (SCC Online version); *Carter v. Carter Coal Company*, 298 US 238 (1936) (SCC Online version).

67   Michael E Parrish, 'The Great Depression, The New Deal, and the American Legal Order', *Washington Law Review*, vol. 59 (1984): p. 731 [hereinafter Parrish, 'New Deal'].

68   *Morehad v. New York ex rel. Tipaldo*, 298 US 587 (1936) (SCC Online version).

69   Id., para 28.

70   William E Leuchtenburg, 'The Origins of Franklin D Roosevelt's 'Court-Packing' Plan', *The Supreme Court Review* (1966): p. 377.

71   Gregory A Caldeira, 'Public Opinion and The US Supreme Court: FDR's Court-Packing Plan', *The American Political Science Review*, vol. 81 (1987): pp. 1140–1141.

72   Barry Cushman, 'Rethinking the New Deal Court', *Virginia Law Review*, vol. 80 (1994): pp. 208–209. In 1937, the Court comprised Chief Justice Charles Evan Hughes, Justices Willis Van Devanter, James McReynolds, Louis Brandeis, George Sutherland, Pierce Butler, Harlan Stone, Owen Roberts, and Benjamin Cardozo. Justices Van De Vanter, McReynolds, Sutherland and Butler were of a conservative bent, while Justices Brandeis, Stone and Cardozo were of a liberal bent. Chief Justice Hughes and Justice Roberts were the 'swing justices.' See William H Rehnquist, *The Supreme Court: How It Was, How It Is* (New York: William Morrow & Co., 1987), p. 222; Parrish, 'New Deal', pp. 730–731.

73   Sandra Day O'Connor, *Out of Order: Stories from the History of the Supreme Court* (New York: Random House, 2013), p. 137.

74   Some maintained that it was erroneous to assume that the Court Packing Plan had influenced a change in Justice Roberts' voting pattern. See, Felix Frankfurter, 'Mr. Justice Roberts', *University of Pennsylvania Law Review*, vol. 104 (1955): p. 313.

75   Daniel E Ho and Kevin M Quinn, 'Did a Switch in Time Save Nine', *Journal of Legal Analysis*, vol. 2 (2010): 70. Also see, William E Leuchtenburg, 'FDR's Court-Packing Plan: A Second Life, a Second Death', *Duke Law Journal*, vol. 1985 no. 3/4 (1985): 673.

76   *West Coast Hotel Co. v. Parrish*, 300 US 379 (1937) (SCC Online version).

77   Id., para 21–22.

78   Id., para 23.

79   *NLRB v. Jones & Laughlin Steel Corporation*, 301 US 1 (1937) (SCC Online version).

80   Id., paras 15–18, 26–30, 33–34.
81   *United States v. Darby*, 312 US 100 (1941) (SCC Online version).
82   Id., para 4. Justice Stone held that the Act was supported by the Constitution's authorization allowing Congress to regulate inter-state commerce, and that a law regulating payment of minimum wages and hours of work, was not a violation of the due process rights contained in the 5th Amendment and the 14th Amendment. Id., paras 14–17, 22–27, 36.
83   See Stone et al., *Constitutional Law*, pp. 754–755.
84   CAD, vol. II, p. 323.
85   Id., p. 324.
86   Id., pp. 328–333.
87   B Shiva Rao, *The Framing of India's Constitution: Select Documents*, vol. I (New Delhi: Indian Institute of Public Administration, 1966), pp. 209–218 [hereinafter B Shiva Rao, *Framing of India's Constitution*, vol. I].
88   Id., p. 213.
89   Id., p. 216.
90   CAD, vol. II, pp. 347–349.
91   B Shiva Rao, *The Framing of India's Constitution: Select Documents*, vol. II (New Delhi: Indian Institute of Public Administration, 1967), pp. 65–67 [hereinafter B Shiva Rao, *Framing of India's Constitution*, vol. II]; Minutes of the first meeting of the Advisory Committee, 27 February 1947.
92   Ibid. The members of the Fundamental Rights Sub-Committee were Acharya JB Kripalani, MR Masani, KT Shah, Rajkumari Amrit Kaur, Alladi Krishnaswami Ayyar, KM Munshi, Sardar Harnam Singh, Maulana Abul Kalam Azad, Dr Ambedkar and Jairamdas Daulatram.
93   Id., pp. 67–69.
94   Id., pp. 68–69.
95   Id., p. 68.
96   Id., pp. 69–80.
97   Id., p. 71.
98   Id., pp. 73–80.
99   Id., p. 75.
100 Id., p. 71.
101 Id., pp. 79–80.
102 Id., p. 80.
103 Id., pp. 36–55.

104 Id., p. 55.

105 Id., pp. 84–114.

106 Arvind Elangovan, *Norms and Politics: Sir Benegal Narsing Rau in the Making of the Indian Constitution, 1935–50* (New Delhi: Oxford University Press, 2019), p. 206 [hereinafter Elangovan, *Norms and Politics*].

107 B Shiva Rao, *Framing of India's Constitution*, vol. II, p. 86.

108 Elangovan, *Norms and Politics*, p. 211.

109 B Shiva Rao, *Framing of India's Constitution*, vol. II, pp. 114–137.

110 Id., p. 116. Minutes of the Fundamental Rights Sub-Committee's Meeting dated 24 March 1947. The minutes record the following: It was decided to take up Mr. Munshi's draft and examine it in conjunction with the other drafts.'

111 Elangovan, *Norms and Politics*, p. 212.

112 B Shiva Rao, *Framing of India's Constitution*, vol. II, pp. 121–124.

113 Id., p. 122. Although nine members were in attendance at this meeting, the minutes record that Article V(4) was adopted by a 5:2 vote, which means seven members voted. The minutes of this meeting do not indicate why this occurred. ('During the discussion of sub-clause (4), it was pointed out to the committee that the expression "due process of law" has been judicially interpreted to cover not merely procedure but also substantive rights. If sub clause (4) were included as a fundamental right, tenancy legislation which takes away certain rights from landlords and transfers them to tenants without payment of compensation may become invalid except on payment of compensation which the court regards as just. To this extent the enactment of this clause might go further than the Government of India Act, 1935. After discussion it was decided, by a majority of 5 to 2, that the clause should be retained.')

114 Id., p. 124.

115 Id., pp. 137–143.

116 Id., p. 139.

117 Id., p. 141.

118 Id., pp. 163–169. Minutes of the Meetings of the Sub-Committee dated 14–15 April 1947.

119 Id., p. 163.

120 Id., p. 164.

121 Id., pp. 166–169.

122 Id., p. 167.

123 Id., pp. 169–198.
124 Id., p. 173.
125 Id., p. 210.
126 Id., pp. 240–242.
127 Id., p. 240.
128 Id., pp. 240–241.
129 Id., p. 241.
130 Id., p. 242.
131 Ibid.
132 Ibid.
133 Ibid.
134 Id., p. 241.
135 Ibid.
136 Id., p. 242.
137 Id., p. 243.
138 Ibid.
139 Ibid.
140 Id., pp. 241, 243.
141 Id., p. 243.
142 Ibid.
143 Ibid.
144 Id., pp. 243–244.
145 Id., p. 244. Dr Ambedkar was perhaps referring to Clause 30(3) of the draft of Fundamental Rights submitted by the Fundamental Rights Sub-Committee along with its 'Report of the Sub-Committee on Fundamental Rights.' According to Clause 30(3), the fundamental right to move the Supreme Court seeking the enforcement of fundamental rights 'shall not be suspended unless when, in cases of rebellion or invasion, or other grave emergency, the public safety may require it.' See Id., p. 175.
146 Id., p. 244. (Emphasis added.)
147 Ibid.
148 Ibid.
149 Id., p. 245.
150 Id., p. 247. ('I think there are many here who share my sentiment that the legislature or the executive should not be placed in absolute power to dispose of people's life and liberty.')
151 Id., p. 246.
152 Id., p. 241.
153 Id., p. 243.

154 B Shiva Rao, *The Framing of India's Constitution: A Study* (New Delhi: Indian Institute of Public Administration, 1968), p. 234 [hereinafter B Shiva Rao, *A Study*].

155 B Shiva Rao, *Framing of India's Constitution*, vol. II, p. 245.

156 Ibid.

157 Ibid.

158 Id., pp. 245–246.

159 Id., p. 246.

160 Ibid. The modified version of the clause on due process proposed by C Rajagopalachari read as follows: 'No person shall be deprived of his life or liberty without due process of law nor shall any person be denied the equal treatment of the laws within the territories of the Union provided that this shall not prevent the enactment of laws in the interest of public order and security.' Also see, Austin, *The Indian Constitution*, pp. 107–108.

161 B Shiva Rao, *Framing of India's Constitution*, vol. II, p. 246. Also see, B Shiva Rao, *A Study*, p. 235.

162 B Shiva Rao, *Framing of India's Constitution*, vol. II, p. 247. Also see, Tripathi, 'Perspectives', p. 84.

163 B Shiva Rao, *Framing of India's Constitution*, vol. II, p. 246.

164 Id., pp. 246–247.

165 Id., p. 247.

166 Id., p. 288. At this point in time, the due process clause was enumerated in Clause 12. The numbering would change in the final report of the Advisory Committee. Also see, B Shiva Rao, *A Study*, p. 233.

167 CAD, vol. III, pp. 437–444.

168 Id., p. 437.

169 See B Shiva Rao, *Framing of India's Constitution*, vol. II, pp. 304–306.

170 CAD, vol. III, p. 437.

171 Id., pp. 440–444.

172 Id., p. 441.

173 Id., pp. 440–441.

174 Id., pp. 399–400.

175 Id., p. 400.

176 Id., p. 443.

177 Ibid.

178 Id., pp. 409–410.

179 Id., p. 410.

180 Id., p. 468.

'CLAUSE 9-RIGHTS OF FREEDOM

Mr. President: Then we come to Clause 9.

Mr K.M. Munshi: I move that for the words "the equal treatment of the laws" the words "equality before the law" be substituted.

The amendment was adopted.

Mr President: As regards the proviso there is a formal amendment to drop it. Then there are some amendments of which notice has been given.

(Messrs. Diwakar, Mohanlal Saksena and Mahavir Tyagi did not move their amendments.)

Mr. President: Then I come to the amendment saying that the proviso be dropped.

Mr. K.M. Munshi: I move that the proviso be dropped.

The amendment was adopted.

Mr. President: I put Clause 9 as amended.

Clause 9, as amended, was adopted.'

181 B Shiva Rao, *Framing of India's Constitution*, vol. II, p. 301. Property rights were housed in Clause 19, an entirely separate fundamental right. See Id., p. 303.

182 B Shiva Rao, *Framing of India's Constitution*, vol. II, pp. 240–242. ('The decisions therefore of the U.S. Supreme Court have not been uniform on the interpretation of the due process clause. There have been frequent oscillations and adjustments… During the previous discussion, I drew attention of the committee to the course of decisions in America and the committee arrived at the decision after attention was drawn by Sir B.N. Rau and myself. Let us maintain the decision with full knowledge of the implications. I am for retention of the clause.') Id., p. 242.

183 See CAD, vol. III, p. 468.

184 Id., p. 525.

185 B Shiva Rao, *Framing of India's Constitution*, vol. II, p. 303.

2

Due Process

The Middle-Path Solution of BN Rau

————◆————

BN Rau as Constitutional Advisor

THE POST OF CONSTITUTIONAL ADVISOR WAS HELD BY SIR BENEGAL Narsing Rau.* Just before the Constituent Assembly convened in December 1946, BN Rau had in his 'Outline of an Organisation for the Constituent Assembly' of 5 June 1946, presented his ideas for creating the administrative structure and support system for the Assembly's smooth functioning.[1]

In presenting the outline, Rau accepted the invitation of George Abell, Viceroy Wavell's Private Secretary, to serve as the future Constituent Assembly's Constitutional Advisor but on the condition that he would serve in an honorary capacity.[2] This offer

———————————

*   In the interest of full disclosure, I must state here that I am related to
     BN Rau on my maternal side.

49

was readily accepted and in his letter to Rau dated 8 June 1946,[3] George Abell indicated that the Viceroy was 'glad to hear of your willingness to act as Constitutional Advisor, and to do so in an honorary capacity.'[4]

On 14 August 1947, on the eve of India's Independence, Jawaharlal Nehru moved a motion by which each member of the Constituent Assembly was to take a pledge to dedicate themselves to the service of the nation. In moving this Resolution, Nehru delivered his famous 'Tryst with Destiny' speech.[5] After the motion was adopted, members waited for the 'stroke of the midnight hour',[6] the moment of Indian Independence, to take the pledge that they had just adopted.[7] With midnight having come and gone, the President of the Assembly conveyed to Louis Mountbatten, the Viceroy at the time, that the Constituent Assembly had taken over the governance of India, and that Mountbatten would, from 15 August 1947, be the Governor-General of India.[8]

After attaining independence, the Constituent Assembly, which now functioned under Section 8(1) of the Indian Independence Act, 1947, a law of British vintage, was responsible for expeditiously presenting a new constitution that would govern free India.[9]

On 29 August 1947, Satyanarayan Sinha moved a motion for the Assembly to constitute a Drafting Committee. As per this motion, the Drafting Committee, which would consist of seven members, would prepare a Draft Constitution after critically analysing the decisions the Assembly had already taken. The names of Alladi Krishnaswami Ayyar, N Gopalaswami Ayyangar, Dr Ambedkar, KM Munshi, Saiyid Mohd Saadulla, BL Mitter and DP Khaitan were proposed for the Drafting Committee.[10]

BG Kher sought to amend this motion and create a new method for drafting the constitution. According to him, since the Constituent Assembly had already discussed a large number of reports and recommendations,[11] it would be better if the Constitutional Advisor created a draft constitution which reflected the various decisions taken by the Assembly, and included all such provisions which must necessarily be part of the constitution, first. Thereafter the Drafting Committee would use this draft constitution as a template, scrutinize it thoroughly and submit the final draft of the Constitution to the Assembly for its consideration.[12]

Some members, however, opposed such a course of action. For instance, Tajamul Hussain resisted the idea of 'doing work piecemeal' and felt it would be wisest if all the reports were first debated by the Constituent Assembly.[13] Jaipal Singh opposed the motion since he felt that the Drafting Committee would 'pry into things which we have not yet decided.'[14]

Supporting Sinha's motion, Alladi Krishnaswami Ayyar was confident that the Drafting Committee had a limited role. For him, it was clear that the Drafting Committee could not make any recommendations contrary to what the Constituent Assembly had already decided on, since the Assembly's decisions were binding. Under the scheme of the motion, the Drafting Committee had to prepare a constitution consistent with the decisions the Assembly has already taken.[15] As Ayyar saw it:

> Sir, on a matter like this it is as well we are sure as to what exactly the import of the resolution is. *One thing must be made quite clear, namely that in regard to decisions already reached, they will be treated as binding, though if errors are discovered or unforeseen difficulties arise, it will always be open to the House to review the decisions.*[16]

Ayyar went on to reiterate:

> There has been a Fundamental Rights Committee, the
> Union Powers Committee, and the Union Constitution
> Committee and they have considered and placed their
> decisions before this House. In regard to matters which
> have already been considered by this Assembly and *in
> regard to which decisions have been reached, the scope of
> review at a later stage must naturally be limited.*[17]

Ayyar's speech acquires enormous importance because in it he
maintained that the duty of the Drafting Committee (of which
he was to be a member) would be to remain respectful of all the
previous decisions that the Assembly had taken. As we shall see
in the subsequent chapters, Ayyar would end up disregarding this
note of caution which he sounded. He would come to play a key
role in, and would staunchly defend, the Drafting Committee's
repudiation of the due process guarantee—a fundamental right
which the Assembly had approved and voted upon on 30 April
1947.

After this brief debate, the Constituent Assembly in quick
succession voted to adopt BG Kher's amendment as well as the
amended motion.[18] Now, it would fall on the Constitutional
Advisor, to draft a full-length constitution and incorporate all the
decisions of the Assembly as well as introduce provisions to make
the constitution a workable document.

BN Rau: A Brief Boswell

Before serving as the Constitutional Advisor, Rau had a
distinguished career in the Indian Civil Service. After graduating

with a Tripos from Trinity College, Cambridge, Rau joined the Indian Civil Service in 1909, being the only Indian to be selected in that year.[19]

Incidentally, at Trinity College, Rau happened to be a student at the same time as Jawaharlal Nehru. In a letter to his father, written on 28 May 1908, Nehru writes of Rau as being 'frightfully clever' and one who 'certainly works hard enough.' All that Nehru seemed to have seen of Rau was him attending his lectures and spending his time studying.[20] Neither of them could have possibly foreseen that their paths would intertwine when India's Constitution was to be founded.

Soon after being inducted into the civil service, Rau in 1910, was posted as Assistant Magistrate and Collector in Burdwan, Bengal. In 1921, Rau was appointed as District and Sessions Judge in Assam and in 1925 he was appointed as the Legal Remembrancer and Secretary to the Assam government.[21]

In 1935, Rau served as judge of the Calcutta High Court, but only for a short while as his services were called for in the Reforms Office. That year, the Government of India Act had come into force which necessitated the overhaul of all the laws, both at the federal and provincial level, in order to align them with the new scheme of the 1935 Act. Rau oversaw this exercise and was able to complete it in less than two years.[22] For these services, Rau was knighted in 1938.[23]

Rau rejoined the Calcutta High Court in 1939. He did so because the then Indian Federal Court's Chief Justice, Sir Maurice Gwyer was keen to induct Rau to the Federal Court. But to be eligible for appointment, Rau needed to serve as a judge of a High Court for at least five years.[24] During his time as a High Court judge, Rau authored several landmark judgments including in *GP Stewart v. BK Roy Chaudhury*,[25] which defined the doctrine of repugnancy when applied to legislative relations. In 1956, this decision was treated as having high precedential value by a Constitution Bench of the Supreme Court in *Tika Ramji*'s case.[26]

As a High Court judge, Rau also served as chairman of various committees. The most notable being that in 1941 when he was appointed as chairman of the committee looking into the reform of Hindu law. It was Rau's report which would later serve as the basis of the laws enacted to reform Hindu law in 1955.[27] Although Rau was to retire from the civil service in 1944, his services were still called for.

In 1944 itself, Rau agreed to become Prime Minister of Kashmir, but he had a short-lived tenure. He resigned in June 1945.[28] Thereafter, Viceroy Wavell appointed him as Secretary in the Governor General's Secretariat's Reform Office, since Rau preferred this post over being appointed as a permanent judge of the Calcutta High Court.[29]

Rau's legal acumen was also called for in an entirely different setting—the Indian National Army (INA) Trials which took place in the Red Fort in New Delhi in 1946. As Arvind Elangovan tells us in his magisterial biography of BN Rau, three officers of the INA, which was founded by Subhas Chandra Bose, were on trial for their daring attacks against the British. The soldiers were represented by Bhulabhai Desai, the legendary lawyer from Bombay[30] and also by Tej Bahadur Sapru and Jawaharlal Nehru who appeared in defence of the soldiers. But it was Rau who devised the defence strategy.[31]

In 1948, Rau was dispatched to the United Nations to present India's case on the integration of Hyderabad with India and soon thereafter, he was elected by the UN General Assembly to the International Law Commission.[32]

Rau was appointed as India's Ambassador to the Security Council of the United Nations in 1949, but by that time Rau's health began to deteriorate on account of cancer. However, that did not stop him from ably discharging his duties in the United Nations, where he was recognized for his acumen and diplomacy.[33] It is believed that during that time, Rau was considered a leading candidate for being appointed the Secretary General of the United Nations.[34]

In 1952, Rau was elected as a judge to the International Court of Justice but the resurgence of his cancer meant he served as a judge only till 1953. Rau was unable to fight off his illness and he passed away in Zurich, Switzerland on 30 November 1953.[35]

BN Rau and the Reshaping of the Due Process Guarantee

Under the motion which the Constituent Assembly had adopted on 29 August 1947, the first step towards drafting a constitution was to be taken by BN Rau who would compile a constitution reflective of the Assembly's prior decisions and deliberations. Soon after the adoption of this motion, Rau began to work rapidly and within a few months, by October 1947, Rau's Draft Constitution was ready. This was a voluminous document which had 240 clauses in addition to also consisting of thirteen schedules.[36]

In Part III of the Draft Constitution, Chapter II contained the clauses on Fundamental Rights running from Clauses 11–30. Importantly, Clauses 11–14 pertained to the 'Right to Equality', Clauses 15–19 pertained to the 'Rights of Freedom', Clauses 20–23 pertained to 'Right Relating to Religion', Clause 24 pertained to 'Cultural and Educational Rights', Clauses 25–27 pertained to

'Miscellaneous Rights' and Clauses 28–30 pertained to 'Rights to Constitutional Remedies.'[37]

In Chapter II, the clause on due process was contained in Clause 16, which read:

> *No person shall be deprived of his life or personal liberty without due process of law*, nor shall any person be denied equality before the law within the territories of the Federation.[38]

To ensure that rights were enforceable as well as justiciable, the Draft Constitution contained two layers of protection. The first layer of protection was provided in Chapter I of Part III of the Draft Constitution. In it, Clause 9 provided that laws which violated fundamental rights would be invalid. The last part of Clause 9 presented an expansive definition of what would constitute as law; it ranged from legislation to ordinary rules. This was important because with this broader meaning of 'law', even ordinary regulations made by government departments would be treated as law and could be scrutinized for their compliance with fundamental rights.[39]

BN Rau was careful to ensure that all the rights enumerated in Chapter II were enforceable in courts of law. For that reason, Rau's Draft Constitution contained a separate section on 'Right to Constitutional Remedies.'[40] This was the second layer of protection.

Clause 28(1) provided that the right to move the Supreme Court for the enforcement of fundamental rights would itself be a fundamental right. Under Clause 28(2), this right to move the Supreme Court could only be suspended when an emergency was declared. What this essentially meant was that in times of disruption or an emergency alone, the Supreme Court could not be moved for enforcement of fundamental rights.

In Part III of the Draft Constitution, Chapter III contained the Directive Principles of State Policy, which were enumerated in Clauses 31–41.[41] The Directive Principles contained several goals that the State must strive to achieve in order to promote social good, public welfare and the improvement of the conditions in which Indians lived.

With respect to Directive Principles, the Draft Constitution contained an important stipulation. In Chapter I of Part III, Clause 10 stipulated that the Directive Principles of State Policy were principles which were to guide the policies of the State. They were to be treated as the goals which state policy must strive to achieve. And although it would be the duty of the State to make laws to give effect to them, Directive Principles would not be enforceable in courts of law.[42] This meant that unlike with Fundamental Rights, proceedings could not be instituted, under Clause 28, to seek their enforcement.

In respect of the due process guarantee, it is immediately noticeable that BN Rau in drafting Clause 16 and retaining the phrase 'due process' carried forward the Constituent Assembly's decision of 30 April 1947, when it voted to accept the due process guarantee as a fundamental right. However, Rau made certain modifications. He prefixed the word 'personal' before the word 'liberty' and he replaced the word 'Union' with the word 'Federation.'[43]

Rau was aware that the chapters on Fundamental Rights and Directive Principles were to reflect the decisions the Constituent Assembly had already taken on them.[44] But using the phrase 'personal liberty' along with the due process guarantee, instead of 'liberty', in Clause 16 of the Draft Constitution was a major deviation from the Assembly's previous decision on the due process guarantee.

What led BN Rau to use the phrase 'personal liberty' in Clause 16 of his Draft Constitution whilst still retaining the phrase 'due process'? And what did he hope to achieve by making this modification, or rather what controversy did Rau seek to avoid by incorporating such a clause on due process? To answer these questions, one needs to delve into the concerns Rau had repeatedly raised over the proper form which the due process guarantee must take in the Indian Constitution.

BN Rau's Early Conception of Due Process: Shield Against an Oppressive State

The Constituent Assembly had begun its deliberations on 9 December 1946, pursuant to the Cabinet Mission Statement of 1946. Much before the Assembly had convened, BN Rau had submitted his 'Notes on Fundamental Rights' on 2 September 1946.[45] The purpose of the Notes was to present the Assembly with certain views on how other countries had dealt with the issue of incorporating fundamental rights. It is in this document that BN Rau first highlighted some of the controversies which surrounded due process rights.

BN Rau began his Notes by observing that although many constitutions enumerated fundamental rights, some considerations must be reviewed in determining how to structure them. He noted that in countries with written constitutions such as the USA, USSR and Ireland, several fundamental rights were enumerated relating to the rights of equality, free speech and religious freedom, to name a few.

Even in countries such as England which did not have a written constitution, charters such as the *Magna Carta* had influenced the creation of a tradition of constitutionalism. What would, therefore, be required of the Constituent Assembly, in respect of fundamental rights would be to define the contours of the rights and to formulate methods for safeguarding them.[46]

Focusing first on the issue of defining the contours of rights, Rau took the example of Germany to demonstrate how *not* to structure rights. He used Article 153 of the 1919 Constitution of Germany, which related to property rights to show that if the limits of a fundamental right were contingent entirely on how the Legislature chose to define them, then fundamental rights were essentially meaningless. According to Rau, 'rights of private property are said to be inviolable except where the law otherwise provides, which means that the rights are not inviolable.'[47]

Rau also took the example of Article 115 of the German Constitution where the fundamental right of treating a citizen's residence as a sanctuary was subject to enacted laws. According to Rau, such an approach allowed states to easily make laws to override rights which effectively meant that 'there is no constitutional guarantee against an oppressive Legislature.'[48] For him, therefore, the model of broadly defining rights and then leaving it to Legislatures to define their scope was not worthy of emulation, for it invited the State to act in an oppressive manner.

The second issue which Rau focused on was of devising effective methods for protecting the enforcement of rights. As he saw it, the ability to protect rights had a direct correlation with how the rights were defined. Ideally, in Rau's conception, rights should not be defined at broad levels of generality since it could lead to uncertainty of how courts understood such rights, rendering them susceptible to endless forms of interpretations.

To guard against this, three possible solutions were presented: first, allow courts to enforce fundamental rights regardless of the structure of the rights; second, make rights non-justiciable and unenforceable, akin to directive principles, thus completely ousting the court's jurisdiction; or, third, allow only a category of rights which are well defined, to be justiciable.[49]

To show how generally defined rights could be susceptible to varying interpretations, Rau turned his attention to the jurisprudence of the US Supreme Court on the due process clause contained in the 5th and 14th Amendments, as well as the jurisprudence on the equality clause contained in the 14th Amendment.[50] Rau began by noting that the due process guarantee had attracted an outpouring of judgments and had become the 'most important single basis of judicial review today'.[51]

Rau expounded that due process, which now covered not only procedural due process rights but also substantive due process, meant that rights cannot be interfered with 'without just cause' and that the courts alone were arbiters of what constitutes 'just cause'. The fallout of this, according to Rau, was that individual liberty was affected by virtually every law with a public welfare goal. And all laws of such nature could be judicially reviewed and in fact be invalidated for encroaching on the liberty right contained in the 5th and 14th Amendments, without just cause. As Rau noted:

At first it was regarded as a limitation on procedure and not on substance of legislation; but it has now been settled that it applies to matters of substantive law as well. In fact, the phrase 'due process of law' appears to have become synonymous with 'without just cause' the courts being the judge of what is 'just cause'; and since the object of most legislation is to promote the public welfare by restraining and regulating individual rights of liberty and property, the court can be invited, under this clause, to review almost any law.[52]

What primarily concerned Rau was that, in his view, an examination of the US Supreme Court decisions revealed that doctrinal coherence was absent and the outcome of cases suggested that there was no discernible uniform legal or constitutional principle. Paying close attention to cases of laws concerning public good and public welfare and the due process guarantee, Rau concluded that at different time periods, the due process guarantee was used to both invalidate as well as uphold labour welfare legislation, depending on the US Supreme Court's conception of the liberty right at that point of time.

As he noted, in *Lochner*, a New York legislation regulating the work hours of workers in bakeries was invalidated by the US Supreme Court for interfering with due process and the liberty to contract. But within over a decade, legislation regulating work hours in factories was upheld. In respect of minimum wages, Rau noted that in 1923, the US Supreme Court invalidated legislation which fixed minimum wages for women and children. But in less than fifteen years the US Supreme Court reversed this decision and ruled in favour of minimum wage laws.[53]

BN Rau used the development of American constitutional law and particularly the development of the due process guarantee to demonstrate the perils of a constitution containing generally defined rights. For Rau, a generally defined liberty right along with the due process clause would mean that the Indian Constitution appoints the courts as having the final say on which law is good or bad. In his view, adopting such an approach was rife with deleterious consequences since the enactment of laws would be affected; courts would be inundated with petitions challenging all forms of legislations and arguably, the courts may not adopt a discernible standard of review in all such cases. Finally, to invest in an 'irremovable judiciary' the power to strike down laws made by a Legislature, which is sensitive to public needs and public welfare, would be too high a price to pay. For Rau, rights must not be structured in a manner that results in courts trying to constantly divine the meaning of such generally defined rights.[54]

So far as BN Rau's scepticism about following the US model on the due process guarantee was concerned, some observations are worth considering.

Rau's scepticism was based on a sampling of cases decided by the US Supreme Court. Rau's Notes only partially recounted the history of substantive due process starting from 1905. In decrying the incorporation of due process, Rau relied only on decisions of the US Supreme Court handed down in the early part of the 20th century. This was used to paint a grim picture of welfare measures being under threat, which was done without discussing the then contemporary statement of the law on due process in that time period.[55]

Furthermore, as we saw in Chapter 1, up until 1937, several decisions of the US Supreme Court upheld laws which were motivated by public interest.[56] In fact, in a 1949 decision it had been emphatically asserted that the US Supreme Court had begun to reject challenges to laws which were motivated by a socially ameliorative goal as early as 1934.[57] At any rate, after 1937, the year in which the decision in *West Coast Hotel Co.* was handed down, the US Supreme Court ruled in favour of public welfare laws.[58] Therefore, long before Rau had even been appointed as Constitutional Advisor, the jurisprudential understanding of the due process guarantee in the US Constitution had transformed so fundamentally that it no longer bore any link with the *Lochner* era.

Rau authored his Notes in 1946, by which time the law on substantive due process was no longer in a state of flux, but rather on the contrary, it had been applied in a uniform manner in several decisions.[59] To stop his discussion of due process and the American Constitution with what occurred till 1937, and use older decisions as the basis of fearing due process is problematic because if by the early 1930s itself, *Lochner* was disfavoured in America,[60] there was no reason to raise its bogey in India in 1946.

Moreover, in the 1920s itself, the US Supreme Court had understood the liberty right broadly, which led it to hold that it included the liberty to lead a full and wholesome life and make intimate choices about one's family and the upbringing of one's children. This meant that substantive due process was applied not only to cases of liberty of contract but also to instances involving innate human interests.[61]

In a pair of cases—*Meyer*[62] and *Pierce*[63]—decided in the mid–1920s, the US Supreme Court held that the autonomy of parents to decide on their child's upbringing was protected by the liberty right of the 14th Amendment, and that laws which compelled families to have their children taught in a particular language (*Meyer*), or in a particular form of school system (*Pierce*), unconstitutionally infringed the liberty right and due process guarantee of the 14th Amendment.

Therefore, Rau ought to have also discussed these early cases to show that when laws invaded an individual's ability to make deeply personal choices, without an overriding public interest consideration, the due process guarantee could be used as a shield against such laws and state action.

Rau seemed to have harboured an apprehension that the legitimacy of judicial review was reduced when fundamental rights are not interpreted in a uniform manner. An important reason to avoid the American Constitution's model of the due process guarantee was due to the variations in the way in which the US Supreme Court applied due process, which reduced predictability and certainty in the decision-making process.[64] However, to reject the inclusion of a fundamental right on the proffered ground that its application had not been uniform or that the outcome of cases did not present a predictable and standardized doctrine, would be to reject the autonomy inherent in the process of judicial review.

When adjudicating a legal question, although a court may be presented with a past precedent as possibly answering the question, it still retains freedom and flexibility in deciding how to answer the legal question as well as how much weight is to be accorded to the precedent. After all, judges, in some measure 'have significant latitude in how they view, define, and apply inconsistencies and ambiguities in such prior decisions.'[65] To demand that courts function only along a linear pattern would be to reduce judicial review to a formulaic exercise.

Historically, in deciding cases involving fundamental rights, constitutional courts sometimes over a course of time, reach a different conclusion based on an evolved and more nuanced understanding and appreciation of a fundamental right. Rau perhaps did not fully account for the fact that variations in adjudicatory outcomes occasioned by a transformed understanding of the constitution was an integral and inexorable part of the judicial process.

It is worthwhile to note, that in the USA itself, and just before Rau had begun to express his views on the structure of rights, other fundamental rights also witnessed variations in judicial outcomes, for instance, as is noticeable in the 'Flag Salute' cases.

In *Gobitis*[66] the US Supreme Court held that children belonging to minority religions could be compelled to salute the American flag, even if it were contrary to their religious beliefs. But within three years, in 1943, the US Supreme Court in *Barnette*[67] overruled *Gobitis*, and came to the opposite conclusion that it was unconstitutional to force those whose religious beliefs do not allow it, to salute the flag.[68]

This variation in judicial outcome and a changed understanding of liberty and religious freedom, which occurred within a few years, did not lead Rau to argue that on this score, India must abandon all efforts to promote religious freedom and autonomy or that the Constitution must promote religious orthodoxy on this ground. In fact, Rau's Draft Constitution contained fundamental rights which prohibited religious discrimination[69] as well as detailed fundamental rights which promoted religious freedom.[70]

Therefore, to peg the rejection of due process on the fact that courts can have variations in outcome was not a principle which was applied uniformly to the entire Constitution or, for that matter, treated as the guiding principle to determine the incorporation of fundamental rights. What truly makes Rau's position intriguing is that he was a former judge, but did not really pin any hopes on the judiciary.[71] Perhaps familiarity did breed contempt.

To be sure, BN Rau most certainly did not want to give life, liberty and due process rights a complete go by or couch rights in language which permitted legislatures to violate them at will, or for that matter create a judiciary which would not enforce fundamental rights.

When Rau turned to analyse the Irish Constitution of 1937, he noted that certain fundamental rights were structured in a manner which would perhaps allow courts to declare a law unconstitutional, if it contravened a fundamental right. But some of the other rights barely qualified as fundamental rights, in the sense of protecting persons from certain forms of state action. Rau examined the personal liberty right contained in Article 40(4)1° of the Irish Constitution and was convinced that such a formulation was not a fundamental right at all.[72] Article 40(4)1° read: 'No citizen shall be deprived of his personal liberty save in accordance with law.'[73]

According to Rau, such language in a right, even if enforceable through courts, served no useful purpose since a valuable right concerning personal liberty was entirely subject to a law made by the *Oireachtas* (Irish Legislature). What this meant was that by enacting a law, the State could easily restrict the right to personal liberty without the right itself affording any checks. For Rau, in the most extreme conception, the Irish Legislature could, by law, tcar the personal liberty right asunder. Therefore, making the fundamental right of personal liberty subservient to legislative will rendered the right meaningless and conferred no protection against state actions. This model of rights was unworthy of emulation.[74] As Rau put it:

> But a provision such as 'No citizen shall be deprived of his personal liberty save in accordance with law' occurring in section 40(4)1° cannot invalidate any law and is really meaningless as a guarantee against oppressive laws after enactment.[75]

For Rau, making a valuable right such as the one protecting life and liberty contingent entirely on legislative action meant that the right was nothing more than a moral precept. What also drove Rau to reject the model of the Irish Constitution was the fear that once a fundamental right dealing with personal liberty was entirely dependent upon the law-making powers of the State, then all that an oppressive State needs to do is to pass a law which restricts the fundamental right—a situation in which fundamental rights afford neither safety nor security to the people.

It is also crucial to note that Rau was also critical Article 40(4)1° of the Irish Constitution, for it entirely disabled courts from conducting any inquiry into a law which truncated the personal liberty right. For Rau, Article 40(4)1° could not at all be classified as a fundamental right.[76]

We can thus see that in 1946, the message that BN Rau conveyed was that when the Constituent Assembly deliberated on enumerating Fundamental Rights, the choice must not be made between two extremes.

On the one hand was the case of the American Constitution which in defining the due process right in general terms had allowed courts to determine what was right or not, with the result that even the court's approach in interpreting and protecting rights was haphazard. On the other, the approach of the Irish Constitution, as evidenced by Article 40(4)1° was not worth emulating. A fundamental right on personal liberty was rendered virtually meaningless and incapable of receiving judicial protection, if the legislature could, without the slightest difficulty, encroach on it and render enforceability a mirage.

Therefore, Rau suggested that when the Constituent Assembly deliberated on enumerating fundamental rights, the choice must not be made between two extremes. It must adopt a middle path. In 1946, he proposed that a justiciable Bill of Rights may be a necessity for India, but the fundamental rights will have to be structured very carefully.[77]

The central message projected by Rau in his Notes was that the Constituent Assembly must neither enumerate fundamental rights which are amorphous in their meaning nor structure them as mere incantations. Equally, Rau proposed a systematized process by which courts would have the jurisdiction to question legislation and enforce fundamental rights. But the powers of the court ought not to extend to questioning laws meant to promote social welfare and the public good. In Rau's conception, the structure of rights would have an inextricable link with the scope of judicial review as well as the attainment of the common good.

BN Rau and the Advisory Committee

As part of the drafting process from the early days and as Constitutional Advisor, BN Rau participated in the deliberations of the Sub-Committee on Fundamental Rights as well as in the deliberations of the Advisory Committee, when it discussed the Sub-Committee's Reports. In the proceedings before both these committees, Rau provided a careful analysis of the move towards incorporating a due process guarantee as a fundamental right.

Note of 8 April 1947

As we saw in Chapter 1, the Fundamental Rights Sub-Committee had submitted its Draft Report of the Sub-Committee on 3 April 1947. This was the first version of the report which the Sub-Committee would submit to the Advisory Committee. In that Draft Report, the clause on due process was contained in Clause 11.[78] After the Draft Report had been submitted, BN Rau submitted two sets of notes, in which, amongst other things, he voiced his concern over the language used in Clause 11.

In his 'Notes on the Draft Report' of 8 April 1947, Rau in reference to Clause 11 simply noted: 'Adapted from the USA Constitution, Amendment V and Amendment 14, Section 1.'[79]

Accompanying the Notes on the Draft Report was a 'Note by the Constitutional Advisor *(BN Rau) on the Effect of Some of the Proposed Clauses.*'[80] The purpose of this second note was to outline the 'possible effect of certain provisions of the draft.'[81] Here Rau critically examined the feasibility of including a due process clause, such as Clause 11 as part of Fundamental Rights.

Rau posited that since Clause 11 was a blend of the due process clause contained in the 5th and the 14th Amendment to the US Constitution, all the controversies which had arisen in America over the interpretation and meaning of due process would also arise in India. And since the Sub-Committee proposed that all laws, including laws enacted prior to the Constitution, were to be tested against fundamental rights (see Clause 2 of the Draft Fundamental Rights),[82] India would witness an enormous rise in litigation pertaining to the due process guarantee.[83] According to Rau:

> The result is likely to be a vast flood of litigation immediately following upon the new Constitution. Tenancy laws, laws to regulate money lending, laws to relieve debt, laws to prescribe minimum wages, laws to prescribe maximum working hours of work etc. will all be liable to be challenged; and not only those which may be enacted in future but also those which have already been enacted.[84]

As he saw it, the incorporation of the due process guarantee as envisaged by the Fundamental Rights Sub-Committee was not a moment of celebration but a cause for deep concern. For Rau, use of the word 'liberty' in conjunction with 'due process' would spell doom for all efforts made towards social welfare, public good and redistribution efforts. In so speaking, Rau echoed a concern that he had voiced previously in 1946: for a nation such as India, it was impractical for the judiciary to have the final say on matters of public welfare and social good, and to second-guess legislative wisdom. But this was exactly what the Constitution would achieve by enumerating a clause on liberty with due process, at its broadest level of generality.[85]

On the issue of property rights, Rau observed that protection against the taking of property was not only protected by the due process guarantee in Clause 11, but also in Clause 27. As per Clause 27, no property of any kind belonging to anyone could be taken for public use, unless legislation for that purpose 'provides for the payment of just compensation.'[86]

According to Rau, affording such heightened due process protection against the taking of property by the State would mean that apart from protecting persons against 'predatory legislation', laws affecting property redistribution would not pass muster in a court of law. Rau believed that both these clauses would 'stand in the way of beneficial social legislation.'[87] What he feared was that such an approach would render the goal of achieving social progress and equality in property rights nearly impossible.

To chart a course out of this difficulty, Rau suggested a 'middle course'[88] akin to Article 43(2) of the Irish Constitution, an article which attenuated property rights to the extent that they may not prevail over what is essential for the common good.[89] Taking a lead from this, Rau recommended the incorporation of a new provision, Clause 27A, which would not allow property rights to prevail over the 'common good' for society.'[90] It would guard against expropriation of property by the State, but at the same time allow the State to enact laws for achieving the common good.

It is worth noting that in this second Note, what mainly seemed to concern Rau was that strong due process protection was accorded both to the liberty interest as well as to property rights. However, for Rau, even though the use of 'liberty' in the due process guarantee could result in similar controversies as the US had witnessed, he did not recommend its deletion. Rather, he used this second Note as an opportunity to warn the Fundamental Rights Sub-Committee of what the possible fallout would be if a broadly worded due process guarantee were to be recommended as a fundamental right for property rights.

For Rau, protecting a person's life and liberty was an important goal to be achieved through the medium of fundamental rights, but he differed from the Sub-Committee on Fundamental Rights on the mode of achieving that protection. So far as property rights were concerned, Rau believed that such rights must ideally not be entitled to any due process protection, which is why in respect of property rights alone, Rau suggested the inclusion of the proposed Clause 27A.

As we saw in Chapter 1, the Fundamental Rights Sub-Committee submitted its 'Report of the Sub-Committee on Fundamental Rights' along with the draft fundamental rights, for the second time around on 16 April 1947. In that, the clause on due process which was contained in Clause 12 of the Report, had been redrafted to now also include a clause on equal protection, thus taking it much closer to the language of the 14th Amendment to the US Constitution. Further, a separate clause on property rights was also contained in Clause 26.[91] When the Advisory Committee took up this second Report of the Sub-Committee of 16 April 1947 for discussion, one of the primary concerns which arose was that due process protection was granted to property rights.

To a large extent, BN Rau's warning about the fallout of including 'property' in the clause on due process, in addition to having a standalone clause which protected property rights, seemed to have presaged the concern which the Advisory Committee was voicing. Alarmed that such robust protection for property rights might derail the land reform project which India was to embark upon, the Advisory Committee eventually decided to delete the reference to 'property' in the clause on due process and deal with property as a separate subject.

As we saw, it was for this reason that the Advisory Committee in its Interim Report, provided a clause on due process in Clause 9 which extended due process protection only to 'life' and 'liberty', and not for 'property'. In Clause 19 of the Interim Report, which carried forward the Sub-Committee's draft clause as contained in Clause 26 of their second Report,[92] property was dealt with as a separate subject.[93] In the Interim Report, the Advisory Committee did not recommend a provision such as Rau's proposed Clause 27A.[94]

Now although the due process guarantee did not apply to property rights, there still remained the issue of 'liberty' being used in the due process guarantee. The focus of BN Rau's attention would now shift to incorporating a narrower version of the liberty right in the due process guarantee.

From 'Liberty' to 'Personal Liberty'

On 30 April 1947, the Constituent Assembly voted to resolve that in the new Constitution, people would have the fundamental right of not being deprived of their life or liberty without due process. Since the word 'liberty' had been used, Rau's concerns about the due process guarantee's feasibility for a nation such as India still remained.

For Rau, liberty would become not only a shield against state intervention, but would be used as a sword to invalidate any legislation which affected the liberty of the people, whether directly or remotely. As a result, a variety of legislations such as laws concerning social welfare, public good, equality of payment of wages, labour welfare would all be open to challenge.

Until now, Rau's role was confined to advising the Constituent Assembly, which was free to reject his advice. Now in August 1947, with Rau tasked with the responsibility of drafting the Draft Constitution, he was able to play a more direct role in the shaping of the due process guarantee, which meant he was in a position to ensure that the due process guarantee did not suffer the same fate in India, as it did in the US.

We can now begin to see why Clause 16 in Rau's Draft Constitution departed from the due process guarantee as agreed upon by the Assembly during its vote on 30 April 1947. Rau's concern was that using the word 'liberty' in the due process clause would create havoc and potentially endanger a host of laws which dealt with public good and social welfare; a concern that the neither the Fundamental Rights Sub-Committee nor the Advisory Committee heeded.

However, in a bid to control the clause on due process, Rau did not believe in rendering the liberty right effete, ineffectual or inconsequential. As we have seen, Rau did not want fundamental rights to completely abdicate their fidelity to protecting the life and liberty of the person. Rau also did not want to empower the State to infringe on a person's liberty without any checks, or render the judiciary completely incapacitated when laws affecting a person's life and liberty were questioned in the court of law.

In Rau's conception, creating a fundamental right which enabled the State to be oppressive was not the price to be paid for tempering the due process guarantee. The task before Rau, therefore, was to properly reconcile due process rights which were justiciable, and which granted courts adequate powers to check the violation of fundamental rights, with the State's ability to make laws on matters of social welfare and public good.

The formula Rau thus devised, for a balanced clause on due process in his Draft Constitution, was to blend the 14th Amendment to the US Constitution with Article 40(4)1° of the Irish Constitution, and arrive at an entirely new version of the due process guarantee. This blend was represented in the language of Clause 16 of Rau's Draft Constitution, a fact which is borne out by the marginal note to Clause 16 in it.[95] For Rau, it was the appropriate middle path between two extreme versions of rights pertaining to life and liberty.[96]

This middle path would strengthen the individual's hand in protecting their life and personal liberty, and at the same time strengthen the State's hand in achieving social welfare. By taking the phrase 'personal liberty' from the Irish Constitution and the phrase 'due process' from the American Constitution, what Rau perhaps envisaged was that when state actions affected the individual personally in their sense of 'being' and 'freedom', then the due process guarantee could be triggered to repel such state action.

However, since the phrase 'personal liberty' was used, courts perhaps would not be able to enact a '*Lochner* era' like scenario in India, and laws pertaining to social and economic welfare could not be questioned under the clause on due process. Rau thus conceived that prefixing the word 'personal' before the word 'liberty' in Clause 16 would avoid the controversies that arose over due process in America.

It is important to note that despite his scepticism, Rau retained the phrase 'due process' in Clause 16 of his Draft Constitution. This was seemingly done because, when Rau had analyzed the Irish Constitution's fundamental right on personal liberty in his Notes on Fundamental Rights dated 2 September 1946,[97] he had concluded that if the fundamental right to personal liberty was subservient to legislative will, the Constitution would have enacted nothing more than a moral code. This is something that Rau did not wish to follow in India, which is what explains Rau retaining the phrase 'due process' in his Draft Constitution.

If Rau had believed that the State must have the final say over all fundamental rights and courts have no role to play in their enforcement, then he could have easily achieved that by deleting 'due process' altogether. That is something that he did not do. Crucially, for Rau, the cornerstone for preserving and protecting life and personal liberty, was justiciability, which would be the most appropriate means of ensuring that the State could always be kept in check.

That this was Rau's vision for the due process guarantee is brought out in his 'Note on Certain Clauses by the Constitutional Advisor' dated 7 October 1947. In it, Rau noted that in reference to Clause 16 of his Draft Constitution, he had prefixed 'personal' before 'liberty' or else 'liberty might be construed very widely unless qualified.'[98]

To illustrate the point, Rau gave an example in a starred footnote to this note on Clause 16. If the word liberty were to be used without any reservations or limitations, then under the clause on due process 'even price-control might be regarded as interference with liberty (of contract between buyer and seller)'.[99]

Interestingly, at the time the new version of due process contained in Rau's Draft Constitution was presented, it did not raise much controversy with the Drafting Committee. In response to Rau's Draft Constitution, KM Munshi, Alladi Krishnaswami Ayyar and DP Khaitan prepared detailed notes and memoranda in which they recommended several changes, but none of them had anything to say on due process.[100] This perhaps suggests that other members of the Drafting Committee were satisfied with Clause 16 since the due process guarantee had still been retained by Rau in his Draft Constitution.

The BN Rau–Justice Felix Frankfurter Discussions on Due Process

With his Draft Constitution now prepared, BN Rau travelled to America, Canada, Ireland and the UK meeting leaders from these nations to seek their advice on constitution making.[101] After completing his visits, Rau submitted a Report to Dr Rajendra Prasad which chronicled his discussions with these world leaders.[102] In this Report, Rau noted that when he went to America, he had the opportunity of meeting several justices of the US Supreme Court.

After arriving in New York City on 26 October 1947, Rau travelled to Washington, DC, where he met with the Chief Justice of the US Supreme Court (Fred M Vinson), and the former Chief Justice, Charles Evan Hughes. Rau also met with several justices of the US Supreme Court such as Justice Frankfurter, Justice Murphy and Justice Burton.[103]

Rau and Justice Frankfurter seemed to have had spirited discussions, with each having a great impact on each other.

Impressed with BN Rau's erudition, Justice Frankfurter famously remarked:

> If the President of the U.S.A. were to ask me to recommend
> a judge for our Supreme Court on the strength of his
> knowledge of the history and working of the American
> Constitution, B.N. Rau would be first on my list.[104]

During their discussions, Justice Frankfurter appears to have advised BN Rau that the new Indian Constitution must be extremely tentative towards due process. He told Rau that the incorporation of a due process guarantee was riddled with problems since it was contrary to democratic norms and encumbered the working of the judicial branch. As Rau records:

> Indeed, Justice Frankfurter considered that the power
> of judicial review implied in the due process clause of
> which there is a qualified version in clause 16 of our Draft
> Constitution was not only undemocratic (because it gave
> a few judges a power of vetoing legislation enacted by the
> representatives of the nation) but also threw an unfair
> burden on the judiciary.'[105]

Justice Frankfurter also advised Rau on other aspects including that the Constitution must ensure that the Supreme Court hears its cases *en banc* (a judicial system in which all the justices decide all the cases together, rather than in smaller and separate benches), apart from drawing his attention to legal developments in New York on the issue of removal of judges from office.[106]

BN Rau also met another great legal luminary, Judge Learned Hand, who at that time served on the United States Court of Appeal for the Second Circuit and was strongly opposed to the idea of a constitution even containing fundamental rights. According to Rau, Hand suggested that 'it would be better to have all fundamental rights as moral precepts than as legal fetters in the Constitution.'[107]

Justice Frankfurter has been much celebrated in India for the advice he gave BN Rau.[108] However, the nature of his advice on due process has been faulted, for he relied primarily on a set of antiquated decisions of the US Supreme Court to influence Rau against the perils of due process and used the body of law which pertained to the liberty of contract to condemn substantive due process in its entirety.[109]

Moreover, Justice Frankfurter purportedly belonged to the school of thought which believed courts must not question legislative will.[110] But despite his ideological leanings, his espousal of courts needing to be non-interventionist is tendentious given that Justice Frankfurter was no shrinking violet when it came to cases in which he believed that the law in question ought to be struck down.[111] This is of particular importance given how Justice Frankfurter had attempted to influence Rau against the idea of courts being empowered to invalidate legislations.

Rau had carefully chosen the language of Clause 16 of his Draft Constitution in order to reconcile the need for a due process guarantee with the need for the Constitution to allow the implementation of laws with a public welfare aim without being impeded by constitutional challenges. That reconciliation was achieved in the form of Clause 16 using the phrase 'personal liberty.'

A standard tale that has often been recounted is that after meeting Justice Frankfurter and Judge Learned Hand, Rau recommended that there be no due process guarantee at all and it is this which caused the 'due process' guarantee to disappear from what would later become Article 21 of the Indian Constitution.[112]

That does not seem to be the case. On the other hand, from available sources, it appears that after meeting them and hearing their concerns over due process, Rau nevertheless decided to retain the due process guarantee in Clause 16 of his Draft Constitution, rather than recommending its deletion.

Nonetheless, perhaps due to the fact that legal luminaries in the US who were steeped in the culture of interpreting the Constitution viewed the due process guarantee with some trepidation, Rau aimed to neutralize the threat of a constitutional challenge directed at public welfare and social progress measures. This much is clear from Rau's writings itself on this matter.[113]

Rau's solution was to place Directive Principles of State Policy not only above the due process guarantee, but above all Fundamental Rights. To that end, Rau recommended the introduction of an amendment to Clause 9 and Clause 10 in his Draft Constitution.

In his Air Letter of 11 November 1947, sent to the Constituent Assembly from Washington, DC, Rau outlined that after his meetings in Washington, DC, and Ottawa (Canada), he was recommending some amendments to his Draft Constitution.[114] First, Rau recommended that Clause 9(2) must be made secondary and contingent to Clause 10. The proposed amendment to Clause 9(2) was intended to read as follows:

> Subject to the provisions of section 10, Nothing in this Constitution shall be taken to empower the State to make any law which curtails or takes away or which has the effect of curtailing or taking away any of the rights conferred

by Chapter II of this Part except by way of amendment of this Constitution under section 232 and any law made in contravention of this sub-section shall, to the extent of the contravention, be void.[115] (Underlining denotes the proposed amendment.)

The second recommendation was that in Clause 10, a new paragraph must be added which would read:

The principles of policy set forth in Chapter III of this Part are intended for guidance of the State. While these principles are not cognizable by any court, they are nevertheless fundamental in the governance of the country and it shall be the duty of the State to apply these principles in making laws.

No law which may be made by the State in the discharge of its duty under the first paragraph of this section and no law which may have been made by the State in pursuance of these policies now set forth in Chapter III of this part shall be void, merely on the ground that it contravenes the provisions of section 9, or is inconsistent with the provisions of Chapter II of this Part.[116] (Underlining denotes the proposed amendment.)

In the same Air Letter, Rau presented the reasons which justified these amendments. As he noted, laws enacted to give effect to a directive principle are meant for the benefit of the entirety of the people but fundamental rights are meant to be enjoyed by individuals in their personal capacity. Therefore, when faced with a situation where a law meant to further a directive principle collides with a fundamental right, it is the fundamental right which must cede ground to the directive principle. Rau offered two rationales for this new vision for the Constitution.

As Rau saw it, Clause 10 of his Draft Constitution stipulated that Directive Principles of State Policy are fundamental to governance and meant for the greater good of society. Rau believed that it would then be essential to ensure that laws made to give effect to them must continue to retain their standing in the face of a legal challenge. Otherwise, making such laws would be imprudent if not an entirely wasteful exercise since fundamental rights would render directive principles of little use. For him, this line of reasoning was justified on the ground that 'general welfare should prevail over the individual right'.[117]

Furthermore, Rau noted that in America, courts had fashioned the doctrine of 'police powers' to determine circumstances under which it was constitutional for a law to affect a fundamental right. In order to avoid a case-by-case development of the conditions under which a public welfare law could survive constitutional scrutiny, Rau believed that with the proposed amendment to Clause 9, it would be clear to all courts that when a law was in furtherance of a Directive Principle of State Policy, it would be *per se* in the public interest and for the welfare of the people.[118]

Despite there appearing to be a causal link between Rau's meetings with Justice Frankfurter and Judge Learned Hand and Rau's proposed amendments, it is interesting to note that these proposed amendments were not by any means brand new. Rather they had always been churning at the back of Rau's mind.

When Rau submitted his Draft Constitution in October 1947, he had also submitted a 'Note on Certain Clauses' dated 7 October 1947. In discussing the chapter on Directive Principles of State Policy, Rau had noted that as per his Draft Constitution, a law which was in furtherance of a directive principle could be invalidated for violating a fundamental right. At that time, Rau had wondered whether it would be prudent to enumerate in the Constitution that laws giving effect to a directive principle ought to be immune from judicial review entirely:

> It is therefore a matter requiring careful consideration whether the constitution might not expressly provide that no law made and no action taken by the State in the discharge of its duties under Chapter III of Part III (which deals with directive principles of State policy) shall be invalid merely for reason for its contravening the provision of Chapter II of the same Part (which deals with fundamental rights); clause 9(2) of the draft would then need consequential modifications.[119]

We can now see that in October 1947 itself, Rau had been exploring the idea of introducing some change in the Draft Constitution to protect laws giving effect to a directive principle, but had not yet acted on it.

Thus, the amendments which he recommended in his Air Letter of 11 November 1947 were to give effect to an idea that Rau had already conceived of, and his world travels only convinced him to act on an instinct he already had about the interplay between fundamental rights and directive principles. But above all, it must be remembered that Rau did not recommend that the due process guarantee be deleted.

Regardless of the motives which compelled Rau to propose these amendments in November 1947 after his travels (which were no doubt well meaning), their combined effect was far-reaching and essentially imbalanced the Constitution. Rau had started out by recognizing that fundamental rights must be justiciable and enforceable. But after his visit to America, Rau was convinced that fundamental rights though justiciable, must be subordinate to directive principles. Even if such laws giving effect to directive principles violated fundamental rights, the law would pass muster and courts would be barred from invalidating such laws. Importantly, these proposed amendments immunized laws giving effect to directive principles from all fundamental rights, rather than only from the due process guarantee contained in Clause 16 of the Draft Constitution.

Moreover, these two proposed amendments to the Draft Constitution had the effect of depriving individuals of the right to petition the Supreme Court to enforce their fundamental rights. Since Rau believed that the Directive Principles of State Policy contained principles which were meant to achieve social and public good, preventing judicial review of laws enacted to give effect to them was critical. His proposed amendments created a safe harbour provision to ensure that fundamental rights (including the due process guarantee) would never be a threat to state action aimed at giving effect to the directive principles.

For Rau, the ultimate goal of achieving public good would merit the negation of not only due process rights but of the whole chapter on fundamental rights. With these proposed amendments, a second instance was sought to be created in which fundamental rights would remain in suspended animation and be unenforceable. The first instance was contained in Clause 28(2) of Rau's Draft Constitution, where the right to move the Supreme Court for the enforcement of fundamental rights could be suspended during a period of disturbance or emergency.

Despite these proposed amendments to his Draft Constitution, Rau did not recommend the deletion of Clause 16 and the due process guarantee was still retained. Seen in this light, Justice

Frankfurter and Judge Learned Hand did not successfully persuade Rau to abandon due process altogether.

So, what did Clause 16 ultimately promise? According to Granville Austin, the preeminent historian of the Indian Constitution, Rau had intended that Clause 16 will preserve only procedural due process rights and not extend any substantive due process rights.[120] However, Austin's view only partially captures what Rau intended. Clause 16 Rau's Draft Constitution had a different purpose altogether.

In the original version of the Draft Constitution, Rau had intended on retaining due process protection, including substantive due process, against all measures which did not partake of the character of economic and public welfare laws. Rau was not opposed to due process in its entirety and this meant that substantive due process could be pressed into service in all of those situations in which state action was for a purpose other than public welfare. What was absent, however, from Clause 16, was the fact that such a limiting principle had not been expressly stipulated.

In a bid to enumerate this limiting principle—that the due process guarantee must not affect laws promoting public welfare—as an article in the Constitution itself, Rau recommended the introduction of his proposed amendments to Clause 9 and Clause 10 of his Draft Constitution. For Rau, this would have clarified beyond doubt what had always been implicit in the meaning of Clause 16: that the due process guarantee ought not to be used to test the validity of laws giving effect to Directive Principles of State Policy.

For all other laws and state action, the due process guarantee in the form of both substantive due process and procedural due process, could be availed by a person complaining of a violation of their right to life or personal liberty.

Rau had outlined numerous reasons for being tentative towards the due process guarantee in its relationship with public welfare laws, which led him to truncate its meaning in his Draft Constitution. But his unwavering commitment towards a constitution robustly protecting the right to life and personal liberty ensured that the due process guarantee was not removed. Rau had attempted to reduce the due process guarantee's scope of operation but leave a semblance of it, since Clause 16 could still be pressed into service against a law which did not deal with a Directive Principle of State Policy.

Nevertheless, when the Drafting Committee would begin discussing Rau's Draft Constitution, the due process guarantee would once again come under sharp focus, and in the due course of time, eventually disappear from the Constitution, without so much as leaving a footprint in the sands of time.

Endnotes

1   B Shiva Rao, *Framing of India's Constitution*, vol. I, pp. 360–361.
2   Id., p. 361.
3   Id., pp. 362–363.
4   Id., p. 362.
5   CAD, vol. V, pp. 3–5.
6   Id., p. 4.
7   Id., p. 9.
8   Id., pp. 9–10.
9   Under the Indian Independence Act, 1947, the Constituent Assembly would additionally perform legislative functions till such time a Legislature was elected in accordance with the Constitution. See 'Report of Committee on the Functions of the Constituent Assembly under the Indian Independence Act', CAD, vol. V, 25 August 1947, pp.

289–291. The Indian Independence Act was finally repealed by Article 395 of the Indian Constitution.

10   Id., pp. 293–294.

11   Incidentally, after Independence, the Constituent Assembly would for some days discuss other reports such as that of the Union Constitution Committee and the Report of the Advisory Committee on Minorities. See CAD, vol. V, pp. 69–285.

12   Id., pp. 294–295.

13   Id., p. 303.

14   Id., p. 306.

15   Id., pp. 301–302. (Emphasis added.)

16   Id., p. 301. (Emphasis added.)

17   Ibid. (Emphasis added.)

18   Id., p. 309.

19   Kanchan Karopady Bannerjee, *The Benegal Brothers: The Story of a Family and its Times 1864–1975* (India: Ameya Prakashan, 2010), pp. 55–56 [hereinafter Bannerjee, The Benegal Brothers].

20   S Gopal, *Selected Works of Jawaharlal Nehru*, vol. I (New Delhi: Orient Longman, 1972), p. 56. In Nehru's words: 'The Brahmin boy who is alluded to in such complimentary terms is the brother of Rau who just failed to get through to the I.C.S. last year. He came here the same term as I did and is going to take the maths trip next year. I did not know before reading this letter that he was so frightfully clever. He certainly works hard. The only times I ever see him is in hall or going to hall or lectures. I believe he works all the rest of the time. The other Rau to whom Nehru referred to was B Rama Rau who went on to join the Indian Civil Service in 1919. B Rama Rau had a storied career and has the distinction of being the longest serving Governor of the Reserve Bank of India, from 1949 to 1957. See Bannerjee, *The Benegal Brothers*, pp. 68–76.

21   Elangovan, *Norms and Politics*, pp. 17–18.

22   Sir Benegal Narsing Rau, *India's Constitution in the Making*, ed. B Shiva Rao (Madras: Allied Publishers, 1960), p. xix [hereinafter Rau, *India's Constitution in the Making*].

23   Elangovan, *Norms and Politics*, p. 19.

24   Rau, *India's Constitution in the Making*, p. xix.

25   AIR 1939 Cal 628.

26   Justice ES Venkataramiah, *B.N. Rau: Constitutional Advisor* (New Delhi: NM Tripathi Pvt. Ltd., 1987), pp. 6–7 [hereinafter Venkataramiah,

Rau]. The judgment of the Supreme Court is reported at 1956 SCR 393.

27 Bannerjee, *The Benegal Brothers*, pp. 61–62.

28 Id., p. 62; *Elangovan, Norms and Politics*, p. 22.

29 Rau, *India's Constitution in the Making*, pp. xxii–xxiii.

30 Venkataramiah, *Rau*, pp. 17–18.

31 Elangovan, *Norms and Politics*, p. 33, note 69. Also see, Rau, *India's Constitution in the Making*, p. xxvi.

32 Rau, *India's Constitution in the Making*, pp. xxx–xxxi.

33 Id., p. xxxii.

34 The Editors of Encyclopaedia Britannica, 'Sir Benegal Narsing Rau: Indian Jurist', Encyclopaedia Britannica, 22 February 2021(available at https://www.britannica.com/biography/Benegal-Narsing-Rau).

35 Rau, *India's Constitution in the Making*, p. xxxiii; Bannerjee, *The Benegal Brothers*, p. 66.

36 B Shiva Rao, *Framing of India's Constitution: Select Documents*, vol. III (New Delhi: Indian Institute of Public Administration, 1967), pp. 3–197 [hereinafter B Shiva Rao, *Framing of India's Constitution*, vol. III].

37 Id., pp. 7–12. (Emphasis added.)

38 Id., p. 9. (Emphasis added.)

39 Id., p. 7.

40 Id., p. 12.

41 Id., pp. 12–14.

42 Id., p. 7.

43 Also see, Austin, *The Indian Constitution*, p. 129; Abhinav Chandrachud, 'Due Process', in *The Oxford Handbook of the Indian Constitution*, ed. Sujit Choudhry, Madhav Khosla and Pratap Bhanu Mehta (New Delhi: Oxford University Press, 2016), p. 780 [hereinafter Chandrachud, 'Due Process'].

44 Rau, *India's Constitution in the Making*, p. 127.

45 B Shiva Rao, *Framing of India's Constitution*, vol. II, pp. 21–36.

46 Id., pp. 21–22.

47 Id., p. 22.

48 Ibid.

49 Ibid.

50 For a critical examination of Rau's analysis of the controversies surrounding the 14th Amendment to the US Constitution and the fundamental right to equality see Elangovan, *Norms and Politics*, pp. 176–179.

51   B Shiva Rao, *Framing of India's Constitution*, vol. II, p. 29.

52   Ibid.

53   Id., p. 30. These cases have been discussed in Chapter 1.

54   Id., pp. 30–31.

55   This objection has been raised previously by scholars, but only in passing. See Austin, *The Indian Constitution*, p. 110, note 12; TR Andhyarujina, 'The Evolution of Due Process of Law by the Supreme Court', in *Supreme but not Infallible: Essays in Honour of the Supreme Court of India*, ed. BN Kirpal, Ashok H Desai, Gopal Subramanium, Rajeev Dhavan, and Raju Ramachandran (New Delhi: Oxford University Press, 5th Impression, 2008), p. 196 [hereinafter Andhyarujina, 'Evolution of Due Process'].

56   See for instance the decisions of the US Supreme Court in *Mueller, Blaisdell,* and *Nebbia.* These decisions are discussed in Chapter 1.

57   *Lincoln Federal Labour Union v. Northwestern Iron & Metal Co,* 335 US 525 (1949) (SCC Online version), para 17. ('This Court beginning at least as early as 1934, when the Nebbia case was decided, has steadily rejected the due process philosophy enunciated in the Adair–Coppage line of cases. I[n] doing so it has consciously returned closer and closer to the earlier constitutional principle that states have power to legislate against what are found to be injurious practices in their internal commercial and business affairs, so long as their laws do not run afoul of some specific federal constitutional prohibition, or of some valid federal law ... Under this constitutional doctrine the due process clause is no longer to be so broadly construed that the Congress and state legislatures are put in a strait jacket when they attempt to suppress business and industrial conditions which they regard as offensive to the public welfare.')

58   See Chapter 1.

59   See *Day-Brite Lighting Inc v. State of Missouri,* 342 US 421 (1952) (SCC Online version), para 6. ('But if our recent cases mean anything, they leave debatable issues as respects business, economic, and social affairs to legislative decision. We could strike down this law only if we returned to the philosophy of the Lochner, Coppage, and Adkins cases.)

60   Abhinav Chandrachud, *Due Process of Law* (Lucknow: Eastern Book Company, 2011), p. 58 [hereinafter, Chandrachud, *Due Process of Law*].

61   See John Heart Ely, 'The Wages of Crying Wolf: A Comment on Roe v. Wade', Yale Law Journal, vol. 82 (1973): p. 938. Ely suggests that

even the decided cases of the US Supreme Court concerning the 'liberty to contract' were cases which in one sense involved a '"human" dimension."' Ibid.

62 *Meyer v. State of Nebraska*, 262 US 390 (1923) (SCC Online version).

63 *Pierce v. Society of Sisters*, 268 US 510 (1925) (SCC Online version).

64 See Madhav Khosla, *India's Founding Moment: The Constitution of a Most Surprising Democracy* (Cambridge, Massachusetts: Harvard University Press, 2020), pp. 66–67.

65 Michael J Gerhardt, 'The Role of Precedent in Constitutional Decisionmaking Process and Theory', The George Washington Law Review, vol. 60 (1991): p. 90 (internal citation omitted).

66 *Mineresville School Dist v. Gobitis*, 310 US 596 (1940) (SCC Online version).

67 *West Virginia State Board of Education v. Barnette*, 319 US 624 (1943) (SCC Online version).

68 See Melvin I Urofsky, 'The Flag Salute Case', OAH Magazine of History, vol. 9 (1995): 30.

69 B Shiva Rao, *Framing of India's Constitution*, vol. II, pp. 7–8. See Clause 11(1) and Clause 12(2).

70 Id., p. 10. See Clause 2 and Clause 21.

71 Elangovan, *Norms and Politics*, p. 179.

72 B Shiva Rao, *Framing of India's Constitution*, vol. II, pp. 31–32.

73 Id., p. 32.

74 Ibid.

75 Ibid. (Italics in the original.)

76 Ibid.

77 Id., p. 36.

78 Clause 11: No person shall be deprived of his life, liberty, or property without due process of law. See B Shiva Rao, Framing of India's Constitution, vol. II, p. 139.

79 Id., p. 148.

80 Id., pp. 151–153.

81 Id., p. 151.

82 Clause 2: Any law or usage in force within the territories of the Union immediately before the commencement of the Constitution and any law which may hereafter be made by the State inconsistent with the provisions of this Chapter/Constitution shall be void to the extent of such inconsistency. See B Shiva Rao, *Framing of India's Constitution*, vol. II, p. 138.

83 Id., p. 151.

84 Ibid.

85 Ibid.

86 Id., p. 141.

87 Id., p. 151.

88 Ibid.

89 Id., p. 152.

90 Ibid. Clause 27A read as follows: 'The State may limit by law the rights guaranteed by sections 11, 16 and 27 whenever the exigencies of the common good so require.'

91 Id., pp. 172, 174.

92 See 'Report of the Sub-Committee on Fundamental Rights' (16 April 1947). B Shiva Rao, *Framing of India's Constitution*, vol. II, p. 174.

93 Clause 19 read as follows: 'No property, movable or immovable, of any person or corporation including any interest in any commercial or industrial undertaking, shall be taken or acquired for public use unless the law provides for the payment of compensation for the property taken or acquired and specified the principles on which and the manner in which the compensation is to be determined.' See CAD, vol. III, p. 443. Clause 19 recommended by the Advisory Committee in its Interim Report was debated by the Constituent Assembly on 2 May 1947, and adopted on the same day, without any amendments being made to it. See CAD, vol. III, pp. 511–522.

94 In fact, at the stage of the Fundamental Rights Sub-Committee itself, Rau's proposed Clause 27A did not find approval amongst the members and it was thus not recommended to the Advisory Committee. See B Shiva Rao, *Framing of India's Constitution*, vol. II, p. 166. Minutes of the Meetings of the Sub-Committee dated 15 April 1947. ('Clause 27. Accepted. The committee by a majority decided not to accept the suggestion of Sir B.N. Rau to insert a new clause 27(A) contained in his note dated 8-4-47.')

95 B Shiva Rao, *Framing of India's Constitution*, vol. III, p. 9. 'Protection of life and liberty and equality before law [Cf. U.S.A. Constitution (1868), Art. XIV, S. 1, Irish Constitution Arts. 40(1) & 40(4)].'

96 See BN Rau, Notes on Fundamental Rights dated 2 September 1946 discussing these two extremes.

97 B Shiva Rao, *Framing of India's Constitution*, vol. II, pp. 21–36.

98 Id., p. 199. 'Clause 16: The word "liberty" might be construed very widely unless qualified. Hence the insertion of "personal."' (Italics in the original.)

99 Ibid.

100 'A Note by KM Munshi on Certain Clauses, October 1947.' Id., pp. 205–206; 'A Note on Certain Clauses by Alladi Krishnaswami Ayyar.' Id., pp. 206–214; 'Suggestions and Amendments by DP Khaitan.' Id., pp. 214–216.

101 Rau, *India's Constitution in the Making*, pp. 328–341.

102 B Shiva Rao, *Framing of India's Constitution*, vol. III, pp. 217–234.

103 Id., pp. 217–218.

104 Rau, *India's Constitution in the Making*, p. xxviii.

105 B Shiva Rao, *Framing of India's Constitution*, vol. III, p. 218.

106 Id., pp. 219–220.

107 Id., p. 218.

108 See Upendra Baxi, 'Who Bothers About the Supreme Court? The Problem of Impact of Judicial Decisions', *Journal of the Indian Law Institute*, vol. 24 (1982): 850 [hereinafter Baxi, 'Who Bothers'].

109 Manoj Mate, 'The Origins of Due Process in India: The Role of Borrowing in Personal Liberty and Preventive Detention Cases', Berkeley Journal of International Law, vol. 28 (2010): p. 222 [hereinafter Mate, 'The Origins'].

110 Austin, *The Indian Constitution*, p. 130.

111 Tara Leigh Grove, 'The Supreme Court's Legitimacy Dilemma: Book Review', review of *Law and Legitimacy in the Supreme Court*, by Richard H Fallon Jr, *Harvard Law Review*, vol. 132 (2019): pp. 2264–2265 (internal citations omitted).

112 See B Shiva Rao, *A Study*, p. 235. ('This view [of Justice Frankfurter] was communicated by B.N. Rau to the Drafting Committee which introduced a far-reaching change in the clause by replacing the expression "without due process of law" by the expression "except according to procedure established by law."'); Tripathi, 'Perspectives', p. 85. ('The upshot of it was that he persuaded the Drafting Committee to remove the expression "due process" altogether from the draft to be placed before the Constituent Assembly.'); Baxi, 'Who Bothers', p. 848. ('IN INDIA, the hero-worship of Justice Felix Frankfurter began rather early with the making of the Constitution when Sir B.N. Rau and others were persuaded to drop the phrase "due process" from the chapter on fundamental rights. Many interpreters of the Constitution including the justices of the Indian Supreme Court have admired Frankfurter not just for the felicity of his style; they have held his self-restraint with unabashed admiration and converted his work into a kind of judicial role-model of reticence apt for the Indian appellate judiciary.'); Vijayashri Sripati, 'Towards Fifty Years of Constitutionalism

and Fundamental Rights: Looking Back to See Ahead (1950–2000)',
American University International Law Review, vol. 14 (1998): p. 434.
('Despite the tremendous influence of the United States Bill of Rights
in framing the Indian Constitution's Part III provisions, the absence of
a due process clause is conspicuous. Why is this so? Ironically, it was
the advice of an American jurist, Felix Frankfurter, that contributed
to the demise of this clause in the Constitution.') (internal citation
omitted) [hereinafter Sripati, 'Fifty Years']; HM Seervai, *Constitutional
Law of India*, vol. 2 (Delhi: Universal Traders, 4th edition, 1999), p.
970. ('However, the abuse of substantive due process by the U.S. Sup.
Ct. produced second thoughts, and "due process" was replaced by
"procedure established by law". This change was a result the result of
a discussion which the Constitutional Adviser, Sir B.N. Rau had with
Frankfurter J. of the U.S. Sup. Ct.') (italics in the original) [hereinafter
Seervai, *Constitutional Law of India*]; Andhyarujina, 'Evolution of Due
Process', pp. 197–198. ('Rao (sic) proposed an amendment to the draft
Constitution to eliminate the due process of law clause, in favour of the
expression 'according to procedure established by law.') Id., p. 198. In
narrating the sequence of events, however, Andhyarujina mistakenly
claims that it was the Constituent Assembly which formulated the
Draft Constitution in October 1947. According to Andhyarujina: 'The
Constituent Assembly had favoured due process of law in personal
liberty, and it had been included in the draft Constitution published
in October 1947. However, it was strongly opposed by B.N. Rao (sic).'
Id., p. 197; Chandrachud, *Due Process of Law*, p. 62. ('Perhaps B.N.
Rau's meetings with Frankfurter J, and other American justices had
provided the nail for the due process coffin in India.'); Chandrachud,
'Due Process', pp. 777–778. ('Following Rau's meeting with Frankfurter,
the term 'due process of law' was deleted from the text of India's Draft
Constitution, and replaced with the words 'procedure established by
law.') Id., p. 777. Also see, Id., pp. 780–781 (internal citations omitted
throughout).

113 See Rau, *India's Constitution in the Making*, pp. 328–329. ('As the result
of these discussions, I have proposed two amendments to India's draft
Constitution. The first of them is designed to secure that when a law
made by the State in the discharge of one of the fundamental duties
imposed upon it by the Constitution happens to conflict with one
of the fundamental rights guaranteed to the individual, the former
should prevail over the latter: in other words, the general welfare

should prevail over the individual right.') Id., p. 328. Also see, Austin, *The Indian Constitution*, p. 130.

114 B Shiva Rao, *Framing of India's Constitution*, vol. III, p. 226. In the same letter, Rau proposed amendments to certain other articles as well but those are not being discussed here.

115 Id., p. 226.

116 Ibid.

117 Ibid.

118 Ibid.

119 Id., p. 199.

120 Austin, *The Indian Constitution*, p. 130. ('Rau's emphasis at this time— and it remained so in the future was on the substantive meaning of due process, not the procedural aspect.') This view of Austin has its share of supporters. See Sripati, 'Fifty Years', pp. 435–436.

3

Slings and Arrows

From 'Due Process' to 'Procedure Established by Law'

———◆———

T HE SEVEN-MEMBER DRAFTING COMMITTEE, WHICH HAD BEEN constituted in terms of the Constituent Assembly's resolution of 29 August 1947, met for the first time on 30 August 1947. In its first meeting, the members elected Dr Ambedkar as the Chairman. After working out the modalities of how the Drafting Committee must function in order to settle on a Draft Constitution, it decided to reconvene once BN Rau had submitted his Draft Constitution.[1] After Rau had done so, the Drafting Committee met on 27 October 1947.[2] From this point on, the focus of creating the first version of the Constitution for free India would shift entirely to the Drafting Committee.

In this meeting, only six members were in attendance since BL Mitter was no longer a member of the Constituent Assembly and therefore not a part of the Drafting Committee. After taking a few decisions, including that it was unnecessary to have Rau's Draft Constitution published for comments, and that only the Drafting Committee's draft version should be published,[3] the Committee commenced its clause-wise deliberation of Rau's Draft Constitution.[4] On 5 February 1947, Dr Rajendra Prasad nominated TT Krishamachari to the Drafting Committee owing to the demise of DP Khaitan. And on 5 December 1947, Dr Prasad would appoint N Madhava Rao as a member of the Drafting Committee, to fill the vacancy left by BL Mitter.[5]

On 30 October 1947, the Drafting Committee discussed various clauses including Clause 9 (the provision which stipulated laws which violate fundamental rights are unconstitutional) and Clause 10 (the provision which stipulated that Directive Principles of State Policy although unenforceable ought to guide the State's activities) of Rau's Draft Constitution.[6] On that day, DP Khaitan did not attend the Drafting Committee's meeting.[7] In respect of Clause 9, it was decided to retain the provision as contained in Rau's Draft Constitution but with slight modifications to its structure, without disturbing its content.[8] The Drafting Committee also decided that it would be better if Clause 10 of Rau's Draft Constitution was made a part of the chapter pertaining to Directive Principles of State Policy, rather than it appearing in the chapter on Fundamental Rights.[9] As a consequence of these decisions, the Drafting Committee rejected Rau's recommendations sent to the Constituent Assembly from Washington, DC, in which he had had advised that amendments must be made to these two clauses to ensure that the laws giving effect to the Directive Principles of State Policy should enjoy complete immunity.

On 31 October 1947, the Drafting Committee took up for discussion, amongst other clauses, Clause 16 of Rau's Draft Constitution, which contained the clause on due process.[10] On that day too, DP Khaitan did not attend the Drafting Committee's meeting. When it came to due process, the Drafting Committee was mostly happy with it and in favour of retaining the phrase 'personal liberty', since the Drafting Committee felt that using 'liberty' would mean that it 'might be construed too widely'.[11] To this extent, Rau's views on due process seemed to have prevailed.

KM Munshi disapproved of the phrase 'personal liberty' essentially because the Constituent Assembly had already voted to approve the due process guarantee as a part of fundamental rights on 30 April 1947 (when the Assembly was debating on the fundamental rights which were recommended in the Advisory Committee's Interim Report), without the phrase 'personal liberty'.[12] As we saw in Chapter 1, during those debates, the Assembly had advisedly and after careful deliberation settled on the language of the due process guarantee. But in light of Munshi's opposition, it was decided that the proper course would be to present the justification for using the phrase 'personal liberty' in the Drafting Committee's final report.[13]

On the question of the part of Clause 16 containing the right to equality, the Drafting Committee decided to add the phrase 'equal protection of the laws' after the phrase 'equality before the law'.[14] Thus, on 31 October 1947, Clause 16 read:

> No person shall be deprived of his life or personal liberty without due process of law, nor shall any person be denied equality before the law or the equal protection of the laws within the territory of India.[15]

A few months later, on 19 January 1948, the Drafting Committee once again took up Clause 16 of Rau's Draft Constitution for discussion.[16] On that day a quorum was not reached since only

Dr Ambedkar and N Madhava Rao were present. BN Rau, who had begun attending the Drafting Committee's meetings from 6 December 1947,[17] was also present in his capacity as Constitutional Advisor.

In this meeting, the Drafting Committee noted that the footnote to Clause 16 had been modified.[18] In respect of the phrase 'personal liberty', the first starred footnote read:[19]

> *The, committee is of [the] opinion that the word 'liberty' should be qualified by the insertion of the word 'personal' before it for otherwise it might be construed very widely.[20]

This footnote clearly showed that in substance it was a complete reiteration of the view BN Rau had put forth on Clause 16 in his Note on Certain Clauses which accompanied his Draft Constitution.[21] Evidently, the rationale presented by Rau in October 1947 was accepted by the Drafting Committee as correctly stating the position on the use of the phrase 'personal liberty.'

Another footnote was settled on by the Drafting Committee to justify the modification of Clause 16 insofar as it related to the fundamental right to equality, the modification being that the phrase 'equal protection of the laws' must also be incorporated. The singular purpose of inserting this phrase, according to the Drafting Committee was to replicate the part of the 14th Amendment to the US Constitution pertaining to the right of equality. According to the second double starred footnote:

> **The committee is also of opinion that the words 'or the equal protection of the laws' should be inserted after the words 'equality before the law' as in section (1) of Article XIV of the U.S.A. Constitution (1865).[22]

We can now see that from these meetings when due process was discussed, few important points emerge.

The Drafting Committee was agreed that the due process guarantee should be retained in the form recommended by BN Rau in his Draft Constitution. This is important because till January 1948, 'due process' had not been a point of contestation. Rather, the only point over which differences arose was on whether the word 'liberty' or the phrase 'personal liberty' ought to be used.

In any case, the Drafting Committee thought it advisable to use the phrase 'personal liberty' to ensure that it would be understood in a limited manner and would not stand in the way of measures implemented to achieve public good and social welfare. But the fact that the Drafting Committee had decided not to adopt Rau's proposed amendments in respect of Clauses 9 and 10, recommended in his Air Letter of 11 November 1947, is important. It demonstrated that at least textually in the Constitution, the due process guarantee was not subservient to the laws made to implement the Directive Principles of State Policy.

This is of critical importance, for without Rau's proposed amendments being approved by the Drafting Committee, the possibility of the due process guarantee being available against all forms of laws and state action still remained.

Moreover, the Drafting Committee's intent had been to follow the language and structure of the 14th Amendment to the US Constitution, with some modifications such as avoiding reference to 'property' and using the phrase 'personal liberty'. The purpose of these two modifications was to narrow the scope of the due process guarantee. In fact, the intent of following the language of the 14th Amendment is confirmed by the fact that the Drafting Committee replicated in Clause 16, the entirety of the equal protection clause contained in the 14th Amendment to the US Constitution.[23]

Furthermore, the elaboration provided in the footnote regarding preference for the phrase 'personal liberty' only provides an explanation regarding the ambit of the term, but does not *justify* why the Drafting Committee was going against the express decision of the Constituent Assembly, which voted to adopt the due process guarantee as a fundamental right on 30 April 1947, without the phrase 'personal liberty' in it.

At a normative level, this was problematic because when the Constituent Assembly had debated the resolution constituting the Drafting Committee, it was clear that the Constitutional Advisor was to prepare a Draft Constitution in accordance with the decisions taken by the Assembly and the Drafting Committee was to scrutinize and revise this draft.[24] In all likelihood then, when Rau's version of the due process guarantee did not conform with the previous decision of the Constituent Assembly, it was the Drafting Committee's bounden duty to revise Clause 16 of Rau's Draft, to bring it closer to the version of the due process guarantee accepted by the Assembly on 30 April 1947.

As we have seen in Chapter 2, this idea had been reinforced by Alladi Krishnaswami Ayyar in his speech of 29 August 1947, in the Constituent Assembly, when speaking on the constitution of the Drafting Committee. The narrow remit of the Drafting Committee was to give effect to the decisions that the Assembly had already taken, and not to go against them.[25] Undoubtedly then, the Drafting Committee's decision to use the phrase 'personal liberty' was an express abnegation of the Assembly's previous decision of 30 April 1947 to use 'liberty' along with the due process guarantee. What exacerbates it further is that when the Advisory Committee had settled on the language of the due process guarantee, its decision was a result of detailed debate and made with full knowledge of the potential implications which would arise if the due process guarantee were to have the word 'liberty.'

The decision of the Advisory Committee and thereafter the act of the Constituent Assembly voting in favour of using 'liberty' in the due process guarantee was neither made in haste nor without proper discussion. Factually, too, the Drafting Committee had neither expressed any fault with the prior decision of the Assembly on the due process guarantee, nor had the Drafting Committee concluded that the Assembly's decision was in any way erroneous or riddled with faults. This, to recall Ayyar's speech from 29 August 1947, had been the only two grounds on which the Drafting Committee could depart from the previous decision of the Constituent Assembly.

To, therefore, reject the Constituent Assembly's past decision on the due process guarantee on the cryptic ground that using 'liberty' would mean that it 'might be construed too widely' was to not only summarily reject the Assembly's vote on the due process guarantee, but to subvert the trust the Assembly reposed in the Drafting Committee.

Interestingly, and this is a point which we shall return to in Chapter 8, on 19 January 1948, when the explanation for using 'personal liberty' was approved by the Drafting Committee, only two members were in attendance. This meant that the restructuring of the due process guarantee occurred without a proper debate, and without fully addressing the concerns raised by KM Munshi in the Drafting Committee's meeting of 31 October 1947. What is more, when the wording of Clause 16 was being settled on, even a quorum was not reached for the Drafting Committee's meeting since only Dr Ambedkar and N Madhava Rao were present on that day.[26]

Slings and Arrows

On 21 February 1948, Dr Ambedkar as Chairman of the Drafting Committee submitted the Draft Constitution to the President of the Constituent Assembly. In the report which accompanied the Draft Constitution,[27] Dr Ambedkar began by pointing out that although the remit of the Drafting Committee was to prepare a Draft Constitution, which reflected the decisions that the Constituent Assembly had already taken on a number of issues, the Committee had departed from the Assembly's decisions, wherever it was felt necessary to do so. As Dr Ambedkar wrote:

> In preparing the Draft the Drafting Committee was of course expected to follow the decisions taken by the Constituent Assembly or by the various committees appointed by the Constituent Assembly. This the Drafting Committee has endeavoured to do as far as possible. There were however some matters in respect of which the Drafting Committee felt it necessary to suggest certain changes. All such changes have been indicated in the Draft by underlining or side-lining the relevant portions. Care has also been taken by the Drafting Committee to insert a footnote explaining the reasons for every such change.[28]

With respect to Fundamental Rights, Dr Ambedkar stated that the Drafting Committee had endeavoured to enumerate the rights along with the grounds on which they could be restricted, in a bid to ensure that rights would be understood in a definitive manner by the courts when they would inevitably be called upon to expound on their meaning.[29]

A glance at the Draft Constitution which was submitted by the Drafting Committee[30] reveals that Part III contained the 'Fundamental Rights' which were from draft Articles 7–27.[31] Conspicuous by its absence was the due process guarantee and the language of Clause 16 from BN Rau's Draft Constitution, that had been approved by the Drafting Committee on 19 January 1948.

In its stead was an entirely new fundamental right pertaining to 'life' and 'personal liberty', which was now enumerated in draft Article 15:

> *No person shall be deprived of his life or personal liberty except according to procedure established by law*, nor shall any person be denied equality before the law or the equal protection of the law within the territory of India.[32]

Only when the Drafting Committee submitted its version of the Draft Constitution to the President of the Assembly on 21 February 1948, did it come to light that 'due process' had been defenestrated from the Draft Constitution. Draft Article 15 followed the pattern of Clause 16 of Rau's Draft Constitution in the first part (by reciting 'life' and 'personal liberty'). But now the phrase 'without due process of law' was replaced with the phrase 'except according to procedure established by law.'

With regards to the fundamental right to equality, the latter part of draft Article 15 followed the language and structure which had been settled on by the Drafting Committee during its meetings.

The explanation for such a radical overhaul, where the robust phrase 'due process' was replaced with the supine phrase 'procedure established by law', was provided in the footnote accompanying draft Article 15. The first part of the footnote explained why the phrase 'personal liberty' was being used:

> The committee is of [the] opinion that the word 'liberty' should be qualified by the insertion of the word 'personal' before it, for otherwise it might be construed very widely so as to include even the freedoms already dealt with in article 13.[33]

The second part of the footnote to draft Article 15 presented the reason for using the phrase 'except according to procedure established by law':

> The committee has also substituted the expression 'except according to procedure established by law' for the words 'without due process of law' as the former is more specific (c.f. Art. XXXI of the Japanese Constitution, 1946). The corresponding provision in the Irish Constitution runs: 'No citizen shall be deprived of his personal liberty save in accordance with law.'[34]

The third part of the footnote to draft Article 15 was relatively uncontroversial. It provided that in the latter part of draft Article 15, the phrase 'equal protection of the laws' must be inserted to reflect the language of the 14th Amendment to the US Constitution.[35]

As we have seen, in the Drafting Committee's meetings, the deliberations over the due process guarantee had been confined primarily to discussions over using the phrase 'personal liberty' and it did not extend to deleting 'due process' itself.

According to available sources, the Drafting Committee had settled on Clause 16 of Rau's Draft Constitution in their meeting of 19 January 1948. Thereafter, the Drafting Committee met nine more times in January[36] and eight times in February, with the last meeting held on 13 February 1948.[37]

A reading of the minutes of these subsequent meetings indicate that Clause 16 of Rau's Draft Constitution was not discussed further by the Drafting Committee. It would seem that on 19 January 1948, the Drafting Committee had agreed to incorporate into the Draft Constitution, the version of Clause 16 as settled on that day with due process very much part of it. That apparently was not to be.

Alladi Krishnaswami Ayyar's Switch in Time That Saved Nothing

What transpired between 19 January 1948, when the due process guarantee was still tentatively to be a part of the Draft Constitution and 21 February 1948, when the Draft Constitution was submitted to Dr Rajendra Prasad, wherein draft Article 15 made no reference to due process at all?

Granville Austin speculates that after BN Rau's proposed amendments (to Clauses 9 and 10 of his Draft Constitution) were not accepted by the Drafting Committee, Rau attempted to have the phrase 'according to procedure established by law' replace the due process guarantee.[38] Austin attempts to reconstruct the events leading to the incorporation of draft Article 15 by relying mainly on an interview with KM Munshi and certain other individuals who Austin does not name.[39]

Reportedly, Munshi told Austin that Rau had attempted to persuade a member of the Drafting Committee to rethink their position on due process.[40] Austin's reconstruction of events, which is based only on Munshi's recollection, is as follows:

> The Drafting Committee took up the matter again during its meeting of January 1948, and at some time after 19 January the members decided to omit due process. *It is not clear precisely what happened, but some reconstruction of the event is possible.* Of the seven members of the Drafting Committee at that time (Ambedkar, the chairman, Munshi, Ayyar, N.G. Ayyangar, D.P. Khaitan, N. Madhava Rau [sic], and Mohammed Saadulla), *four had been supporters of due process* – Munshi, Ayyar, Ambedkar and Saadulla. Ayyangar apparently did not support it; *N.M. Rau's* [sic] *views are not known* and Khaitan, a Marwari who was close to Patel, may be presumed to have opposed it. *To eliminate due process, one of the four supporters had to change sides. Apparently this was A.K. Ayyar.* B.N. Rau had several times met Ayyar since his return and had convinced him of the dangers inherent in [the] substantive interpretation of due process. And, as we shall see, Ayyar later became one of the most outspoken opponents of the clause. It is doubtful if Ambedkar or Saadulla also changed sides; certainly Munshi did not. But Ayyar's vote was sufficient.[41]

Let us take a moment to appreciate the unique position Austin was in. In reconstructing the events leading to the abandonment of due process, he was in a position which no scholar can ever aspire to be in: he had access to those who were most familiar with the inner workings of the Constituent Assembly. Austin qualified this narrative by stating that this may not be an exact account of what actually transpired.[42] We have to probe this reconstruction of events with the knowledge that this particular narrative of how due process came to be deleted is largely speculative in nature.

Austin's reconstruction of events raises some questions. He acknowledges that 'NM Rau's' (sic) views on due process were unknown. It is then difficult to discern with any certainty whether or not N Madhava Rao voted to support draft Article 15. Munshi himself provides no account of the voting pattern and as per the available sources, there are no minutes of any meeting of the Drafting Committee which record the precise votes cast in favour of incorporating draft Article 15. It is therefore presumed, speculatively, that 'NM Rau' (sic) opposed due process.

Furthermore, it is also speculated that DP Khaitan opposed the inclusion of the due process guarantee. But, the transcripts of the Drafting Committee's meetings show that Khaitan did not attend the meetings on the two days when the due process guarantee was discussed, and indeed confirmed by the Drafting Committee. So, there is nothing on record, at least officially, to show that Khaitan objected to the inclusion of a due process clause. Even Austin has not speculated that Khaitan had ever opposed due process in the past. Seen in this light, it is difficult to fully understand why it came to be presumed that Khaitan opposed due process, merely due to his proximity to Sardar Patel.

Moreover, it is worth noting that Austin's narrative shows that in deciding whether the due process guarantee was to be part of the Draft Constitution, it was only the seven *members* of the Drafting Committee who could have *decided*, and indeed did decide on it and not those *advising* it. As we saw in Chapter 2, the members of the Drafting Committee were drawn from amongst those who were members of the Constituent Assembly. Therefore, it is only the appointed members of the Drafting Committee, who were first and foremost members of the Assembly, who could have voted to delete due process from the Draft Constitution.

With regard to BN Rau, he was not a member of the Constituent Assembly and thus did not participate in the decision-making process in the same capacity as the members of the Assembly did. Rather, he served the Constituent Assembly in an honorary capacity. Rau's role as Constitutional Advisor extended to matters in which his counsel and advice were sought by the Assembly.[43] So was the case with the Drafting Committee of which Rau was not a member, since the Drafting Committee drew its members from those who were members of the Constituent Assembly.

Seen in this light and irrespective of what influenced him, it is vital to note that as per Munshi's account, it was Ayyar who was the swing vote—the member of the Drafting Committee who at the critical moment, switched from being a proponent of due process to being its opponent. It is this 'switch' that resulted in the deletion of the due process guarantee and led to the introduction of the phrase 'procedure established by law.'[44]

It is also worth noting that Austin's reconstruction of events, based on Munshi's recollections, may not completely square up with BN Rau's consistent stand on retaining some form of due process protection in the Constitution.

BN Rau had throughout preferred the incorporation of a due process guarantee albeit with certain modifications. Even after his world travels and meeting Justice Frankfurter and Judge Learned Hand, Rau did not recommend the deletion of the due process guarantee. He only proposed two amendments to his Draft Constitution to safeguard laws with a public welfare aim and keep them out of the purview of a constitutional challenge; something that even Austin acknowledged.[45] That the Drafting Committee in 1947–1948, had been discussing Clause 16 of Rau's Draft

Constitution which included due process, only confirms the fact that Rau was in favour of the people having robust protection, in other words, due process protection to preserve their life and personal liberty.

In fact, all along Rau had preferred to read the right to life and personal liberty in conjunction with due process. He had done so to avoid couching this fundamental right in language akin to Article 40(4)1° of the Irish Constitution, which in his view weakened the personal liberty right by rendering its existence contingent on the meaning which the State wished to give this right.

Therefore, it seems curious that Rau would suddenly recommend the incorporation of a phrase that was remarkably like the one contained in Article 40(4)1° of the Irish Constitution, when he had in the past consistently opposed the incorporation of such language in a fundamental right. In any case, Rau had not specifically alluded to drawing any inspiration from Article 31 of the Japanese Constitution, when recommending the fundamental right on life and personal liberty in his Draft Constitution.

Ayyar's switch in voting against due process, however, was only one contributing factor which led to its deletion. As Austin speculates, there was another extraordinarily compelling reason which swayed the Drafting Committee against due process: the gruesomely violent aftermath of Indian Independence coupled with the assassination of Mahatma Gandhi on 30 January 1948. According to Austin:

> An added reason for removing due process may have been an increasing conviction that preventive detention provided the best weapon against communal violence that had racked North India during the past year. This view, if existed, could only have been strengthened by the

cataclysm of Gandhi's assassination a few days later on 30
January, 1948.[46]

In the immediate aftermath of Independence, India was ravaged
by a humanitarian crisis and extreme violence. According to the
noted historian Bipin Chandra, Independence and the Partition
of India had resulted in a mass exodus, with approximately six
million people pouring into new India. The joy of Independence
was darkened by acts of extreme communal violence during
which 'nearly 500,000 people were killed and property worth
thousands of millions of rupees was looted and destroyed.'[47]
Indian Independence had left in its wake a humanitarian crisis of
incalculable proportions, with violent outbreaks only increasing
after Independence.

As Austin seems to suggest, it was in these circumstances that
the Drafting Committee was impelled to reconsider its move to
incorporate a due process guarantee.[48]

It should be recalled that the fear that due process would thwart
all efforts at curtailing acts of mindless violence which India
was witnessing in the days before Independence was something
Govind Ballabh Pant had voiced during the proceedings of the
Advisory Committee in April 1947, while debating the feasibility
of recommending the due process guarantee as a fundamental
right.[49] This had been one of the grounds on which Pant had
objected to the due process guarantee.

The fact that external events had a great influence on the
outcome of the Drafting Committee's deliberations was something
that a member of the Drafting Committee alluded to a few years
later. Speaking on 21 November 1949, a few days before the
Indian Constitution would be voted upon for a final time by the
Constituent Assembly, Syed Muhammad Saadulla, acknowledged
that the members of the Drafting Committee were not immune

from the happenings which had taken place around them and that many articles of the Draft Constitution were incorporated under the strain of such events.

In fact, Saadulla acknowledged that several articles in the Constitution which 'jar against the sense of democracy, even of the members of the Drafting Committee, had to be embodied here on account of forces which were superior to that of the Drafting Committee.'[50] Saadulla did not elaborate on which precise events impacted the work of the Drafting Committee, but in light of the above discussion it is not difficult to gather what he may have been alluding to.

All of this indicates that the incorporation of draft Article 15 was not a result of careful deliberation and discussion, but rather the combined effect of the sudden switch by Alladi Krishnaswami Ayyar, from being a supporter of due process to becoming its opponent, coupled with the violent aftermath of Indian Independence and the assassination of Mahatma Gandhi.

These developments appear to have exerted enormous pressure on the Drafting Committee, resulting in the eventual deletion of the due process guarantee as a fundamental right. However, it must be noted that the Drafting Committee, for its part, did not outline the reasons which led to the incorporation of draft Article 15 and the rationale for rejecting the incorporation of the due process guarantee.

Ultimately, the formulation of the right to life and personal liberty without due process was an act of impulsive spontaneity unsupported by strong reasons justifying a departure from the due process guarantee; an act which was given the veneer of a carefully calibrated decision.

At any rate, once the Drafting Committee had agreed that Clause 16 (the due process clause) in Rau's Draft Constitution was a perfectly acceptable fundamental right on due process, there was no conceivable justification to so drastically alter the language of the right that it no longer bore any resemblance to a due process guarantee. The better course of action would have been to either incorporate Clause 16 from Rau's Draft Constitution into the Drafting Committee's Draft Constitution or recommend the version of the due process guarantee as had been voted upon by the Constituent Assembly. This would have allowed the Assembly to decide if it wished to include the due process guarantee in the final Constitution.

This course of action would have been the prudent choice to make since recommending a due process guarantee would have been respectful of the Constituent Assembly's previous decision on due process. It is imperative to remember that the mandate of the Drafting Committee, when it was constituted had been to reduce the past decisions of the Assembly to articles in the Draft Constitution unless that decision seemed erroneous. If the Drafting Committee had demonstrated fidelity to its responsibility, it would have enumerated a due process guarantee in the chapter on fundamental rights. After all, to follow this course of action was by no means a Sisyphean or gargantuan task. Most notably though, in August 1947, it was Ayyar who in a long speech highlighted this role of the Drafting Committee. But in 1948, in rejecting due process, Ayyar seemingly abandoned the advice that he had himself given the Constituent Assembly—less than a year ago—on the proper role of the Drafting Committee.

The New Reason for Personal Liberty

In the first part of the footnote to draft Article 15, an *entirely new reason* was presented for using the phrase 'personal liberty.' Thus far, the word 'liberty' was avoided only to ensure that the liberty right was not generously interpreted to interfere with social welfare legislations and state action aimed at achieving public good. But now a curious shift occurred.

In the Drafting Committee's Draft Constitution, draft Article 13 enumerated seven civil liberty rights such as the freedom of speech and expression; the freedom of movement throughout India; and property rights, to name a few.[51] The Drafting Committee now favoured the phrase 'personal liberty' only as a means of preventing the incorporation of other fundamental rights, specifically the seven rights enumerated in draft Article 13 into draft Article 15.[52] This was an entirely new reason in defence of 'personal liberty' which made an appearance for the first time, and as a footnote in 1948.

Regarding this particular reason for using the phrase 'personal liberty', the acclaimed jurist HM Seervai has reasoned that the approach of the Drafting Committee was correct since the civil liberty rights enumerated in draft Article 13 applied *only* to citizens whereas draft Article 15 applied to *all* persons (which included non-citizens).[53] Be that as it may, this newly minted reason for using 'personal liberty' raised more questions than it answered.

If the only aim of the Drafting Committee was to prevent the incorporation in draft Article 15 of the fundamental rights enumerated in draft Article 13, then that could have been achieved by using 'liberty' instead of 'personal liberty.' In doing so, the Drafting Committee could have then appended to draft Article 15 an explanatory article clarifying that it does not incorporate the rights enumerated in draft Article 13.

The incorporation of rights in draft Article 15 was not intrinsically connected to 'personal liberty', in the sense that this phrase alone is not a constitutional device which presented a frame of reference for the incorporation of rights. If the aim now was to prevent other enumerated rights from being incorporated into draft Article 15, then the Drafting Committee was well placed to use 'liberty' with the above-mentioned clarification on the issue of incorporation of rights; using 'liberty' would have been an ideal choice. Moreover, nothing in the footnote to draft Article 15 stipulated that fundamental rights other than draft Article 13 could not be incorporated in draft Article 15. Several other fundamental rights in the Draft Constitution related to 'persons' while some others neither mentioned 'persons' nor 'citizens.' Viewed on its own, this new explanation provided in the footnote made it possible for fundamental rights, other than those enumerated in draft Article 13, to be incorporated in draft Article 15.

What was also concerning was that prior to this new explanation being offered in favour of 'personal liberty' it would have been arguable that draft Article 15 allowed for the incorporation of all fundamental rights. It is critical to note that the incorporation of rights usually occurs under the rubric of judicial interpretation of constitutional rights,[54] but by this new explanation, the Drafting Committee endeavoured to foreclose any discussion or judicial interpretation on the incorporation of fundamental rights in draft Article 15.

It would have been a different matter altogether if the Drafting Committee had stipulated in the Constitution itself, by way of an article, that courts cannot incorporate other fundamental rights into the language of draft Article 15. Then, there would have been an article in the original Constitution to that effect, which courts would have heeded. But here, the Drafting Committee attempted to control judicial review and the future development of a fundamental right not by a stipulation in the Draft Constitution but by a mere footnote, which was just an explanatory statement on the merits of using 'personal liberty.'

Procedure Established by Law: Probing the Japanese and Irish Influences

The second part of the footnote to draft Article 15 suggested that the phrase 'without due process of law' was replaced by the phrase 'except according to procedure established by law' borrowed from Article 31 of the Constitution of Japan, 1946. The footnote also noted that a corresponding provision was contained in the Irish Constitution [referring to Article 40(4)1° of the Irish Constitution of 1937]. The proffered justification of the Drafting Committee for using this new phrase was to introduce precision and specificity of meaning.[55]

This reasoning was inadequate. Article 40(4)1° of the Irish Constitution is not the same as Article 31 of the Constitution of Japan. Article 40(4)1° of the Irish Constitution reads, 'No citizen shall be deprived of his personal liberty save in accordance with law.' Article 31 of the Japanese Constitution reads, 'No person shall be deprived of life or liberty, nor shall any other criminal penalty be imposed, except according to procedure established by law.'[56]

The differences between these two articles are self-evident. Article 40(4)1° of the Irish Constitution applies only to citizens, uses the phrase 'personal liberty', and predicates the deprivation of the right on 'save in accordance with law.' On the other hand, Article 31 of the Constitution of Japan applies to all persons, i.e., not to citizens alone, uses the word 'liberty' and allows for the right to be restricted as per 'procedure established by law.'

Draft Article 15 was thus a blend of Article 40(4)1° of the Irish Constitution from where the phrase 'personal liberty' was borrowed, and Article 31 of the Japanese Constitution from where the phrase 'except according to procedure established by law' was borrowed. If the Drafting Committee had only replicated Article 31 of the Japanese Constitution, then the phrase 'personal liberty' would not be used as Article 31 employs the broader term 'liberty.'

As we have seen in Chapter 2, BN Rau had strongly condemned Article 40(4)1° of the Irish Constitution. In his Notes on Fundamental Rights dated 2 September 1946,[57] Rau had rightly criticized this article as affording little protection against oppressive state action, since all that the state needed to override the personal liberty right was to simply pass a law to that effect. According to Rau, such a right possessed little force. In fact, Rau had used Article 40(4)1° to demonstrate a counter-model of rights; a right which *must not* be emulated since the valuable right of personal liberty ought not to be subservient to legislative will, unchecked by courts.[58] The marginal note in Rau's Draft Constitution to Clause 16 (the due process clause) clearly indicated that the *only* part of Article 40(4)1° of the Irish Constitution which was being borrowed was the phrase 'personal liberty' and the remainder of the text of Clause 16, including the phrase 'without due process of law' was borrowed from the 14th Amendment to the US Constitution.[59]

Another inference that can be drawn is, when Rau presented his Draft Constitution in October 1947, the Japanese Constitution had already come into force. Despite that, Rau did not replicate the language of Article 31 of the Japanese Constitution in his Draft Constitution, choosing rather to retain the due process guarantee with the phrase 'personal liberty.'

A reason for this could perhaps have been that the phrase 'procedure established by law' is markedly similar to the phrase 'save in accordance with law' which appears in Article 40(4)1° of the Irish Constitution. Perhaps, noting the similarities between the two articles, Rau chose to retain the due process guarantee in Clause 16 especially since he had been extremely critical of Article 40(4)1° of the Irish Constitution and did not want to include in the Constitution any right on personal liberty akin to it. This, as we shall see in Chapter 4, was a point which was repeatedly raised in the Constituent Assembly during the debates on draft Article 15.

Furthermore, the explanation of the Drafting Committee— that the phrase 'procedure established by law' was specific—does not comport with the reason presented by the Drafting Committee for using the phrase 'personal liberty.'

During its meetings, the Drafting Committee followed the justification presented by BN Rau and defended the use of 'personal liberty' since this would ensure that the due process guarantee was not interpreted too broadly. With this, there seemed to be no compelling reason to delete due process itself since as per the Drafting Committee's own reasoning, the presence of 'personal liberty' would operate as a device which would limit and control the scope and extent of operation of the due process guarantee.

For both Rau and the Drafting Committee, 'personal liberty' sufficiently truncated the due process guarantee. In fact, by using 'personal liberty' and confirming Clause 16 from Rau's Draft Constitution in 1947–1948, the Drafting Committee had been confident that they had indeed ensured a specific meaning for the due process guarantee. Seen in this light and given the Drafting Committee's early preference for this model of due process, the sudden move towards deleting the due process guarantee altogether on the proffered justification that 'procedure established by law' was more specific was curious to say the least.

At this juncture it is important to briefly appreciate the structure of the Japanese Constitution. The Japanese Constitution was drafted under the supervision of the Supreme Commander of the Allied Powers, General Douglas MacArthur, at the end of the Second World War. Under Section 12 of the Potsdam Proclamation of 26 July 1945, framing a constitution for Japan was not one of the main tasks of the Allied powers.[60] However, on 3 February 1946, worried that the Matsumoto Committee was not making much headway in terms of framing a constitution, General Douglas MacArthur decided that it would be wisest if a model constitution was framed for Japan, which the Japanese government could then discuss further. To carry out these orders, General MacArthur's deputy, General Whitney asked the Government Section to draw up a model constitution.[61]

On 4 February 1946, twenty-five officers—of which five officers were lawyers by training—from the Government Section began the process of drafting the model constitution.[62] By 10 February 1946, the Government Section submitted the model Draft Constitution to General MacArthur and on 13 February 1946, the Japanese government was presented with the model Constitution.[63] The model Constitution went through several revisions and was 'formally promulgated on 3 November 1946.'[64]

Since the original framework of the Japanese Constitution was provided by the office of the Supreme Commander of Allied Powers, it appears that the Government Section in drafting the Constitution avoided incorporating a clause on due process to avoid substantive due process from germinating in Japan. This, in part, could be since many of the members of the Government Section drafting the Constitution were 'New Dealers.'[65] But the Japanese Constitution did not abandon due process altogether:

Articles 32–40 provided detailed and adequate safeguards to protect due process rights in the realm of criminal law.[66]

Thus, the Japanese Constitution had in fact incorporated due process guarantees, which was a radical move, since Japan—which was earlier influenced by German law—did not really have such guarantees.[67] And although Article 31 did not endeavour to incorporate substantive due process, as understood in American Constitutional law at that time,[68] the Japanese Constitution attempted to provide many of the rights which formed part of due process, such as a separate provision dealing with property rights in Article 29 but with some innovation.[69]

Conceptually and structurally, the meaning of the rights enumerated in the Japanese and Irish Constitutions was different. Article 31 of the Japanese Constitution differed from the language of Article 40(4)1° of the Irish Constitution in important respects. Article 31 was to be read along with the fundamental rights which followed it; the subsequent rights afforded strong due process rights, something that Article 40(4)1° of the Irish Constitution did not provide. But the real reason for using language from Article 31 of the Japanese Constitution in draft Article 15 of the Draft Constitution seems to have been driven by an effort towards ensuring that the doctrine of substantive due process did not raise its head in India.

However, in choosing to follow the language of Article 31 of the Japanese Constitution, the Drafting Committee either did not appreciate the Japanese Constitution as a whole or did not fully appreciate why Article 31 was worded the way it was. The problem with simply emulating Article 31 of the Japanese Constitution was that the Drafting Committee did not also replicate the charter of rights contained in Articles 32–40 of the Japanese Constitution.[70] In a bid to avoid substantive due process, the Drafting Committee ended up forgoing all the important rights which are otherwise part of due process. In fact, nothing prevented the Drafting Committee from enumerating the rights contained in Articles 32–40 of the Japanese Constitution which included rights such as access to courts (Article 32); prohibition against torture and cruel punishment (Article 36); and even the right to seek compensation for being wrongly arrested (Article 40).

The series of rights which Chapter III of the Japanese Constitution enumerates, in addition to Articles 32–40, are considered so detailed and varied that it has been termed as representing 'what is perhaps the world's most extensive constitutional guarantees on civil rights.'[71] Unfortunately, the full panoply of rights which the Japanese Constitution guarantees were not incorporated by the Drafting Committee. And in their absence, draft Article 15 ended up providing the most minimal safeguards against State encroachment on a person's life or personal liberty. This would become a point of enormous debate, and a source of eternal consternation amongst many members of the Constituent Assembly.

In substance, draft Article 15 followed the spirit of Article 40(4)1° of the Irish Constitution, something that BN Rau had been keen to avoid, even though some language from Article 31 of the Constitution of Japan was reflected in draft Article 15. With the adoption of the phrase 'procedure established by law' the Drafting Committee did not give due process a coherent vision and a systematized structure. Rather, the proffered justification—that the phrase 'procedure established by law' was 'more specific'—was a red herring, for its use marked nothing but the total abandonment of due process.[72]

That draft Article 15 had been weakened considerably is not difficult to see. Here was a fundamental right which had eliminated due process, confined protection only to personal liberty rather than the broader liberty right, and shut out the possibility of draft Article 15 incorporating other fundamental rights. Added to all of this was the phrase 'procedure established by law', which as we shall see, was really a step backwards.

The Drafting Committee had attempted to refine the explanation for using 'personal liberty', but in a bid to present a stronger justification, it ended up weakening its case against 'liberty'. If the Drafting Committee fervently wanted to prevent the incorporation of the civil liberty rights enumerated in draft Article 13 and Article 15, then there was no need to word the fundamental right to life and personal liberty in a manner that rendered it powerless to check any state action. But perhaps most critically, BN Rau had repeatedly sounded a warning precisely against the Indian Constitution incorporating such a weak fundamental right on the right to life and personal liberty, as far back as in 1946. That warning proved futile.

Introducing the Draft Constitution in the Constituent Assembly

After the Draft Constitution had been submitted on 21 February 1948 to Dr Rajendra Prasad, members of the Assembly were invited to submit their comments, which would then be reviewed by the Drafting Committee.[73] Certain members proposed amendments to draft Article 15.

For instance, B Pattabhi Sitaramayya and a few others wished to replace 'except according to procedure established by law' with 'save in accordance with law'.[74] To this amendment, the Drafting Committee presented a short Note which elaborated on the reason for removing the reference to due process.

As per the Note, due process as originally understood in the American Constitution meant only what was 'due procedure prescribed or established by law.' This original vision of due process was reflected in Article 31 of the Constitution of Japan; a conclusion bolstered by the fact that Japan's Constitution was framed 'under American guidance.'[75] The Note then stated that the phrase 'save in accordance with law' which appears in the Irish Constitution [Article 40(4)1°] possesses the same meaning as the phrase 'except according to procedure established by law' which occurs in the Japanese Constitution; something which the footnote to draft Article 15 already mentioned. In light of the similarity in the meaning of these two phrases, there was no need to consider the amendment which sought to introduce 'save in accordance with law.'[76]

Evidently enthused by the idea that Article 31 of the Constitution of Japan had been drafted under American supervision, the Drafting Committee seemed convinced that the absence of a due process guarantee in that article was a lesson learned on the pitfalls which surrounded due process in the US Constitution. For this reason, the phrase 'procedure established by law' as it appeared in Article 31 of the Japanese Constitution was considered suitable for being replicated in the Indian Constitution. This perhaps suggests that in the Drafting Committee's view, if due process was considered such an important right, then surely it would have been mentioned in the text of the Japanese Constitution.

Thereafter, in response to Upendranth Barman's comments that draft Article 15 must use the phrase 'without due process of law' instead of 'except according to procedure established by law', the Drafting Committee's Note elucidated that the footnote appended to draft Article 15 sufficiently clarified the reasons for introducing the latter phrase. The Note also stated that the footnote sufficiently explained the reason for going against the Advisory Committee's version of the due process guarantee which had been recommended in their Interim Report.[77]

KM Munshi, a strong proponent of due process rights redoubled his efforts in order to resurrect due process. After receiving comments on the Draft Constitution, the Drafting Committee met four times in the last week of March 1948 to review the comments and make changes to the text.[78]

At the meeting of 23 March 1948, KM Munshi rightly mooted the point that the Drafting Committee must 'restore the words "without due process of law"' in draft Article 15, but the Drafting Committee decided against it.[79] At this meeting, apart from Munshi, only Dr Ambedkar and N Madhava Rao were present and thus the decision against restoring due process in draft Article 15 was taken by a majority of two to one.[80] Draft Article 15 was not taken up for discussion again.

After the Drafting Committee had reviewed the Draft Constitution and made changes it thought necessary, it was then reviewed by the Special Committee which met on 10 and 11 April 1948.[81] Thereafter, the Drafting Committee received many more comments which were reviewed, and further changes were made to the Draft Constitution. Finally, on 26 October 1948, Dr Ambedkar presented a copy of the revised Draft Constitution to the President of the Assembly.[82]

As Dr Ambedkar noted in his letter accompanying the Draft Constitution, the Drafting Committee had completed a colossal task between 21 February 1948 and 26 October 1948. After submitting a copy of the Draft Constitution to the President on 21 February 1948, the Drafting Committee had collated and considered the comments and suggestions received on the Draft

Constitution from various quarters, including from the Special Committee.[83] Thereafter, the Drafting Committee reviewed the Draft Constitution in light of the numerous comments received from several quarters including the Provincial Governments and Provincial Legislatures, to name a few. Finally, after completing this mammoth exercise, the revised Draft Constitution was being submitted.[84]

It was this revised Draft Constitution, containing many of the recommended amendments, as well as the changes which the Drafting Committee thought would be appropriate, which was introduced on 4 November 1948 by Dr Ambedkar in the Constituent Assembly.[85]

In moving the resolution that the Constituent Assembly take up for consideration the Draft Constitution, Dr Ambedkar presented a detailed outline of the Constitution in which he described the structure of government, the federal division of power and even presented a defence against the charge that the Drafting Committee had erred in replicating large portions of the Government of India Act, 1935. Dr Ambedkar also spoke on the nature of fundamental rights enumerated in the Draft Constitution, which in his view was the 'most criticized part of the Draft Constitution.'[86]

When Dr Ambedkar's motion was taken up for discussion in the Constituent Assembly, several members expressed disappointment with the manner in which the chapter on Fundamental Rights was drafted, and also with the fact that it did not make any reference to the due process guarantee.

During the debate on Dr Ambedkar's motion, KT Shah emphatically announced that in his view, the chapter on fundamental rights needed to be corrected which he would endeavour to do in the fullness of time.[87] Several others seemed perturbed by the fact that there was nothing in the Draft Constitution which guaranteed that persons would not be arrested on whimsical grounds, and that they would be guaranteed a range of rights when they came into contact with the justice system.[88] As we shall see, this would be the focus of attention when draft Article 15 would be debated in the Constituent Assembly.

After five days of debate, on 9 November 1948 the Constituent Assembly adopted Dr Ambedkar's motion of taking up the Draft Constitution for consideration.[89] On 15 November 1948, the Assembly commenced the clause-wise discussion of the Draft Constitution.[90]

KT Shah's Early Attempt at Incorporating Due Process

Before draft Article 15 came up for debate in the Constituent Assembly, KT Shah attempted to introduce the due process guarantee in the chapter on Fundamental Rights. When Shah spoke in the Assembly, in reply to Dr Ambedkar's motion for taking up the Draft Constitution for consideration, he focused on the fact that the Fundamental Rights contained too many exceptions. Viewing the draft of Fundamental Rights as riddled with errors, Shah declared that he would move amendments to 'redress the omission and correct the distortion this Draft suffers from on this most important subject.'[91]

KT Shah had been an early proponent of fundamental rights which enumerated a due process guarantee. In fact, in 1946, Shah had presented his vision of a due process guarantee in his Note on Fundamental Rights which accompanied the Draft Clauses on fundamental rights prepared by him.[92] In that, Clause 52 provided that 'No one shall be deprived of their life, limb or property except under due process of law.'[93]

Draft Article 15 must have been a cause of some chagrin for him, and in his own way, Shah attempted to have a due process guarantee incorporated in the chapter on Fundamental Rights. To that end, Shah moved an amendment to incorporate a due process guarantee not in draft Article 15, but in draft Article 13.

Draft Article 13(1) in sub-clauses (a)–(g) enumerated seven civil rights with draft Articles 13(2)–(6) enumerating the grounds on which each of the rights in draft Article 13(1) could be restricted. On 1 December 1948, draft Article 13 of the Draft Constitution was taken up for discussion by the Constituent Assembly.[94] On that day, Shah moved Amendment No. 445, which proposed to add a new clause (2) to draft Article 13. Amendment No. 445 read:

> Liberty of the person is guaranteed. No person shall be deprived of his life, nor be arrested or detained in custody, or imprisoned, except according to due process of law, nor shall any person be denied equality before the law or equal protection of the laws within the territory of India.[95]

Amendment No. 445 shows that the proposed clause on due process avoided prefixing 'personal' to 'liberty', and although it spoke of due process it did not propose a due process clause akin to the one the Constituent Assembly had approved on 30 April 1947. Rather, the proposed amendment aimed at ensuring that people received holistic and proper protection from instances of arbitrary detention and arrest, and ensured that the process of imprisonment would be consistent with due process principles.

Speaking on the amendment, Shah launched a scathing attack on the idea that the Constitution would not respect fundamental principles of civil liberty. 'The autocrat, the despot, has always wished' Shah reminded the Constituent Assembly 'just to shut out those who did not agree with him.'[96] A mark of a constitution which tolerated differences in opinion was the extent to which it safeguarded personal liberty. Shah resolutely argued that the ideal of protecting individual liberty was a hallmark of a great many constitutions and like those constitutions, India must also ensure that the liberty of the people is placed on the highest pedestal.[97] As Shah proclaimed in the Assembly:

> It was, therefore, that any time the slightest difference of opinion was expressed, the slightest inconvenience or embarrassment was likely to be caused by any individual, the only course open to those who wanted to exercise autocratic power was to imprison or arrest or detain such a person without charge or trial. It has been in fact in many modern constitutions among the most cardinal articles that the liberty of the person shall be sacred, shall be guaranteed by the Constitution.[98]

Shah also added:

> We are covering new ground and should not omit to incorporate in our Constitution those items which in my opinion ought to be sacrosanct, which would never lose anything by repetition, and which would also add to our moral stature.[99]

Shah was aware that personal liberty had been placed at a lower rung due to the charged environment following Indian Independence and the carnage which India suffered for over a year. In fact, he admitted that in such trying times, violence had to be controlled and that swiftness in response had been the need of the hour, which rigorous compliance with due process may have thwarted.[100]

Nevertheless, as Shah would point out, the unfortunate occurrences of the past must not cloud the Constituent Assembly's judgment on protecting personal liberty. As Shah told the Assembly, such exceptional situations ought not to influence the making of a constitution which would be implemented in otherwise peaceful times—India would not be in a state of permanent emergency which would necessitate the Constitution giving short shrift to important liberty rights.[101]

It was Shah's commitment towards inaugurating for India a progressive constitution which, for him, undoubtedly merited the enumeration of a right where all canons of due process were respected when an individual was placed under arrest.[102] But he could foretell that his amendment would not be approved by the Constituent Assembly particularly since many other amendments to draft Article 13 had not succeeded in obtaining the Assembly's approval. Attempting to have a due process guarantee in draft Article 13, had in Shah's own words, been like 'hurling myself against a blank wall.'[103] But he was committed to the ideal that a constitution must uphold civil liberty rights, which motivated him to move the amendment in the hope that it may persuade the Assembly to take a relook at the civil liberties enumerated in the Draft Constitution.[104]

Shah's premonition for his amendment proved true, for on 2 December 1948, the Constituent Assembly decided not to approve Amendment No. 445.[105]

In its effort to attain specificity of meaning and prevent the incorporation of other fundamental rights into draft Article 15, the Drafting Committee had achieved the unthinkable. It had not only deleted reference to due process in draft Article 15, but also retained a truncated version of the liberty right in the form of 'personal liberty'. Moreover, by succumbing to the pressure exerted by Alladi Krishnaswami Ayyar's switch to the side which opposed due process, and then hurriedly replacing the language of Clause 16 of Rau's Draft Constitution with a newly worded right, the Drafting Committee was not only guilty of patchwork but also of ignoring the Assembly's past unanimous decision of 30 April 1947, to accept a due process guarantee as a fundamental right.

Added to this was the fact that there was an impending deadline for submitting a Draft Constitution to the Constituent Assembly. The Drafting Committee had to hurriedly come up with a new fundamental right on life and personal liberty which would avoid any mention of due process. It was in this manner that the Drafting Committee settled on the language of draft Article 15.

At the hands of the Drafting Committee, due process suffered an unceremonious exit and no efforts were made, in the days leading up to the submission of the Draft Constitution, to bring it back into the Constitution. In a fervent bid to avoid making any reference to due process, the Drafting Committee inverted fundamental rights and ensured that through draft Article 15, the people would have little protection when facing the State. From its heady days in April 1947, due process suffered a stunning collapse.

Nevertheless, the resolve of many members to incorporate a due process guarantee would remain unwavering. When draft Article 15 would be taken up for debate, several members would make strenuous efforts to resurrect due process. The debates on draft Article 15 would demonstrate the bitterly contentious and deeply divided framing of the fundamental right to life and personal liberty. And in those debates, the Constituent Assembly would witness one of the greatest spectacles in oratory, historical insight and constitutional analysis.

Endnotes

1   B Shiva Rao, *Framing of India's Constitution*, vol. III, p. 316.
2   Id., pp. 317–319. Minutes of the Meeting of 27 October 1947.
3   Id., p. 317.
4   Id., pp. 318–319.
5   Id., p. 315. After participating in the first meeting of the Drafting Committee, BL Mitter did not participate at all thereafter because he was no longer a member of the Constituent Assembly. Ibid.
6   Id., pp. 325–327.
7   At many of the Drafting Committee's meetings not all the members were present including when the due process guarantee was being discussed. As we shall see in Chapter 8, the absence of members at these crucial junctures will assume importance.
8   Id., pp. 325, 327.
9   Id., pp. 325, 327.
10 Id., pp. 327–329.
11 Id., p. 328.
12 Ibid.
13 Ibid.
14 Ibid.
15 Id., p. 329. Appendix B to Minutes of the Meeting of the Drafting Committee dated 31 October 1947.
16 Id., pp. 406–409. Minutes of the Meeting of the Drafting Committee dated 19 January 1948.
17 Id., pp. 356–366. Minutes of the Meeting of the Drafting Committee dated 6 December 1947.
18 Id., p. 406.
19 Id., p. 409. Appendix to Minutes of the meeting of the Drafting Committee dated 19 January 1948.
20 Id., p. 409. See starred footnote in Appendix to Minutes of the Meeting of the Drafting Committee dated 19 January 1948.
21 Id., p. 199. Rau's note on Clause 16 read as follows: 'The word "liberty" might be construed very widely unless qualified. Hence the insertion of "personal."'
22 Id., p. 409. See starred footnote in Appendix to Minutes of the Meeting of the Drafting Committee dated 19 January 1948.
23 Ibid.
24 See speech of BG Kher, CAD, vol. V, pp. 294–295.
25 Id., pp. 301–302.

26   The minutes of the meeting record that Dr Ambedkar and N Madhava
      Rao were 'present' and that BN Rau, SN Mukherjee (Joint Secretary)
      and JK Khanna (Deputy Secretary) were 'In attendance' at the meeting.
      This suggests a distinction between how the presence of the members
      of the Drafting Committee and those assisting it were shown. See B
      Shiva Rao, *Framing of India's Constitution*, vol. III, p. 406.

27   Id., pp. 509–517.

28   Id., pp. 509–510.

29   Id., p. 511.

30   Id., pp. 517–675.

31   Id., pp. 520–527.

32   Id., p. 523. (Emphasis added.)

33   Ibid.

34   Ibid.

35   Ibid. The third part of the footnote read as follows: 'The committee
      is also of opinion that the words "or the equal protection of the laws"
      should be inserted after the words "equality before the law" as in
      section 1 of Article XIV of the U.S.A. Constitution (1865).'

36   In January 1948, the Drafting Committee met on January 20, 21, 22,
      23, 24, 26, 28, 29 and 30. See Id., pp. 406–465.

37   In February 1948, the Drafting Committee met on February 3, 4, 5, 6,
      9, 10, 11 and 13. See Id., pp. 465–506.

38   Austin, *The Indian Constitution*, p. 130.

39   Id., p. 131. Also see, Ibid, note 74.

40   Id., pp. 130–131.

41   Id., p. 131. (Emphasis added.)

42   Id., p. 130. Granville Austin makes a passing reference to the fact that
      the Drafting Committee reconsidered the question of due process
      after learning from BN Rau of Justice Frankfurter's thoughts on due
      process. However, to make this point, Austin seems to rely only on a
      correspondence exchanged between the Home Secretary and Nehru's
      Private Secretary, the contents of which are not revealed by Austin;
      Ibid, note 73.

43   Austin, *The Indian Constitution*, p. 25. ('As Constitutional Adviser,
      Rau's advice was heard in the Assembly's inner councils, although he
      was not an Assembly member.'); Upendra Baxi, '"*The Little Done, the
      Vast Undone*": Some Reflections on Reading Granville Austin's The
      Indian Constitution', *Journal of the Indian Law Institute*, vol. 9 (1967):
      p. 328. ('B.N. Rau who though not a member of the Assembly, played
      a crucial advisory role.')

44   Mate, 'The Origins', p. 222.

45   Austin, *The Indian Constitution*, p. 130.

46   Id., p. 131.

47   Bipin Chandra, 'The Initial Years', in *India After Independence: 1947–2000*, ed. Bipin Chandra, Mridula Mukherjee and Aditya Mukherjee (India: Penguin Books, 2000), p. 77.

48   This claim was in fact made as early as 1957 when Charles Henry Alexandrowicz had observed that although the American version of the due process guarantee seemed to have been approved, 'dramatic developments had taken place after independence in consequence of which the whole question was reopened.' See Alexandrowicz, *Constitutional Developments*, p. 23.

49   See B Shiva Rao, *Framing of India's Constitution*, vol. II, pp. 243–244. 'Proceedings of the meetings of the Advisory Committee, 21-22 April 1947.'

50   CAD, vol. XI, p. 733.

51   See B Shiva Rao, *Framing of India's Constitution*, vol. III, pp. 522–523. Draft Article 13 (1) read as follows:
      '13. (1) Subject to the other provisions of this article, all citizens shall have the right—
      (a) to freedom of speech and expression
      (b) to assemble peacefully without arms;
      (c) to form associations and unions;
      (d) to move freely throughout the territory of India;
      (e) to reside and settle in any part of the territory of India;
      (f) to acquire, hold and dispose of property; and
      (g) to practice any profession, or to carry on any occupation, trade or business.'

52   See B Shiva Rao, *Framing of India's Constitution*, vol. III, p. 523; Basu, *Commentary on the Constitution*, p. 3157.

53   Seervai, *Constitutional Law*, p. 970.

54   See William J Brennan, Jr, 'State Constitutions and the Protection of Individual Rights', *Harvard Law Review*, vol. 90 (1977): pp. 493–495 [hereinafter Brennan, 'Individual Rights'].

55   See B Shiva Rao, *A Study*, pp. 235–236; Basu, *Commentary on The Constitution*, p. 3157.

56   The Constitution of Japan (available at https://japan.kantei.go.jp/Constitution_and_government_of_japan/Constitution_e.html).

57   B Shiva Rao, *Framing of India's Constitution*, vol. II, pp. 21–36.

58   Id., p. 32.

59 Id., p. 9.
60 Robert E Ward, 'The Origins of the Japanese Constitution', *The American Political Science Review*, vol. 50 (1956): pp. 983–984 [hereinafter Ward, 'The Origins'].
61 Id., pp. 986, 993.
62 Id., p. 994.
63 Id., p. 995.
64 Id., pp. 1001–1003, 1006.
65 Yasuhir Okudaira, 'Forty Years of the Constitution and its Various Influences: Japanese, American and Europe', *Law and Contemporary Problems*, vol. 53 (1990): p. 30.
66 Id., p. 31
67 Ibid.
68 Nobushige Ukai and Nathaniel L Nathanson, 'Protection of Property Rights and Due Process Law in the Japanese Constitution', *Washington Law Review*, vol. 43 (1968): p. 1135.
69 Id., pp. 1132–1133.
70 Constitution of Japan, 1946:
'Article 32. No person shall be denied the right of access to the courts.
Article 33. No person shall be apprehended except upon warrant issued by a competent judicial officer which specifies the offense with which the person is charged, unless he is apprehended, the offense being committed.
Article 34. No person shall be arrested or detained without being at once informed of the charges against him or without the immediate privilege of counsel; nor shall he be detained without adequate cause; and upon demand of any person such cause must be immediately shown in open court in his presence and the presence of his counsel.
Article 35. The right of all persons to be secure in their homes, papers and effects against entries, searches and seizures shall not be impaired except upon warrant issued for adequate cause and particularly describing the place to be searched and things to be seized, or except as provided by Article 33.
Each search or seizure shall be made upon separate warrant issued by a competent judicial officer.
Article 36. The infliction of torture by any public officer and cruel punishments are absolutely forbidden.
Article 37. In all criminal cases the accused shall enjoy the right to a speedy and public trial by an impartial tribunal.

He shall be permitted full opportunity to examine all witnesses, and he shall have the right of compulsory process for obtaining witnesses on his behalf at public expense.

At all times the accused shall have the assistance of competent counsel who shall, if the accused is unable to secure the same by his own efforts, be assigned to his use by the State.

Article 38. No person shall be compelled to testify against himself.

Confession made under compulsion, torture or threat, or after prolonged arrest or detention shall not be admitted in evidence.

No person shall be convicted or punished in cases where the only proof against him is his own confession.

Article 39. No person shall be held criminally liable for an act which was lawful at the time it was committed, or of which he has been acquitted, nor shall he be placed in double jeopardy.

Article 40. Any person, in case he is acquitted after he has been arrested or detained, may sue the State for redress as provided by law.'

71 Ward, 'The Origins', p. 1000.
72 Generally, see Seervai, *Constitutional Law*, p. 970.
73 B Shiva Rao, *Framing of India's Constitution: Select Documents*, vol. IV (New Delhi: Indian Institute of Public Administration, 1968), p. 3 [hereinafter B Shiva Rao, *Framing of India's Constitution*, vol. IV].
74 Id., p. 39.
75 Ibid.
76 Ibid.
77 Id., pp. 39–40.
78 Id., pp. 392–408. The Drafting Committee met on 23–24 March and then again on 27–28 March 1948. See Id., p. 392.
79 Id., p. 394. Minutes of the Meeting of the Drafting Committee dated 23 March 1948.
80 Id., p. 392.
81 Id., pp. 408–415. Minutes of the meetings of the Special Committee, 10–11 April 1948.
82 Id., pp. 415–416. Letter from the Chairman of the Drafting Committee to the President of the Constituent Assembly.
83 Id., p. 415.
84 Id., pp. 415–416.
85 Speech of Dr Ambedkar, CAD, vol. VII, pp. 31–44.
86 Id., p. 40.
87 Id., p. 245.

88   See speech of Yudhisthir Mishra, CAD, vol VII, p. 282; speech of B
     Pocker Sahib Bahadur, CAD, vol. VII, p. 364.
89   Id., p. 394.
90   Id., p. 398.
91   Id., p. 245.
92   B Shiva Rao, *Framing of India's Constitution: Select Documents*, vol. II,
     pp. 36–55.
93   Id., p. 55.
94   CAD, vol. VII, p. 711.
95   Id., p. 726.
96   Ibid.
97   Ibid.
98   Ibid.
99   Ibid.
100 Id., pp. 726–727.
101 Id., pp. 726–727.
102 Id., p. 727.
103 Ibid.
104 Ibid.
105 Id., pp. 785–786.

4

The Ignominious Retreat
Due Process on the Floor of the Constituent Assembly

———•———

THE CONSTITUENT ASSEMBLY COMMENCED THE CLAUSE-WISE discussion of the Draft Committee's Draft Constitution on 15 November 1948 and by the next month, the Assembly reached draft Article 15. On 3 December 1948, when draft Article 15 was to be taken up for discussion, TT Krishnamachari intervened and requested that debates over draft Article 15 be postponed. The reason for seeking a postponement was that draft Article 15 was still being closely scrutinized by several members.[1] The Vice-President, who was presiding over the deliberations, agreed and moved on to place the next articles for debate.

On 6 December 1948, the Constituent Assembly took up three draft articles for debate. The first order of business was the continuation of the debate over draft Article 19. After completing the debate and voting on Article 19,[2] the Assembly then moved

135

on to draft Article 14, which was debated briefly and then voted on.[3] Thereafter, the Vice-President placed draft Article 15 for the Assembly's consideration, the motion being whether draft Article 15 does 'form part of the Constitution.'[4] With this, the stage was now set for the Assembly to thoroughly examine the scope and breadth of the right to life and personal liberty.

The Proposed Amendments to Draft Article 15

As soon as draft Article 15 was taken up for debate, the Vice-President first invited Brajeshwar Prasad to move his amendments, but Prasad declined to move them.[5] With that, the Vice-President moved on to the first set of amendments, Amendment Nos. 522, 523, 524, 525, 528 and 530, which aimed at replacing the phrase 'except according to procedure established by law' with the phrase 'without due process of law.' Since the Vice-President considered all these amendments to be similar, Amendment No. 523 was to be moved first.[6]

Amendment No. 523 was moved by Kazi Syed Karimuddin. In fact, Karimuddin had moved two separate amendments: one to delete the word 'personal' prefixed before 'liberty' (Amendment No. 523) and another to replace the phrase 'except according to procedure established by law' with the phrase 'without due process of law' (Amendment No. 524). His would be the only amendment which sought deletion of the word 'personal.' Seemingly, due to an error by the Secretariat, both these amendments were clubbed together and shown as Amendment No. 523.[7]

Another set of members, Upendranath Barman, Damodar Swarup Seth and SV Krishnamurthy Rao moved Amendment No. 528 to replace 'procedure established by law' with 'due process of law.'[8] But, according to Karimuddin, Amendment No. 528, could

The Constituent Assembly when it met for the first time on 9 December 1946

Jawaharlal Nehru addressing the Constituent Assembly on 13 December 1946

Jawaharlal Nehru delivering the 'Tryst with Destiny' speech in the Constituent Assembly session of 14–15 August 1947

Louis Mountbatten addressing the Independence Day session on 15 August 1947

A meeting of the Constituent Assembly

Dr Rajendra Prasad addressing the Independence Day session on 15 August 1947

Jawaharlal Nehru addressing a meeting of a committee of the Constituent Assembly. Seated on his left are Dr Rajendra Prasad and Sardar Vallabhbhai Patel.

Sardar Vallabhbhai Patel with Sarojini Naidu in the Constituent Assembly

Photo of Sir BN Rau (from the personal collection of the author)

Family picture of BN Rau (from the personal collection of the author). Sir BN Rau is standing first on the left alongside his brother B Shiva Rao.

Members of the Drafting Committee along with other functionaries:
Sitting (L-R): N Madhava Rao, Saiyd Muhammad Saadulla, Dr BR Ambedkar, Alladi Krishnaswami Ayyar, and Sir BN Rau. Standing (L-R): SN Mukherjee, Jugal Kishore Khanna, and Kewal Krishan

Dr Ambedkar presenting the final draft of the Constitution to Dr Rajendra Prasad on 25 November 1949

Dr Rajendra Prasad signing the Constitution

The Gazette  of India

सत्यमेव जयते

EXTRAORDINARY
PUBLISHED BY AUTHORITY

NEW DELHI, SATURDAY, NOVEMBER 26, 1949

GOVERNMENT OF INDIA

CONSTITUENT ASSEMBLY OF INDIA
NOTIFICATION

New Delhi, the 26th November, 1949

No. CA/83/Cons./49.—The Constitution of India as passed by the Constituent Assembly has been authenticated by the President of the Assembly by affixing his signature thereto this twenty-sixth day of November, 1949, and is hereby published for general information :—

THE CONSTITUTION OF INDIA

WE, THE PEOPLE OF INDIA, having solemnly   Preamble. resolved to constitute India into a SOVEREIGN DEMOCRATIC REPUBLIC and to secure to all its citizens :

JUSTICE, social, economic and political ;

LIBERTY of thought, expression, belief, faith and worship ;

EQUALITY of status and of opportunity ; and to promote among them all

FRATERNITY assuring the dignity of the individual and the unity of the Nation ;

IN OUR CONSTITUENT ASSEMBLY this twenty-sixth day of November, 1949, do HEREBY ADOPT, ENACT AND GIVE TO OURSELVES THIS CONSTITUTION.

[2347]

First page of the Constitution, which was published in *The Gazette of India* on 26 November 1949

Jawaharlal Nehru signing the Constitution

Sardar Vallabhbhai Patel signing the Constitution. Also seen in the picture are John Mathhai and Rajkumari Amrit Kaur.

only be put to vote, as per the settled practice of the Constituent Assembly, since in the agenda, Amendment No. 528 was shown alongside Amendment No. 523.[9]

SV Krishnamurthy Rao objected to the clubbing of Amendment No. 523 with Amendment No. 528, since Amendment No. 523 had sought removal of the word 'personal' prefixed before the word 'liberty', something which Amendment No. 528 did not seek. Overruling this objection, the Vice-President announced that since these amendments were equally important, Amendment No. 528 need not be moved for it would be put straight to a vote.[10]

Amendment No. 525 had been introduced by Naziruddin Ahmed, but due to an error in printing, the proposed amendment was apparently not pressed.[11]

ZH Lari moved Amendment No. 530, intending on putting it to vote.[12] This amendment sought to replace the phrase 'procedure established by law' with the phrase 'due process of law.'[13] Several other members, however, moved amendments which sought to refine the language of draft Article 15.

Mahboob Ali Baig Sahib Bahadur moved Amendment No. 526 which sought to replace the phrase 'except according to procedure established by law' with the phrase 'save in accordance with law.'[14] Since Amendment No. 526 was similar to Amendment No. 524 and Amendment No. 527, the Vice-President had decided that Amendment No. 526 only needed be moved.[15]

Another amendment, Amendment No. 527 had been moved by certain other members to replace the phrase 'except according to procedure established by law' with 'except in accordance with law.'[16]

As we shall see, all these Amendments failed to secure the Constituent Assembly's nod and eventually, draft Article 15 was approved in its original form. But the debates that took place demonstrated the dangers that draft Article 15 brought with it and the mistake of providing an extraordinarily low level of protection against instances of arbitrary and prolonged detention.

The Debates of 6 December 1948

Kazi Syed Karimuddin opened the debate on draft Article 15. He began by expressing his incredulity at the Drafting Committee's move of qualifying 'liberty' with the word 'personal' and using the phrase 'procedure established by law'; since originally, the Advisory Committee had settled on incorporating the due process guarantee as a fundamental right with the words 'life' and 'liberty.' For Karimuddin, this move by the Drafting Committee's would 'open a sad chapter in the history of constitutional law.'[17]

Against draft Article 15, Karimuddin voiced three main grievances. Draft Article 15 would entirely disable the people from interrogating laws which violated personal liberty, since the enactment of a law is the only requirement for the purposes of depriving the people of their life and personal liberty; a wholly unwholesome situation given the hurly-burly of Indian politics. Further, draft Article 15 ought to be fashioned into a due process guarantee to act as a bulwark against state action which limits the operation of fundamental rights. And, finally, in reducing the status of courts and judges to that of passive bystanders, draft Article 15 opened up a dangerous pathway which allowed the State to chip away at fundamental rights. For Karimuddin, it was entirely unwholesome to disallow courts from keeping a check on laws which were 'capricious, unjust or iniquitous.'[18] To guard against all these eventualities, the most appropriate safeguard was the incorporation of a due process guarantee as a fundamental right.

Of the two amendments moved by Karimuddin, one of them was aimed at removing the word 'personal' prefixed to the word 'liberty.' But what concerned him more was having 'except according to procedure established by law' replaced with the phrase 'without due process of law.' Given the fact that the Assembly's Secretariat erroneously combined the two amendments, Karimuddin stated that he would be willing to give up the amendment pertaining to the deletion of the word 'personal.' But he would not budge on his amendment, which sought deletion of the phrase 'except according to procedure established by law.'[19]

Karimuddin, through his short, powerful speech would set the tone for the debates and the subsequent speeches. He laid out succinctly the threats and dangers of draft Article 15. To enumerate a fundamental right which disallowed the people as well as the courts from questioning the wisdom of legislation; to create a framework in which personal liberty could be restricted in the easiest fashion; and to structure fundamental rights which hand over to the State enormous and unquestioned powers to restrict rights, were not the ends which draft Article 15 should aim to achieve.

Mahboob Ali Baig Sahib Bahadur then addressed the Constituent Assembly on draft Article 15. He first introduced his amendment, Amendment No. 526, which sought to replace the phrase 'except according to procedure established by law' with the phrase 'save in accordance with law.'[20] Although different in phraseology, the intent behind moving this amendment was to incorporate a due process guarantee, which Baig had thought could be achieved through the language used in his Amendment.[21]

What concerned Baig was that in choosing the phrase 'except according to procedure established by law' for draft Article 15, the Drafting Committee had apparently followed Article 31 of the

Constitution of Japan since the Drafting Committee felt 'that the expression is more definite.'[22] But there was a glaring lapse in the Drafting Committee's methodology. As he correctly pointed out, the Drafting Committee committed a fundamental error when following the Japanese Constitution. In copying Article 31 from it, the Drafting Committee had inexplicably failed to incorporate the charter of due process rights enumerated in the articles which followed Article 31.[23] According to Baig:

> It is no doubt true that in the Japanese Constitution article 31 reads like this but if the other articles that find place in the Japanese Constitution (viz., articles 32, 34 and 35) had also been incorporated in this Draft Constitution that would have been a complete safe guarding of the personal liberty of the citizen. *This Draft Constitution has conveniently omitted those provisions.*[24]

To bring this unexplained omission under a spotlight, Baig engaged in a detailed analysis of the Constitution of Japan. He argued that Article 32 of the Japanese Constitution stipulated that a person cannot be denied access to courts,[25] but since Article 32 finds no mention in the Draft Constitution, draft Article 15 will be of no avail if an enacted legislation prohibited a person from accessing courts in India to prove they are not guilty of a crime they are charged of committing.

Likewise, Article 34 of the Japanese Constitution provided detailed safeguards and protection of the rights of a person who was arrested.[26] No such companion provision was enumerated in the Draft Constitution. Further, Article 35 of the Japanese Constitution provided persons with a right against unreasonable searches[27] (like the 4th Amendment to the US Constitution)[28] but even this basic right was not mentioned in the Draft Constitution.[29]

Taken together, these articles formed a code in the Japanese Constitution insulating people from state excesses. Pointedly disputing the Drafting Committee's claim that the phrase 'procedure established by law' introduced specificity in draft Article 15, Baig argued that if the Drafting Committee was at all motivated to protect civil liberties, then the articles which followed Article 31 in the Japanese Constitution ought to also have been incorporated in the Draft Constitution. Only then would draft Article 15 of the Draft Constitution have some proper meaning.[30]As Baig put it:

> If for the sake of clarity and definiteness you have imported into this Draft Constitution article 31 of the Japanese Constitution you should in fairness have incorporated the other articles of the Japanese Constitution, which are relevant and which were enacted for safeguarding the personal liberty of the honest citizen.[31]

The fear that drove Baig to seek draft Article 15's amendment was that the article could in fact be used to validate legislations which deprived persons of the opportunity of accessing courts, questioning their detention and proving their innocence. This for him was the most egregious assault that a constitution could inflict on persons who are to exercise fundamental rights under the new Constitution.

Drawing on English history and the law in other countries, Baig argued that the phrase 'without due process of law' had the same connotation as the phrase 'save in accordance with law' which really meant that a person could not be condemned unheard. And it was this phrase which must find mention in draft Article 15 for the phrase 'except according to procedure established by law' inspired very little confidence.[32]

The only logical path to follow was to incorporate in the Indian Constitution, the series of due process guarantees which were enumerated in the Japanese Constitution. As an alternative, he suggested that the Constituent Assembly could consider replacing the phrase 'except according to procedure established by law' with a more definitely worded phrase which would ensure entitlement to the right to a free and full hearing in a court of law. For him, the Constitution had to emphatically state that a person's liberty could not be curtailed without a court hearing.[33]

Indeed, the fear of the Constitution creating a state machinery which would continue, rather than break, the tradition of arresting people in the most arbitrary fashion and without a chance of a fair hearing, appears as a common thread in several of the speeches. It is this fear which also motivated Pandit Thakur Dass Bhargava to speak in favour of draft Article 15 incorporating a due process guarantee.

In fact, on a previous occasion, on 1 December 1948 during the debates on draft Article 13, Bhargava had pointed out to the Constituent Assembly that draft Article 15, which in the pantheon of fundamental rights was the 'most important', was inadequate for it was a right which was virtually unenforceable.[34]

Now in the Constituent Assembly, Bhargava supported Karimuddin's amendment to the extent that the phrase 'without due process of law' was to replace the phrase 'except according to procedure established by law'; he did not really object to the use of the phrase 'personal liberty'.[35] In his speech, Bhargava would mainly focus on the utility of the Constitution incorporating the due process guarantee to allow for the substantive review of laws so as to test their constitutional propriety. He would go a step further, and present a strong defence of judicial review, for in his view the success of the due process guarantee could only be ensured by making the right justiciable in courts of law.

Bhargava commenced by stating that he held a broad conception of the meaning of 'law', rather than narrowly interpreting it to mean only legislations. But, the enactment of the law was but only an initial step. Due process, according to Bhargava, was necessary in order to empower courts to investigate the appropriateness of laws, both in their substantive and procedural aspects, the justness and need of the law, and its effect on the liberty rights of the people. For Bhargava, if the inquiry revealed that the law was constitutionally suspect, then the courts ought to declare it constitutionally invalid.[36]

Recalling the collective suffering endured by hundreds of nationalists under the 'Black Law' (Act XIV of 1908), Bhargava argued that under that law, by a simple notification the Government could declare an organization to be illegal.[37] And although the law was universally denounced, no one could question the legislation, and much less a court which would never enter into such questions. Such a law, according to Bhargava, showed the 'need of the powers of "due process".[38]

For Bhargava, use of the phrase 'due process of law' would signal the truly transformational impact of the Constitution for it would usher in an era of rights for the people of free India which heretofore had, under colonial rule, only been in the realm of hopes and demands.

To bolster his case in favour of due process, Bhargava adopted a creative argument. He put forth the idea that when the Constituent Assembly had debated draft Article 13 and voted to incorporate it as a fundamental right, the Assembly agreed that those rights can be subjected to only such restrictions which are reasonable. To appreciate the significance of this argument, an aside is necessary.

Draft Article 13 [draft Articles 13(1)(a)–13(1)(g)] enumerated seven civil liberties such as the freedom of association, freedom of movement and property rights. For each liberty right enumerated in draft Article 13(1), there was a corresponding clause enumerating the grounds on which the State could impose restrictions [draft Articles 13(2)–13(6)].[39] In the Drafting Committee's version, the State was empowered to impose restrictions on these rights on certain specified grounds.

This had been a cause of concern for Bhargava, since draft Article 13 did not specify any limits on the nature and extent of the restrictions which could be imposed. So, when draft Article 13 was debated by the Constituent Assembly, he successfully moved amendments to prefix the word 'reasonable' to 'restrictions' in draft Articles 13(3) to 13(6). As a result of this, for each of the civil liberty rights enumerated in draft Article 13 (except for the freedom of speech and expression) the restriction had to be a reasonable one. And it would be the judicial branch which would decide whether the restriction in question was reasonable.[40] For Bhargava, the introduction of the idea of 'reasonable restrictions' meant that the highest court of the land would become the 'ultimate arbiter of the liberties of the people.'[41] By empowering courts to examine the reasonableness of a restriction, Bhargava believed he was 'putting the soul' in what some believed was a 'lifeless article.'[42]

Using the debates on draft Article 13 to bolster his argument, Bhargava argued that with the adoption of the amendments at that time, the Constituent Assembly had approved of the principle that courts can inquire into the reasonableness of a law restricting fundamental rights, which was a form of substantive review of laws. Now therefore, when it came to the question of personal liberty—a right which was of far greater import—it was obligatory on the part of the Assembly to adopt the selfsame principle for draft Article 15.[43] As Bhargava put it:

> The House has already accepted the word 'reasonable' in article 13 … *The House is now estopped from adopting another principle. In regard to personal property and life the question is much more important. So far as the question of life and personal liberty are concerned they must be also under the category of subjects which are within the jurisdiction of the courts.*[44]

The novelty of this analogically reasoned argument was its simplicity. For Bhargava, in structuring the civil liberty rights enumerated in draft Article 13, the Constituent Assembly had struck a balance—civil liberty rights could be restricted only through the means of reasonable restrictions, with courts having the final say of what constitutes as 'reasonable.' Seen in this light, it would not be out of place to infuse this identical requirement in draft Article 15 too.[45] After all, if draft Article 13 did not allow the imposition of open ended and maximal restrictions, why then must draft Article 15?

As a means of settling the controversy, Bhargava proposed that either the due process rights mentioned in the Japanese Constitution be made a part of the Indian Constitution, or the phrase 'due process' be made a part of draft Article 15. The effect of this would be to provide guarantees to the people which the State cannot violate, and to create a system where the Supreme Court will have the final say on the meaning and scope of rights.[46]

Bhargava was a strong proponent of judicial review and believed that the due process guarantee would provide a firm basis for courts to launch an inquiry into the correctness of laws. On the specific issue of the relationship of due process and judicial review, Bhargava placed his faith in a constitutional schema in which courts would have all powers to question the sanctity of laws, which would be strengthened by a due process guarantee. It would be the duty of the judicial branch to have the final word on the meaning of fundamental rights.[47]

If due process was made a part of draft Article 15, then that along with the test of reasonableness contained in draft Article 13 'will be a *Magna Carta*' for the Indian Constitution.[48] Even otherwise, according to Bhargava, the survival of liberty needed two pillars—the courts and the legislature—and in times when the legislature is swayed by narrow and partisan considerations, the courts would rescue the people of India.[49]

In the ultimate analysis, Bhargava concluded that the amendment seeking to induct the due process guarantee in draft Article 15 must be accepted, for it would be the best way in which the judicial branch could be empowered to 'save us from tyranny of the legislature and the executive.'[50] For Bhargava, avoidance of the due process guarantee would result in the unwholesome diminution of the position and importance of the judicial branch; a branch in which the Constitution ought to repose its faith.[51]

Chimanlal Chakkubhai Shah was next to speak on draft Article 15, and he too extended support for the amendment to replace 'except according to procedure established by law' with the phrase 'without due process of law.'

Shah began by focusing on the development of due process in American constitutional law and the lessons that India could draw from it. There the due process guarantee had been used to not only implement procedural safeguards, but to also review laws to see that they were 'fair and just and not unreasonable or oppressive or capricious or arbitrary.'[52] This power to substantively review legislations became a cause for concern, for it contributed 'to uncertainty in legislation.'[53] For avoiding these problems, in India, it had been decided that the due process guarantee must be retained, but without reference to property, and by qualifying 'liberty' with the phrase 'personal liberty.'[54]

Deleting the reference to property in the due process guarantee was done on the recommendation of the Advisory Committee in its Interim Report, and the use of 'personal liberty' along with the due process guarantee was first proposed in Clause 16 of BN Rau's Draft Constitution of October 1947. For Shah, these two changes in the due process guarantee were well advised and would ensure that the due process guarantee did not 'lead to any uncertainty in legislation or unnecessary interference by the judiciary in reviewing legislation.'[55]

Shah then turned his attention to the importance of judicial review. As he put it, the point of departure between the English legal system and the federal constitutions of the world was that the latter empowered the judiciary to rule on the constitutional validity of legislations. He also raised an intriguing point. India needed judicial review for an additional reason: during times of emergency, there would be a tendency on the part of the central executive to appropriate more powers for itself.

To keep a check on this unique form of state excesses identified by Shah, it was paramount to ensure that courts were vested with strong powers of judicial review to ensure that legislative powers were not exercised arbitrarily and that in times of emergency, the courts could keep a check on the powers which the legislature grants to the executive.[56]

In Shah's vision, the due process guarantee had to be coupled with judicial review, and despite the attendant issues that due process may bring with it, an uncompromising feature of the Constitution ought to be that individuals use the due process right to keep law–making in check and ensure that laws are consistent with the Constitution.[57] As he put it:

> But it has happened at times that the law is so comprehensive that the individual is deprived of life and liberty without any opportunity of defence. What is the worst that can happen in an article like this if we put in the words 'without due process of law'? Some man may escape death or jail if the judiciary takes the view that the law is oppressive. Sir, is it not better that nine guilty men may escape than one innocent man suffers? That is the worst that can happen even if the judiciary takes a wrong view.[58]

Shah then turned to another troubling feature of draft Article 15. Was it much closer to the right on personal liberty contained in the Irish Constitution, than to Article 31 of the Constitution of Japan? Shah seemed to think so and was emphatic that it is only the phrase 'due process of law' which must replace the phrase 'procedure established by law.'

In that respect, Shah pointed out that Baig's amendment, which sought to replace 'procedure established by law' with the phrase 'save in accordance with law' was not a phrase that could be treated as the functionally operative equivalent of due process. The language of the amendment proposed by Baig to draft Article 15 was really taken from the Irish Constitution and had the same meaning as the phrase 'procedure established by law.' On this, Shah noted:

I therefore fully support the amendment which seeks to substitute the words 'without due process of law' in place of the words which have been used in the Article. As Mr. Mahboob Ali Baig has rightly pointed out, these words are taken from the Japanese Constitution but the Drafting Committee has omitted the other provisions which give meaning to these words. Mr. Baig's amendment which seeks to substitute the words 'save in accordance with law', I am afraid, will not serve his own purpose.[59]

Shah then went on to add:

If he has in mind that the full import of all the provisions of the Japanese Constitution read along with the one which the Drafting Committee has put in, should be brought out here, it is better that he accepts the words, 'without due process of law', *rather than the words 'save in accordance with law' which are taken from the Irish Constitution and which probably have the same meaning as the words put in by the Drafting Committee.* I therefore fully support amendment No. 528.[60]

It is critical to note that through this argument, Shah expressed the same concern, of the dangers of personal liberty being subject to and becoming secondary to laws, that BN Rau had raised several years ago, over the language of Article 40(4)1° of the Irish Constitution. In Chapter 2, we have seen that in his Notes on Fundamental Rights of 2 September 1946[61] Rau had been supremely critical of that Article. Rau firmly believed that such a fundamental right was no right at all, for if the right of personal liberty was dependent entirely on laws for its survival, then such a right afforded little protection against an oppressive state. Therefore, he had been quite clear about the fact that when the Constituent Assembly seeks to incorporate fundamental rights in the Indian Constitution, the model of Article 40(4)1° of the Irish Constitution must not be followed.[62]

However, it is also interesting to note that although Baig believed that the phrase 'save in accordance with law' had a much wider meaning than the phrase 'except according to procedure established by law', that was not the case. As we have seen, BN Rau deplored the phrase 'save in accordance with law' being used in respect of a fundamental right on personal liberty, which is what had led him to avoiding its use in his Draft Constitution of October 1947, preferring rather to retain the due process guarantee in Clause 16 of his Draft Constitution. This perhaps also lends credence to the argument that for this reason, Rau did not propose that the phrase 'except according to procedure established by law' make an appearance in his Draft Constitution.

From the speeches of Baig and Shah, it then perhaps appears quite unlikely that BN Rau would have wanted to use the phrase 'except according to procedure established by law' in respect of the fundamental right to life and personal liberty which, as the debates in the Assembly have shown, was considered even narrower than its counterpart in the Irish Constitution.

For Shah, the phrase 'procedure established by law' was the equivalent of 'save in accordance with law', which is why his stand was that only the phrase 'due process of law' must replace the phrase 'procedure established by law.' Ending his speech by declaring his support for Amendment No. 528, Shah's solution for reforming draft Article 15 was that the Constitution enumerate a due process guarantee which would also take within its stride all of the due process rights which were contained in the Japanese Constitution.[63]

Krishna Chandra Sharma spoke next in favour of amending draft Article 15, and replacing the phrase 'except according to procedure established by law' with the phrase 'without due process of law.' He conceived the due process guarantee as affording a set of minimum standards for the protection of individuals when they are brought before a court of law.

Sharma deployed his knowledge of history to argue in favour of due process by highlighting that the due process guarantee traced its origins to the *Magna Carta*, where the phrase '*Per Legum terrea*' meant 'without due process' and that in Chapter 39, due process rights were recognized.[64] From that, due process was then recognized during Edward III's rule in Statute No. 28 which also spoke of rights akin to due process rights.[65]

Sharma then turned to the American Constitution. Analysing the import of the 5th Amendment, he posited that 'four fundamental principles' could be gleaned from it: right to a fair trial; a court trying a person has been empowered to do so by a valid law; the person being tried has a full and fair opportunity of defending themselves against the charge levelled against them and; in order to ensure that the right to defend oneself is a wholesome right, the person must have full means of defending themselves such as the right of access to counsel and the right to examine witnesses. For him, it was crucial, if not paramount, that these four principles must be guaranteed in the form of fundamental rights.[66]

Like the previous speakers before him, Sharma too was driven by the fear that draft Article 15 would authorize a regime in which persons would find it hard to demand and enforce the basic rights which ought to inhere in individuals, and which must as a minimum guarantee be applicable in all cases where a person is brought before a court of law. For Sharma, draft Article 15 could hardly be called a fundamental right if the applicability of these basic rights was itself doubtful. To ensure that such doubts never loomed, the due process guarantee ought to become a part of draft Article 15.[67]

HV Patskar spoke after Sharma and in a short speech expressed his support for Amendment No. 528. Patskar essentially wanted the phrase 'without due process of law' to replace the phrase 'except according to procedure established by law.' He, too, was chiefly concerned with the absence of due process in draft Article 15. In its absence, it would not be too long before governments started making laws which rendered fundamental rights nugatory and virtually a spent force.[68]

For Patskar, the presence of due process in draft Article 15 would be a guarantee ensuring that individuals could not be routinely detained for indefinite periods, without any chance of respite. As he noted, this would become all the more important since some states had already made laws pertaining to detention in the short period since Independence, which had been roundly condemned in the court of public opinion.[69] Thus, freedom from such scenarios was 'very essential from the point of view of the right of personal liberty' which would be achieved with the introduction of a due process guarantee in draft Article 15.[70] In Patskar's conception, the essence of personal liberty demanded the existence of a minimum set of safeguards, a due process guarantee, to guard against instances of prolonged detention.

The KM Munshi–Alladi Krishnaswami Ayyar Debate

Following Patskar, KM Munshi and Alladi Krishnaswami Ayyar would address the Constituent Assembly, on draft Article 15.

This would be a rare occasion when two important members of the Assembly, who had had a shared history, vision and passion of promoting the incorporation of a due process guarantee as a fundamental right from the early days when the Assembly had begun its proceedings in 1946, would now find themselves on opposite sides of the debate on draft Article 15, and indeed due process itself. Addressing the Assembly, but also speaking to each other in equal measure, Munshi and Ayyar used this moment as an opportunity to present their theories on due process.

For Munshi, his speech largely reflected his ideology on due process which he had laid out, from his days as a member of the Advisory Committee and in fact even before that. For Ayyar, however, his speech would mark an important turning point. Essentially, he would now formally break from all that he had stood for in the past, on due process. He would use his speech to launch a scathing attack against those who felt that draft Article 15 ought to contain a due process guarantee. The fact that this moment was laden with irony would not be lost on the Assembly.

KM Munshi: Due Process as Ennobling Democracy

From the outset, KM Munshi had been a strong proponent of due process rights. In Chapter 1, we saw the process by which the Advisory Committee, and thereafter, the Constituent Assembly, had settled on a fundamental right which prohibited the deprivation of a person's life or liberty without due process. Munshi had played an important role in developing the idea of due process rights. In fact, his Note and Draft Articles on Fundamental Rights of 17 March 1947 which were submitted to the Fundamental Rights Sub-Committee[71] contained a fundamental right on due process,[72] and it was his draft fundamental rights which were used by the Sub-Committee as its template.[73]

When it came to the Drafting Committee, Munshi had unsuccessfully attempted to have the word 'personal' removed as a prefix to 'liberty'. Even when the Drafting Committee met in March 1948, to review the comments and recommendations received on the Draft Constitution submitted by the Drafting Committee on 21 February 1948, Munshi had at the meeting of 23 March 1948, tried to make the phrase 'without due process of law' a part of draft Article 15, but did not succeed.[74] Seen in this background, Munshi's speech was a continuation of his core commitment to civil liberties. In his speech, Munshi would advance an important theory: the democratic justification for due process.

According to Munshi, India was entering an era of freedom in which the electorate would elect its representatives; a democratic experiment in which the governed would choose who to be governed by. And although this was a great stride, it was an essential tenet of democracy that the people be able to check the way in which the government functions. It is here that due process would become an important tool.

For Munshi, due process would have twin objectives: that of providing procedural rights to persons when they came into contact with the justice system; and conferring the power of substantive due process to allow the people and courts, to review the content, merits and justification of a law. As he saw it, at the heart of democracy and the democratic experiment which the Constitution was inaugurating, lay the idea of striking a balance between 'individual liberty' and means of 'social control', and this balance was to be achieved by the due process guarantee.[75]

For Munshi's model of democracy, substantive due process would operate as a means of empowering individuals to enter the system after having cast their vote, keep a check on the state's law-making powers, and invite courts to judge whether the laws are within the four corners of the Constitution. Democracy was a process of continuous engagement between the state and the people, and by failing to incorporate a due process guarantee, this vital facet of democracy would be insufficiently realized.

Key to the idea that democracy was strengthened, rather than weakened, by a due process guarantee, was a second idea: that of creating a judicial system with the power to strike down laws under the due process guarantee, on finding that a law aimed at achieving 'social control' unconstitutionally restricted the liberty right. This was an important advance. In independent India, it would be for the first time that the superior courts would be invested with powers to interrogate state action and strike down laws with the concomitant effect of the state having to respect the lines which a court draws as the boundary for state action.

Indian history is witness to innumerable instances in which judicial decisions, which are supposed to be last word on any controversy, were openly disregarded by the colonial powers. In his book *Famous Judges, Lawyers and Cases of Bombay*, PB Vacha documents numerous skirmishes which occurred between the state and the courts in pre-independent India, since the colonial powers infamously refused to obey judicial decisions which were not to their liking.[76]

An infamous skirmish which Vacha narrates is an incident from 1828, in which Governor Malcolm openly defied a writ of *habeas corpus* issued by the then Supreme Court, located in the city of Bombay (now Mumbai), leading to a situation in which out of sheer frustration and as a measure of expression of his angst at the Governor's recalcitrance, the judge sealed the court for nearly half a year bringing judicial work to a complete stop.

The gravity of this incident resonates even today. In fact, in 2020, in his dissenting judgment in *Kantaru Rajeevaru* (the Supreme Court case on the entry of women into the Sabrimala temple), Justice RF Nariman, in documenting the history of decisions of superior courts being disobeyed, narrates this incident from 1828 as a classic example of the contempt with which the colonial powers treated judicial decisions.[77]

MC Setalvad, a doyen of the Bombay High Court bar who was free India's first Attorney General, in his classic book, *War and Civil Liberties*,[78] had also narrated, through telling instances, of how the British colonial government treated the rule of law as well as the sanctity of judicial decisions with utter contempt. He took the example of *Talpade's* case, in which the Indian Federal Court had come out strongly in favour of civil liberties, by holding that a particular rule under which individuals were detained was not supported by the Defence of India Act, and was therefore invalid. Rather than respecting this decision, the Indian Governor General saw to it that an ordinance was hurriedly passed to nullify its effects.[79] As Setalvad put it: 'Such a course of action could be taken only under a régime *entirely impervious to public opinion and to ideas of constitutional propriety*.'[80]

It was important to create a judicial system which could keep a check on the balance between fundamental rights and the public good by evaluating the wisdom of laws. Thus, Munshi's idea of due process was of coupling it with judicial review to ensure that apart from procedural rights being guaranteed as rights, individuals would use the due process guarantee to engage in a substantive review of laws to ensure that fundamental rights are never subservient to state actions. For Munshi, it was important to unleash the true strength of the due process guarantee by making it justiciable and enforceable.

In some measure, Munshi's democratic justification for due process had a strong counter-intuitive appeal. As we have seen, opponents of due process had viewed it as imposing an unfair burden on a legislature elected by popular will, and if popular will could not be translated into laws, then it was pointless to have elected representatives. For them, a due process guarantee hindered democracy for it was a step towards replacing a popularly elected government with an unelected judiciary. But, through the democratic justification, Munshi turned the proposition around to demonstrate that the due process guarantee was not counter-majoritarian at all.

In Munshi's conception, the due process guarantee would create a *modus vivendi*. It would be used by courts to weigh the individual's interests and freedoms with the state's responsibility of achieving what was needed to ensure public good and social progress. In doing so, the judicial branch would arrive at a decision about whether a constitutionally sound balance was struck between these two competing interests. In this framework, the people would use the due process guarantee to keep a check on law-making and lawmakers, long after they had cast their vote. Importantly, when state action was challenged in courts, the government of the day would be presented with the opportunity of fully and properly defending the measure in question. The due process guarantee's singularly alluring quality would be its role in ennobling democracy.[81]

When Munshi rose to speak, he expressed his support for Amendment No. 528 (which sought to replace 'except according to procedure established by law' with the phrase 'without due process of law'). Perhaps reading the mood of the House, that the Constituent Assembly was not really concerned with the phrase 'personal liberty' appearing in draft Article 15, he focused on the need to bring back the due process guarantee.

Munshi began his speech by laying bare the hollowness of draft Article 15. For him, the fundamental right of due process was an irreducible right, which draft Article 15 had reduced to no right at all. According to Munshi, all that draft Article 15 stipulated as a right was an inquiry as to whether a procedure envisaged by law was followed, and nothing beyond that.

On the contrary, a due process guarantee allowed not only for the examination of the nature of the procedure set out in a law, but also an examination of the larger question: whether the procedure set out, and indeed whether the law itself, was justified. No such inquiry could ever be conducted by courts within the narrow confines of draft Article 15.[82] As Munshi put it:

> This clause would only have meaning if the courts could examine not merely that the conviction has been according to law or according to proper procedure, but that the *procedure as well as the substantive part of the law are such as would be proper and justified by the circumstances of the case.*[83]

What justified, more than anything else, the need for draft Article 15 to include a due process guarantee, was the nature of government that the Constitution had provided for in free India. Munshi highlighted the uniquely Indian version of the due process guarantee which had been formulated after much debate and discussion. This version of due process removed the reference to property, and then presented a truncated version of liberty in the form of 'personal liberty.' What this meant was that the due process guarantee in such form would go on to ensure that before losing one's freedom, the due process of law had been complied with:[84]

> This clause is now restricted to liberty of the person, that is, nobody can be convicted, sent to jail or be sentenced to death without due process of law. That is the narrow meaning of this clause which is now sought to be incorporated by amendment No. 528.[85]

Munshi then returned to his argument of the virtues of the due process guarantee enabling substantive review of legislations, and how this inducted into the Constitution a semblance of balance of power. Rather than being harmed by it, democracy was in fact strengthened by the existence of the due process guarantee. He believed that the due process guarantee had two parts.

In the first part, the due process guarantee allowed courts to examine whether the procedural guarantees have been complied with when a person interacted with the justice system.[86] The second part was that it empowered the people to demand from the state a compelling justification for a law which affected personal liberty. If the state was able to demonstrate such a compelling justification, then for Munshi, a balance between 'individual liberty' and 'social control' was achieved.[87] As Munshi put it:

> In a democracy it is necessary that there should be given an opportunity to the Governments to vindicate the measures that they take. Apart from anything else, it is a wholesome thing that a Government is given an opportunity to justify its action in a court of law.[88]

For Munshi, it was too dangerous a proposition to structure a system in which courts could not examine the content and merits of a law for it was not impossible to imagine a situation in which a democratically elected government would make laws which subverted personal liberty rights. If legislation were to be enacted which conferred on the police extraordinary powers without a system in place which could review the wisdom and purpose of such laws, then personal liberty rights would be nullified.[89]

Munshi also highlighted certain troubling developments which were taking place in different parts of India. He pointed out that there was an increasing trend of laws being made to deprive people of any semblance of rights when they came into contact with the criminal justice system. Munshi used these developments as an example to demonstrate that egregious violations of rights would, in the absence of a due process guarantee, continue unabated:

> We have, unfortunately, in this country legislatures with large majorities, facing very severe problems, and naturally, there is a tendency to pass legislation in a hurry which give sweeping powers to the executive and the police. Now, there will be no deterrent if these legislations are not examined by a court of law. For instance, I read the other day that there is going to be a legislation, or there is already a legislation, in one province in India which denies to the accused the assistance of lawyer. How is that going to be checked? ... This creates tremendous difficulties for the accused and I think, as I have submitted, there must be some agency in a democracy which strikes a balance between individual liberty and social control.[90]

For Munshi, draft Article 15 was a perfidy and would sound the death knell for fundamental rights if such brazen steps could not be challenged in courts by individuals who wished to question the substance and wisdom of such laws and state action. The ability of the people to check state action assumed greater salience since, in the backdrop of these developments, due process would also operate as a deterrent force against legislatures which often hurriedly enact legislations.

Munshi also dealt with another knotty issue. Every time the due process guarantee had been discussed in the past, a recurring complaint had been that in the USA, the due process guarantee has been used to invalidate many laws aimed at achieving social progress. This was used to argue that India can ill-afford such a scenario, where laws that are needed to achieve social progress, income equality, equality in land ownership and laws aimed at promoting public good, might suffer the threat of invalidation.

For his part, Munshi acknowledged that the due process guarantee had been the basis for striking down laws in the USA, but he was quick to point out that in over 90 per cent of such cases the law under challenge had in fact been upheld. Thus, the fact that in a small set of cases, laws had been struck down, was no ground to forever deny to Indians the entire gamut of protection which the due process guarantee offered.[91]

Here it is important to take note of the fact that in defending due process, Munshi advocated for the version of a clause on due process which was enumerated as Clause 16 in Rau's Draft Constitution. In large measure, his speech about how such a clause would enable the development of substantive due process in India goes to confirm the theory advanced in Chapter 2 that even when BN Rau had drafted Clause 16 of his Draft Constitution, the plain text of that clause in fact would have allowed substantive due process to develop in India.

Finally, Munshi recognized that draft Article 15 had in fact been drafted in times of enormous chaos and conflict that had followed Indian Independence, which moved many to oppose the incorporation of the due process guarantee as a fundamental right. Nonetheless, nothing could justify a scheme in which personal liberty was placed at the lowest keel.[92] For him, to accept draft Article 15 would be to commence the process of the eventual destruction of the right to personal liberty. Munshi ended his speech by sounding a note of caution about what draft Article 15 would really mean for India:

> Our emergency at the moment has perhaps led us to forget that if we do not give that scope to individual liberty, and give it the protection of the courts, we will create a tradition which will ultimately destroy even whatever little of personal liberty which exists in this country.[93]

Alladi Krishnaswami Ayyar: Due Process as the Sword of Damocles

After Munshi, Alladi Krishnaswami Ayyar addressed the Constituent Assembly. Now for the first time in the debates on draft Article 15, a member of the Assembly, and no less than a member of the Drafting Committee would defend the incorporation of draft Article 15.[94]

As we saw in Chapter 1, Ayyar had played a key role in persuading the Advisory Committee to appreciate the importance of incorporating a due process guarantee as a fundamental right, since initially, the Advisory Committee had been sceptical of due process rights. However, by the time draft Article 15 reached the floor of the Constituent Assembly, Ayyar had changed his mind about the utility of a constitution incorporating a due process guarantee. A large part of his speech focused on the eternal dangers that the due process guarantee brought with it and why India could ill afford a constitution in which a fundamental right is virtually stopped in its tracks, or any law aimed at achieving social good and public welfare.

What he feared was that welfare laws aimed at achieving social progress would be swept away by the tide of due process. For Ayyar, the incorporation of the due process guarantee would be the constitutional personification of the sword that hung over the head of Damocles. The very presence of the due process guarantee would paralyse law-making and lawmakers, for the validity of such laws would always be cast in doubt.

In his speech, Ayyar would raise several other objections against the due process guarantee such as that the due process guarantee in the USA, had a discursive jurisprudence which was best avoided in India; and that due process results in the inversion of democracy, for courts, and not elected legislatures, ultimately decide what is good for the nation. Ayyar would also argue that even otherwise, using the phrase 'personal liberty' along with a due process clause would not be advantageous in reducing the power of the due process guarantee, for despite the presence of this phrase, the due process guarantee could still be used to engage in substantive due process review and question legislative wisdom.

Ayyar began his speech by pointing out that draft Article 15 had only been a suggestion which was made by the Drafting Committee as an alternative to the due process guarantee, in favour of which most of the previous speakers had spoken. And because the Drafting Committee had recommended draft Article

15 as an alternative, he owed a duty to the Drafting Committee to defend this particular recommendation.[95]

In his discourse on the development of the law of due process, Ayyar pointed out that under English law and as it had evolved in the common law system, due process essentially meant fair and equitable treatment of persons appearing in a court of law, consistent with the principles of natural justice. For him, if this was all that the due process guarantee was supposed to mean in India, then he would not oppose it. [96]

Ayyar added that it is when the due process doctrine was developed in the USA that it began to take on a life of its own— due process had become a ruse for replacing popular will with judicial will, where courts would supplant legislations with their own individual leanings. This was only worsened by the fact that in developing the jurisprudence on due process, the US Supreme Court had 'not adopted a consistent view at all.'[97] Ayyar argued that the American law on due process was unclear and that this legal uncertainty had led to a situation in which it was difficult to divine any clear standard of what constituted a violation of due process.[98]

KM Munshi had distinguished himself as a leading member of the Bombay High Court Bar and in his speech, he had presented a defence of due process and judicial review. He had even argued that in America, the due process guarantee had developed in a coherent manner and had resulted in the invalidation of only a small set of laws. In a pointed riposte aimed at Munshi and to this argument of his, Ayyar had this to say:

> I would challenge any member of the Bar with a deep knowledge of the cases in the United States Supreme Court to say that there is anything like uniformity in regard to

the interpretation of 'due process' ... It all depended upon
the particular Judges that presided on the occasion ...
There is no sort of uniformity at all in the decisions of the
United States Supreme Court.[99]

Ayyar then moved on to counter the idea that the use of 'personal
liberty' would counteract the due process guarantee from being
used to challenge laws. Personal liberty need not be understood
in the limited sense of applying to cases of restraint of persons
such as imprisonment. After all, in the USA itself, courts had
concluded that laws which fixed minimum wages or which
regulated employment were considered as violations of the right
of personal liberty itself. [100]

For Ayyar, this was the most dangerous part of the due process
guarantee and its incorporation would result in virtually the same
sort of pattern in India. Every law, especially those which aimed
to achieve a particular social welfare or public good end, would
in some ways affect liberty or personal liberty rights. When it
came to such laws, it was important for the liberty right to give
way to the social welfare goal. But the presence of the due process
guarantee would be a lurking danger, and such laws would be
treated as constitutionally suspect and susceptible to invalidation.
Added to this, given the fact that there was no clarity about what
the standard of review in a case pertaining to due process was, the
incorporation of a due process guarantee would be a recipe for
disaster. He firmly believed that for the conditions in which India
found herself, it was an unwise course of action to incorporate into
a constitution a right which hung like a threat over laws passed to
achieve demonstrable public good or social welfare ends.[101]

Ayyar then went on to recognize that in the USA, with the
advent of the New Deal, there had been a 'swing of the pendulum';[102]

American courts had begun to avoid the invalidation of laws under the due process guarantee. But even then, the various decisions did not embody a coherent legal principle. If the amendments to draft Article 15 were to succeed, Ayyar noted, then his only pious hope would be that the Indian courts would not follow the path of the American courts when it came to the development of the due process guarantee. For him, Indian courts ought to interpret the due process guarantee, if it were to become a fundamental right, to promote 'the progress and well-being of the country.'[103] For Ayyar, the due process would only then 'prove fairly alright if only the Judges move with the times and bring to bear their wisdom on particular issues.'[104]

Ayyar was clear that even though various speakers had spoken on the assumption that personal liberty meant freedom from restraints and cases of arrest without a trial, the moment personal liberty was used with due process, the meaning of the guarantee would change given how the American courts had understood the relationship between personal liberty and due process. Therefore, the Constituent Assembly must be fully conscious of what it was permitting the Constitution to do, if it decided to accept the amendments to draft Article 15.

What this meant was that the Constitution would need to eventually balance a variety of competing claims to ensure that due process does not become a threat to the Constitution itself. If the amendments were to be approved, Ayyar only hoped that Indian courts would not vacillate on the meaning of due process but contextualize due process to the particular challenges faced by India.[105]

Strikingly, while ending his speech, Ayyar chose to close on a positive note. As he noted, from the outpouring of support that the due process guarantee had received, it seemed that much greater trust was being placed in the judicial branch. But the Drafting Committee had been 'guilty of being apprehensive of judicial vagaries', and had decided to recommend 'procedure established by law' instead of 'due process of law'.[106] The Drafting Committee believed this particular phraseology achieved a balance between the competing claims of individual freedom and issues of security. His positivity led him to, as a parting statement, proclaim that he still held an open mind and if well persuaded, he would perhaps be 'influenced to come to a different conclusion.'[107]

Ayyar's scepticism about the judicial branch was surprising to say the least. He had reached the pinnacle of the legal profession, serving as the Advocate General of Madras from 1929 until 1944. But in his speech, he had wryly noted that from the 'British days we have inherited a kind of faith in lawyers, legal arguments, legal consultations and in courts; I, for my part, having flourished in the law, have no quarrel with those people who believe in the lawyer.'[108]

The fact that Ayyar ended his speech by proclaiming that he was open to changing his position on due process if good reason was shown suggests that he had not absolutely foreclosed the idea of considering the incorporation of the due process guarantee. This raises interesting questions over Munshi's version of events on how due process came to be deleted by the Drafting Committee, which were discussed in Chapter 3.

According to Munshi's recollection, which Granville Austin used as the basis to reconstruct the events of the past, the Drafting Committee decided to delete the due process guarantee and replace it with draft Article 15 because Ayyar had become an opponent of due process. If Ayyar so staunchly opposed due process, it seems curious that he would announce in the Constituent Assembly that he was still open to changing his position and support its inclusion in the Constitution.

However, even though Ayyar ended on this positive note, Granville Austin rates his speech as 'one of the sorriest performances ever put on by the Assembly leadership.'[109] In Austin's estimation, Ayyar's speech was unconvincing and disingenuous. It was unconvincing, given especially the fact that in the past, Ayyar had played a leading role in shepherding the acceptance of the due process guarantee as a fundamental right in the Advisory Committee. And the speech was also disingenuous, for Ayyar did not explain what led him to change his position on due process especially since his speech contained points of argument which he himself had previously been critical of, when speaking in favour of the due process guarantee.[110]

Nevertheless, to fully appreciate the profundity of the change in Ayyar's stance, it is worth examining the sentiment that Ayyar had expressed, on the importance of due process, in the Fundamental Rights Sub-Committee. On 27 February 1947, the newly constituted Sub-Committee had met for the first time. When the Sub-Committee met, the members agreed with KM Munshi's suggestion that a 'preliminary discussion' be had to chalk out the direction of their work.[111]

At that first meeting, Ayyar presented a succinct but truly marvellous defence of due process. He pointed out that so far as the framework of fundamental rights was concerned, it was wiser to have a constitution with justiciable fundamental rights (like the American Constitution) rather than having a constitution which submits fundamental rights to the wishes of the state (like the Irish Constitution did). To reinforce the importance of this point, Ayyar took the example of the due process guarantee contained in the 14th Amendment to the American Constitution. He used it as an instance of a fundamental right which empowered the US Supreme Court to intervene and halt state action aimed at taking away a person's life, liberty or property without due process. Using the specific instance of due process and its endless possibilities of acting as a strong check against unconstitutional measures, Ayyar *advised* the sub-committee to take the United States *as their model* for the *protection of the basic rights* of the citizen.'[112]

The credit for bringing the importance of the due process guarantee to the immediate attention of the Fundamental Rights Sub-Committee goes entirely to Ayyar. But, now in the Constituent Assembly, he adopted a stance which was diametrically opposed to his original position, and here he strongly espoused the case against due process entering the Constitution.

One cannot also help but note that the portion of Ayyar's speech which criticized due process in American constitutional law was, really speaking, a reductive analysis which pressed into service rhetorical flourish rather than offering concrete examples to demonstrate the perils of due process. What makes his speech harder to deconstruct is that when he had spoken on the advantages of incorporating the due process guarantee as a fundamental right in the proceedings of the Advisory Committee, his speech was richly laden with a threadbare analysis of the latest decisions of the American Supreme Court and also contained a remarkable analysis of the advantages and demerits of the due process guarantee.[113]

In his speech in the Advisory Committee, Ayyar had confidently proclaimed that the decision to recommend the due process guarantee by the Fundamental Rights Sub-Committee, had been made after taking into account the 'full implications of that expression' and that he himself was in favour of the due process guarantee and 'not against that clause.'[114] Speaking now in the Constituent Assembly, however, Ayyar attempted to brush aside due process by labelling it a right which confused, confounded and befuddled anyone who attempted to give it a coherent meaning.

Ayyar undoubtedly had committed an about-face on due process, which would not go unnoticed in the Constituent Assembly. ZH Lari would address the Assembly after Ayyar, and express his support for replacing the phrase 'except according to procedure established by law' with the phrase 'without due process of law'.

In a riposte aimed directly at Ayyar, Lari proclaimed that the due process guarantee was necessary not only to secure liberty but to also secure the working of the legislatures.[115] Accusing Ayyar of having a 'fling at the profession of law',[116] Lari argued that legal assistance was paramount for justice.[117] In response to this riposte, Ayyar remonstrated immediately saying, 'I had no fling at the profession of law.'[118]

Moving on to the substance of his speech, Lari wished to clarify that using the phrase 'personal liberty' was not the same as using 'liberty'. This was perhaps necessary since Ayyar had argued that, in the USA, they essentially had the same meaning. Lari pointed out since only the word 'liberty' was used, the due process guarantee became all-encompassing and was used against every sort of law. However, by using 'personal liberty', a phrase which had a limited definition, the scope of its application would be narrowed immediately. Furthermore, as Lari noted, this narrowing of liberty would also mean that a court could not promote liberty at the cost of legitimate ends which the State needed to achieve. For Lari, the judicial branch would be well equipped to balance liberty with what is important for the state.[119]

Lari used this argument to drive home the point that in the USA itself, courts had harmonized due process with legitimate ends which the government hoped to achieve; something which according to Lari, even Ayyar had acknowledged. Seen in this light, there was now no reason to fear that such harmonization would not be undertaken by Indian courts. Lari was confident that the Indian Supreme Court would well harmonize due process with the 'necessities of the state.'[120]

So far as due process was concerned, Lari imagined the due process guarantee as providing two sets of protections: that of having a trial conducted, and that of providing a judgment containing the reasons for the verdict reached. For Lari, if a law provided these two guarantees, then in his view, the due process guarantee was fulfilled.[121]

Lari then turned his attention to the argument that popularly elected legislatures should not have their will thwarted. Deconstructing the scheme of governance that the Constitution intended on inaugurating, he believed that in reality, the Legislature is managed by a Cabinet, which consists of a small group of members, which in turn is really the Executive. And it was to this small group on whom the Constitution would confer great, unchecked powers to violate individual liberty—a dilemma which would be avoided if the amendments to bring back due process into the Constitution (referring to Amendment Nos. 528 and 530) were passed.[122]

Lari also examined the justification provided by the Drafting Committee for using the phrase 'procedure established by law', which was that it was taken from Article 31 of the Constitution of Japan. The justification that the Drafting Committee had provided in the second part of the footnote to draft Article 15, had been that this phrase was 'more specific'. What did this mean? As he pointed out, Article 31 in the Constitution of Japan was certainly more specific since the articles which succeeded it provided a broad range of due process guarantees. Seen in that light, Article 31 was specific in that it stipulated that the right to life and liberty could not be taken away without procedure established by law, and that the guarantees contained in the succeeding articles provided the rights which could not be taken away by law.[123]

Incidentally, Lari had made a similar argument on an earlier occasion. When addressing the Constituent Assembly on 8 November 1948, during the debates which took place when Dr Ambedkar moved the resolution introducing the Draft Constitution, he had argued that comparisons with the Irish and Japanese Constitutions were ill-conceived. This was because those constitutions stipulated the procedures which can be adopted by the State when dealing with the right to life and liberty. But unlike them, the Draft Constitution had said absolutely nothing of the legal procedures to be followed when dealing with the right to life and personal liberty.[124]

According to Lari, the Japanese Constitution was a high watermark in constitutional drafting for two important reasons. The fact that the Americans in guiding the making of the Japanese Constitution nevertheless enumerated a series of due process rights such as the right to access courts (Article 32), showed the universal acceptance of these ideals being guaranteed to the people regardless of the conditions in which the country found itself. Moreover, to enumerate such detailed due process rights for a nation which until the end of the Second World War had been steeped in ideas of fascism, further demonstrated that notwithstanding the prevalence of emergent situations, it was critical to provide due process rights in a constitution.[125] Importantly, the Japanese Constitution's importance lay in articulating the idea that when a nation was to be founded on the basis of a new constitution, freedom of the individual had to coincide and coexist with the State's interest, without the latter completely overawing the former.[126]

In the final part of his speech, Lari addressed the criticism that due process would unsettle legislative will. He was keen to point out that such fears were not only unsubstantiated but were rooted in fear alone. If this fear were to continue to paralyse the drafting of fundamental rights, then the Constitution would be unable to truly provide robust protection against the violation of fundamental rights altogether. For Lari, it was critical to recognize that the enumeration of due process rights was an important goal which the Constitution ought to achieve.[127] Lari ended his speech by sounding a dire warning:

> We should profit by the experience of other countries and by what has been observed for centuries. Or should we go by the *ipse dixit* of X, Y, Z who says that there seems to be some germ of disruption in this clause? … We should not be led away by this bogey into accepting this clause. *If this clause is accepted, then the whole Constitution becomes lifeless. The article, as it stands, is lifeless and it makes also the whole Constitution lifeless.* Unless you accept this amendment, you would not earn the gratitude of future generations.[128]

Dr Ambedkar's Reply

After Lari's speech, the debates on draft Article 15 were to continue on 7 December 1948, but on that day, Dr Ambedkar requested that draft Article 15's consideration be postponed.[129]

The debates on draft Article 15 had been postponed on 7 December 1948, since there was a sense that the many concerns raised by the members during the debates on 6 December 1948, should be addressed and their recommendations be taken heed of. But for a week thereafter, the Constituent Assembly had not heard of any steps being taken to address their concerns, and the Vice-President of the Assembly needed an immediate answer as to what had been done in this respect.[130] It was against this background that nearly a week after that, the Vice-President decided to bring draft Article 15 up for discussion again and asked Dr Ambedkar to address the Assembly.

Dr Ambedkar began by pointing out that the debates on draft Article 15 were deeply divided on the utility of the Constitution incorporating a due process guarantee. On one view, the failure to incorporate a clause on due process meant that draft Article 15 was a spent force. On the other view, draft Article 15 as it stood was perfectly acceptable.[131]

Moving to expound on what due process meant, Dr Ambedkar stated that in a constitution which respected separation of powers there was no controversy if the courts examined whether a law falls within the legislature's legislative competence. What a clause on due process does, however, is to give courts an additional ground of inquiry: which is to inquire whether the law was 'in keeping with certain fundamental principles' so far as fundamental rights were concerned, and whether it 'was good law'.[132]

What this meant was that even though the law was validly enacted, the law may nevertheless fail to pass constitutional muster if the courts concluded, for one reason or another, that the law did not seem justified. Whether or not courts ought to be invested with such powers, was the question that Dr Ambedkar posed to the Constituent Assembly.[133]

For Dr Ambedkar, the answer was not an easy one, and the Constituent Assembly had to make a choice between two options.

The first option was to create a judicial system which would not be allowed to question the wisdom and justness of laws, on the assumption that legislatures will never act in a manner which hurts freedoms. The other option was to invest in courts robust judicial review powers since legislatures may be swayed by 'passion, by party prejudice, by party considerations' and enact legislation which violates the 'fundamental principles' which protect the rights and liberties of the people.[134] But neither could he rule out the possibility that legislatures will act in a manner which is detrimental to the rights of the people nor could he rule out the possibility that a Supreme Court might not examine legislations dispassionately and objectively, and the justices may not prevent their individual viewpoints and beliefs from entering their judgments.[135] As Dr Ambedkar put it:

> For myself I cannot altogether omit the possibility of a Legislature packed by party men making laws which may abrogate or violate what we regard as certain fundamental principles affecting the life and liberty of an individual. At the same time, I do not see how five or six gentlemen sitting in the Federal or Supreme Court examining laws made by the Legislature and by dint of their own individual conscience or their bias or their prejudices be trusted to determine which law is good and which law is bad.[136]

For his part, however, Dr Ambedkar himself was undecided and could not pinpoint which of the options was better. And although a choice had to be made between incorporating a due process guarantee or approving draft Article 15 in the form recommended by the Drafting Committee, it was a choice that the Constituent Assembly had to ultimately make. Dr Ambedkar ended his speech on a sombre note, refusing categorically to guide the Assembly on the choice it must make.[137] He only remarked:

> It is rather a case where a man has to sail between Charybdis and Scylla and I therefore would not say anything. I would leave it to the House to decide in any way it likes.[138]

This uncertainty was an odd change in Dr Ambedkar's stance on the question of incorporating the due process guarantee as a fundamental right. From being the person who first introduced to the Constituent Assembly the concept of due process in 1946 and the idea that the due process guarantee ought to be a part of fundamental rights, Dr Ambedkar had now moved to a position where he would not weigh in on the debates on due process in any substantial measure. Besides, there was no occasion for such ambivalence. After all, as Bhargava had pointed out in his speech on 6 December 1948, once the power of substantive review had been made a part of draft Article 13, where was the occasion to doubt the inclusion of substantive review in draft Article 15, too?

Although an untiring and devoted supporter of due process in the early years, Dr Ambedkar had now decided to leave the Constituent Assembly to its own devices to decide on whether draft Article 15 ought to be incorporated in the form recommended by the Drafting Committee.[139] With the end of Dr Ambedkar's speech, the debates on draft Article 15 drew to a close and the Vice-President then put the amendments to vote. Amendment Nos. 523, 530, 526 and 527 were put to vote, in that order. The Constituent Assembly voted against all of them. As for Amendment No. 528, when the Vice-President put it to vote, SV Krishnamurthy Rao stated that he would no longer press the amendment resulting in the amendment being withdrawn.[140]

Now all that remained for the Constituent Assembly was to vote on draft Article 15, and the Vice-President moved the motion, 'That article 15 stand part of the Constitution.' And the Constituent Assembly voted to adopt the motion.[141]

The vote to incorporate draft Article 15 as recommended by the Drafting Committee, and the rejection of the amendments which sought to incorporate the due process guarantee in it, was a moment of grim irony given that just over a year and a half ago, on 30 April 1947, the Constituent Assembly had voted in favour of including the due process guarantee as a fundamental right.

In draft Article 15, however, the Constituent Assembly approved a right which permitted for laws to provide 'any procedure it cared to prescribe' without the people being guaranteed, as a concomitant right, the ability to question these procedures.[142]

Nevertheless, the void that draft Article 15 left came in for resounding public condemnation,[143] and with the passage of time, the Drafting Committee would begin to explore the idea of filling this void and of introducing some form of substantive due process protection in the Constitution.

In September 1949, Dr Ambedkar would take formal steps to introduce in the Constituent Assembly, and indeed in the Constitution, as a fundamental right, due process protection for persons who came into contact with the criminal justice system. And it would be this move which would ignite in the Constituent Assembly a spirited and renewed debate on the abiding value of the due process guarantee.

Endnotes

1   CAD, vol. VII, p. 797.
2   Id., pp. 823–840.
3   Id., pp. 840–842.

4   Id., p. 840.

5   Id., p. 842.

6   Ibid.

7   Id., p. 843.

8   Ibid.

9   Id., p. 843–844.

10   Id., p. 844.

11   Id., p. 843.

12   Id., p. 844.

13   Id., p. 1001.

14   Id., pp. 844, 1001.

15   Id., p. 844.

16   Id., p. 1001.

17   Id., pp. 842–843.

18   Id., p. 843.

19   Ibid.

20   Id., pp. 844, 1001.

21   Id., p. 845.

22   Id., p. 844.

23   Ibid.

24   Ibid. (Emphasis added.)

25   Constitution of Japan, Article 32: No person shall be denied the right of access to the courts.

26   Constitution of Japan, Article 34: No person shall be arrested or detained without being at once informed of the charges against him or without the immediate privilege of counsel; nor shall he be detained without adequate cause; and upon demand of any person such cause must be immediately shown in open court in his presence and the presence of his counsel.

27   Constitution of Japan, Article 35: The right of all persons to be secure in their homes, papers and effects against entries, searches and seizures shall not be impaired except upon warrant issued for adequate cause and particularly describing the place to be searched and things to be seized, or except as provided by Article 33.

28   US Constitution, Amendment IV: The right of the people to be secure in their persons, houses, papers, and effects, against unreasonable searches and seizures, shall not be violated, and no warrants shall issue, but upon probable cause, supported by oath or affirmation, and particularly describing the place to be searched, and the persons or things to be seized.

29 CAD, vol. VII, pp. 844–845.

30 Id., pp. 844–845.

31 Id., p. 844.

32 Id., p. 845.

33 Id., pp. 845–846.

34 Id., p. 737.

35 Id., p. 846.

36 Ibid. ('By using these words "without due process of law" we want that the courts may be authorised to go into the question of the substantive law as well as procedural law. When an enactment is enacted, according to the amendment now proposed to be passed by this House, the courts will have the right to go into the question whether a particular law enacted by Parliament is just or not, whether it is good or not, whether as a matter of fact it protects the liberties of the people or not. If the Supreme Court comes to the conclusion that it is unconstitutional, that the law is unreasonable or unjust, then in that case the courts will hold the law to be such and that law will not have any further effect.')

37 Pandit Thakur Dass Bhargava was referring to the Indian Criminal Law Amendment Act, 1908 (Act No. 14 of 1908), which came into effect on 11 December 1908. Part II of the Amendment Act pertained to 'Unlawful Associations' and Section 16 empowered the State Government to declare an association unlawful, by notification in the Gazette, if it opined that 'any association interferes or has for its object interference with the administration of the law or with the maintenance of law and order, or that it constitutes a danger to the public peace.' See Indian Criminal Law Amendment Act, 1908 (available at http://legislative.gov.in/sites/default/files/A1908-14.pdf).

38 CAD, vol. VII, p. 847. ('To illustrate this I would refer the House to Act XIV of 1908 called the Black Law under which thousands, if not hundreds of thousands of Congressmen were sent to jail. According to Act XIV of 1908 the Government took to themselves the powers of declaring any organisation illegal by the mere fact that they passed a notification to that effect. This Act, when passed, was condemned by the whole of India … The Courts could not hold that the notification of the Government was wrong. The courts were not competent to hold that any organisation or association of persons was legal though its objects were legal. The objects of the Congress were peaceful. They wanted to attain self-government but by peaceful and legitimate means. All the same, since the Government had notified, the courts

were helpless. This legislation demonstrates the need of the powers of "due process."')

39   See B Shiva Rao, *Framing of India's Constitution*, vol. III, pp. 522–523.
40   See CAD, vol. VII, pp. 735–740, 787.
41   B Shiva Rao, *A Study*, p. 222.
42   CAD, vol. VII, p. 739. In the final Constitution, draft Article 13 after renumbering, became Article 19, which is how we know it today. See, B Shiva Rao, *A Study*, pp. 226–227.
43   CAD, vol. VII, p. 847.
44   Ibid. (Emphasis added.)
45   Tripathi, 'Perspectives', pp. 85–90 (proposing that the presence of the phrase reasonable restrictions in draft Article 13 signalled the incorporation of due process). ('In fact, no constitution which secures liberties by providing for judicial review of executive and legislative action on the basis of judicially supervised standards of reasonableness can simply succeed in avoiding in avoiding the doctrine of "due process" and "police powers." Because as Bhargava and others members of the Constituent Assembly rightly understood, "due process" is none other than the test of "reasonableness" applied by the judiciary in assessing the quality of the legislative measure affecting individual liberty.') Id., p. 90. Also see, Chandrachud, *Due Process of Law*, pp. 78–80 (examining why the principle of reasonableness gained easy acceptance in the Constituent Assembly).
46   CAD, vol. VII, p. 847.
47   Ibid.
48   Id., p. 848.
49   Ibid.
50   Ibid.
51   Ibid.
52   Ibid.
53   Id., p. 849.
54   Ibid.
55   Ibid. ('Secondly, Sir, in the word "liberty" that we have used, we have added the word "personal" and made it "personal liberty" to make it clear that this article does not refer to any kind of liberty of contract or anything of that kind, but relates only to life and liberty of person. Therefore, it would be wrong to say that the words "due process of law" are likely to lead to any uncertainty in legislation or unnecessary interference by the judiciary in reviewing legislation.')

56 Ibid. ('Sir, at times it does happen that the executive requires
    extraordinary powers to deal with extraordinary situations and they
    can pass emergency laws. The legislature, which is generally controlled
    by the executive—because it is the majority that forms the executive—
    gives such powers to the executive in moments of emergency.
    Therefore, it is but proper that we should give the right to the judiciary
    to review legislation.')

57 Ibid.

58 Ibid.

59 Id., p. 850.

60 Ibid. (Emphasis added.)

61 B Shiva Rao, *Framing of India's Constitution*, vol. II, pp. 21–36.

62 Id., p. 32.

63 CAD, vol. VII, p. 850.

64 Id., p. 850. Chapter 39 of *Magna Carta* reads as follows: 'No free man
    shall be taken, or imprisoned, disseised, or outlawed, exiled, or in any
    way destroyed; nor shall we go upon him, not send upon him, but by
    the lawful judgment of his peers or by the law of the land.' Ibid.

65 Id., pp. 850–851. According to Statute No. 28: 'No man of what state
    or conditions so ever he be, shall be put out of his lands or tenements,
    nor taken nor imprisoned, nor indicated, nor put to death, without he
    be brought to answer by due process of law.' Id., p. 850.

66 Id., pp. 850–851.

67 Id., pp. 850–851.

68 Id., p. 851.

69 Ibid.

70 Ibid.

71 B Shiva Rao, *Framing of India's Constitution*, vol. II, p. 71.

72 Ibid.

73 Id., p. 116. Minutes of the meeting of the Sub-Committee on
    Fundamental Rights dated 24 March 1947.

74 B Shiva Rao, *Framing of India's Constitution*, vol. IV, pp. 393–395.

75 CAD, vol. VII, pp. 851–852.

76 PB Vacha, *Famous Judges, Lawyers and Cases of Bombay: A Judicial
    History of Bombay During the British Period* (Bombay: NM Tripathi
    Pvt. Ltd., 1962), pp. 190–214 [hereinafter Vacha, *Famous Judges*].

77 *Kantaru Rajeevaru v. Indian Young Lawyers Association* (2020) 2 SCC
    1, p. 46, para 75 (Sabrimala Entry of Women Review Petition) (citing
    Vacha, *Famous Judges*, pp. 196–198).

78   MC Setalvad, *War and Civil Liberties* (New Delhi: Oxford University Press, 1946).

79   Id., pp. 52–56.

80   Id., p. 56. (Emphasis added.) The ordinance in question did not put matters to an end and a running battle ensued for some years between the courts and the executive. Id., pp. 56–59.

81   CAD, vol. VII, p. 852.

82   Id., p. 851.

83   Ibid. (Emphasis added.)

84   Id. p. 852

85   Ibid.

86   Ibid.

87   Ibid. ('This clause would enable the courts to examine not only the procedural part, the jurisdiction of the court, the jurisdiction of the legislature, but also the substantive law. When a law has been passed which entitles Government to take away the personal liberty of an individual, the court will consider whether the law which has been passed is such as is required by the exigencies of the case, and, therefore, as I said, the balance will be struck between individual liberty and the social control. In the result, Governments will have to go to the court of law and justify why a particular measure infringing the personal liberty of the citizen has been imposed.')

88   Ibid.

89   Ibid.

90   Id., pp. 852–853.

91   Id., p. 852.

92   Ibid.

93   Id., p. 853.

94   B Shiva Rao, *A Study*, p. 237.

95   CAD, vol. VII, p. 853.

96   Ibid. ('The expression "due process" itself as interpreted by the English Judges connoted merely the due course of legal proceedings according to the rules and forms established for the protection of rights, and a fair trial in a court of justice according to the modes of proceeding applicable to the case. Possibly, if the expression has been understood according to its original content and according to the interpretation of English Judges, there might be no difficulty at all.')

97   Ibid.

98   Ibid.

99   Ibid.

100 Id., pp. 853–854. ('Some of my honourable Friends have spoken as if it merely applied to cases of detention and imprisonment. The Minimum Wage Law or a Restraint on Employment have in some cases been regarded as an invasion of personal liberty and freedom, by the United States Supreme Court in its earlier decisions, the theory being that it is an essential part of personal liberty that every person in the world be she a woman, be he a child over fourteen years of age or be he a labourer, has the right to enter into any contract he or she liked and it is not the province of other people to interfere with that liberty. On that ground, in the earlier decisions of the Supreme Court it has been held that the Minimum Wage Laws are invalid as invading personal liberty.')

101 Id., pp. 853–854.

102 Id., p. 854.

103 Ibid.

104 Ibid.

105 Ibid. ('After all the word "personal liberty" has not the same content and meaning as is imported into it by some of our friends who naturally feel very sensitive about people being detained without a proper trial. I equally feel it but that is not the meaning of personal liberty attributed by the American Courts in the context of "due process". I trust that the House will take into account the various aspects of this question, the future progress of India, the well-being and the security of the States, the necessity of maintaining a minimum of liberty, the need for co-ordinating social control and personal liberty, before coming to a decision.')

106 Ibid.

107 Ibid.

108 Ibid.

109 Austin, *The Indian Constitution*, p. 134.

110 Id., pp. 133–134.

111 B Shiva Rao, *Framing of India's Constitution*, vol. II, p. 115.

112 Ibid. (Emphasis added.) The minutes of the meeting record the following in respect of Alladi Krishnaswami Ayyar's statement: 'Alluding to the charter of fundamental rights and guarantees embodied in the Irish and American constitutions, Sir Alladi Krishnaswami Ayyar pointed out that citizens' rights to be embodied in a constitution should consist of guarantees enforceable in courts of law, and that it was no use laying down precepts which remained unenforceable or ineffective. The Supreme Court of the United States,

whenever its power is invoked under the Fourteenth Amendment to the Constitution, prevents a State from depriving any person of his life, liberty or property otherwise than by due process of law. Sir Alladi advised the sub-committee to take the United States as their model for the protection of the basic rights of the citizens.'

113   See B Shiva Rao, *Framing of India's Constitution*, vol. II, pp. 240–243.

114   Id., p. 241.

115   CAD, vol. VII, pp. 854–855.

116   Id., p. 855.

117   Ibid.

118   Ibid.

119   Ibid. ('There the word liberty alone existed and possibly in that state of things, it was possible to interpret it in such a way as to extend the scope of due process of law to other spheres of life but when the word "personal liberty" has been definitely inserted in the clause, I doubt whether any Court which is conscious of the requirements of a State as well as conscious of the necessities of individual liberty, will be so uncharitable to the interest of the State as to interpret in a way to thwart the proper working of the State.')

120   Ibid.

121   Id., p. 855. ('What is the essence of the due process of law? I think they are two. First is, enquiry before you condemn a man. And then there is judgment after trial. If any procedure which is adopted by any legislature provides for the hearing of a person who is suspected or is accused, and then after a proper hearing, enables him to get the benefit of a judgment based on that enquiry, my submission is, that the requirements of the due process of law are complied with.')

122   Id., p. 856.

123   Id., p. 855. ('My friend is right; and the only reason which was given by the Drafting Committee of which the honourable Speaker who preceded me was a member also, was that the words "due process of law" is not specific and the word as was used in the Japanese Constitution is more specific. No doubt the words as they stand in the Japanese Constitution are specific because the procedure is indicated and definitely laid down there.')

124   Id., p. 299.

125   Id., p. 856.

126   Id., pp. 856–857. ('There are two things by which we have to go. One is experience of others. No doubt, every clause can be criticised in one way or other. But we have to be guided by experience. Here is

the experience of other countries, and this has shown that the words "due process of law" can exist without jeopardising the existence of the State. Secondly, we know that not only here, but throughout the world every assembly is likely to misuse its power. It is bound to happen. Power corrupts. We should profit by the experience of other countries and by what has been observed for centuries.') Id., p. 857.

127 Ibid.
128 Ibid. (Emphasis added.)
129 Id., p 859.
130 Id., p. 999.
131 Id., pp. 999–1000.
132 Id., p. 1000.
133 Ibid.
134 Ibid.
135 Id., pp. 1000–1001.
136 Id., pp. 1000–1001.
137 Id., p. 1001.
138 Ibid.
139 Generally, see Alexandrowicz, *Constitutional Developments*, p. 22.
140 CAD, vol. VII, p. 1001. ('Mr. Vice-President: I shall now put the amendments one by one to vote. No. 523.
The question is:— "That in article 15, for the words 'No person shall be deprived of his life or personal liberty except according to procedure established by law' the words 'No person shall be deprived of his life or liberty without due process of law 'be substituted.'"
The amendment was negatived.
'Mr. Vice-President: The question is:—
"That in article 15, for the words 'except according to procedure established by law' the words 'due process of law' be substituted.'"
The amendment was negatived.
'Mr. Vice-President: No. 528.
Shri S. V. Krishnamurthy Rao (Mysore): I do not press it.
The amendment was, by leave of the Assembly, withdrawn.'
'Mr. Vice-President: No. 530.
The question is:—
"That in article 15, for the words 'procedure established by law' the words 'due process of law' be substituted.'"
The amendment was negatived.
'Mr. Vice-President: No. 526
The question is:—

"That in article 15 for the words 'except according to procedure established by law' the words 'save in accordance with law' be substituted.'"

The amendment was negatived.

'Mr. Vice-President: No. 527.

The question is:—

"That in article 15 for the words 'except according to procedure established by law' the words 'except in accordance with law' be substituted.'"

The amendment was negatived.

141 Ibid.

142 Alexandrowicz, *Constitutional Developments*, p. 24.

143 Austin, *The Indian Constitution*, p. 134.

5

Due Process

Abandonment and Atonement

——————•——————

Due Process Reaches an Inflection Point

F ROM THE SPEECHES DELIVERED ON 6 DECEMBER 1948, WITH RESPECT
to draft Article 15, we can discern that the debates on due
process had reached an inflection point. As we have seen, on
all the earlier occasions when the due process guarantee had
been discussed, the principal point of concern had been that
due process would herald the entry of substantive due process
review, which in turn would endanger all efforts that the State
makes to achieve social and economic progress. This is what the
Drafting Committee seemed to have in mind at its meetings of
31 October 1947,[1] and 19 January 1948,[2] when it was finalizing
the incorporation of Clause 16 (the due process guarantee) from
Rau's Draft Constitution as a fundamental right.

When the Constituent Assembly debated draft Article 15, those who participated in the debates were not mainly concerned with substantive due process threatening social progress. What concerned them much more was the impending reality that there was no enumerated fundamental right which could be used to assert basic freedoms in courts of law. There was draft Article 13, which enumerated a set of civil liberty rights (such as the freedom of speech, and freedom of association), and then there was draft Article 15. Apart from these, there was no other fundamental right which spoke of protecting an individual's rights when they came into contact with the criminal justice system.

For this reason, the Drafting Committee's move to remove any reference to due process in draft Article 15 was a cause of considerable alarm. As the debates revealed, numerous members articulated the fear that draft Article 15 would actually be of great assistance to the State to detain and imprison individuals, deny them a fair and open hearing in courts, and prevent them from proving their innocence or even the fact that they had been wrongly arrested. And all of this was achievable by simply enacting a law to that effect, which by the terms of draft Article 15 itself, could not be questioned in the Supreme Court. The main concern was that when an individual is brought before a court of law, they did not have even a modicum of protection extended to them by the Constitution.

In significant measure, these fears were based on historical experience. As FS Nariman has pointed out, in the early 20th century, the British rampantly resorted to 'arbitrary acts [such] as internments, detentions and deportations without trial.'[3] In fact, in its special session of 1918, the Indian National Congress explicitly demanded revocation of all laws which permitted authorities to 'arrest, detain, intern, extern or imprison any

British subject in India outside the process of ordinary civil or criminal law.'[4] However, the demands for fundamental rights and just treatment only translated into the Government of India Act, 1935, providing that a person's property could not be taken without legal backing.[5]

Many members who spoke in favour of amending draft Article 15 and bringing back the due process guarantee, were motivated by the fact that the new Constitution should not continue the tradition of the colonial government—denying people their fundamental rights without a system of robust checks in place. Thus, the regime of 'executive excesses and of repression'[6] which the British had enacted in India, was brought to the fore, for many were convinced that draft Article 15 would not break with this reprehensible tradition.

The check that they hoped for was a clause on due process which would act as a shield against onslaughts on fundamental rights. To be treated fairly and humanely, and to secure a guarantee to that effect was the fundamental demand which draft Article 15 ought to encompass. Unfortunately, draft Article 15 had brought to life the unwholesome idea of conferring on 'Parliament a *carte blanche* to provide for arrest of any person under any circumstances it deemed fit.'[7]

Three Conceptions of Due Process

From the different speeches delivered on 6 December 1948, three distinct conceptions of due process had begun to take shape in the Constituent Assembly.

The first, which was the *Minimalist Conception of Due Process*, focused on the necessity of providing a minimum standard of rights such as to allow a person to question their arrest or detention, have legal representation and answer a charge in a court of law. This was a basic conception of due process which only asked for these safeguards for a person who came into contact with the justice system. For members such as Karimuddin, Chimanlal Shah, Sharma and Patskar, it was really beyond debate that these rudimentary protections ought to be enumerated as rights in the Constitution.

The second, which was the *Intermediate Conception of Due Process*, essentially focused on enumerating a series of due process rights in the Constitution, along the lines of the charter of rights enumerated in the Constitution of Japan. The justification for this was that since draft Article 15 was based on Article 31 of the Japanese Constitution, whatever was enumerated in the latter Constitution with regards to due process rights, must also find a place in the Indian Constitution.

As we have seen, this had proven to be a sharp point of debate since several members could not understand why the Drafting Committee, in following the Japanese Constitution, had not chosen to also enumerate the due process rights which were contained in that Constitution. Therefore, for members such as Baig, Shah, Bhargava, and Lari, the only logical path open to the Constituent Assembly was to put in the Indian Constitution, the due process rights contained in the Japanese Constitution.

The third conception of due process was of substantive due process, which was the *Synergistic Model of Due Process*. In this conception, the due process guarantee could be truly unleashed when coupled with a system in which courts would use the due process guarantee to engage in a substantive review of laws, examine their merits and content, and conclude whether such laws passed constitutional muster. Here, the combined effect of due process and judicial review was stronger than the effect that they could have in their individual capacity. For Munshi, Bhargava, Shah and Baig, the due process model which the Constitution ought to have included was one where the due process guarantee was coupled with robust judicial review. Through it, not only would the people be entitled to retain the panoply of rights which fall under the rubric of due process, but in addition, it would also be utilized to keep a substantive check on laws and state action which affected fundamental rights.

Atonement and the Partial Rebirth of Due Process

In December 1948, the Constituent Assembly had formally disavowed its support for any version of a due process guarantee becoming part of the Constitution. But the juggernaut of criticism that draft Article 15 received did not go unnoticed. The Drafting Committee in time realized the folly of giving short shrift to due process rights.

Its act of atonement came in the form of an entirely new fundamental right on due process which heretofore had not been considered at all[8]—draft Article 15-A—which Dr Ambedkar introduced in the Constituent Assembly on 15 September 1949.[9] Now for the first time, the Constituent Assembly would have before it an honest admission that the wholesale abandonment of due process rights was something that India could ill-afford and amends had to be made.

As introduced in the Constituent Assembly, draft Article 15-A, contained four clauses, and had two parts to it.[10] The first part enumerated the protections which a person was entitled to when they came into contact with the criminal justice system.

Draft Article 15-A(1) provided that any person who was arrested shall be informed of the grounds of arrest and shall also be entitled, as a fundamental right, to avail the services of a lawyer of their own choosing. Draft Article 15-A(2) provided that an arrested person would, within twenty-four hours of their arrest, be presented before the nearest available magistrate, and that any detention beyond this period had to be under the authorization of a magistrate.

The second part of draft Article 15-A, that is draft Articles 15-A(3) and 15-A(4) pertained to the safeguards which were applicable to cases of preventive detention. These clauses provided that preventive detention could not last longer than three months, and an Advisory Board had to authorize such detention. The Advisory Board was an entity comprised of person, who had served as a High Court judge, or were eligible for being appointed as one. The last clause authorized Parliament to make laws providing for situations in which a longer period of detention was possible. An in-depth examination of draft Article 15-A is beyond the scope of this book, but the debates which took place over it are analyzed to demonstrate that for many in the Constituent Assembly, the fears that the Constitution did not fully respect due process rights nevertheless remained, despite the introduction of this new fundamental right.[11]

Through his speech introducing draft Article 15-A, Dr Ambedkar offered rare insight into what transpired after the Constituent Assembly had approved draft Article 15. He began by drawing attention to the vigorous debate that had taken place over due process and draft Article 15. In an honest admission, Dr Ambedkar frankly stated that he along with many other members of the Assembly were 'greatly dissatisfied with the wording of Article 15.'[12] He acknowledged the hard reality that all draft Article 15 required before the State deprived a person of the life or liberty was the enactment of a law, without it prescribing the outer limits of such law-making power. Once the State made a law, no further questions could be raised against any action taken under such a law.

Recognizing the emptiness of draft Article 15, Dr Ambedkar was moved to introduce draft Article 15-A, which in his view was a substantive guarantee against arbitrary detention and illegal arrests.[13] According to Dr Ambedkar:

> It will also be recalled that there is no part of our Draft Constitution which has been so *violently criticised by the public outside* as article 15 *because all that Article 15 does is this, it only prevents the executive from making an arrest. All that is necessary is to have a law and the law need not be subject to any conditions or limitations.* In other words, it was felt that while this matter was being included in the Chapter dealing with Fundamental Rights, we were giving a carte blanche to Parliament to make and provide for the arrest of any person under any circumstances as Parliament may think fit.[14]

Dr Ambedkar then added:

> We are therefore now, by introducing article 15A, making, if I may say so, compensation for what was done then in passing Article 15. In other words, *we are providing for the substance of the law of 'due process' by the introduction of article 15A.*[15]

These statements show that the debates over the fundamental right of life and personal liberty had not been a discussion on an arcane point of constitution making but were being watched closely.

Given the resounding public condemnation of draft Article 15, the Drafting Committee had been rethinking its feasibility, which led it to eventually conclude that standing alone, draft Article 15 was of no assistance to a person facing arbitrary arrest.

As Dr Ambedkar saw it, the value of draft Article 15-A, was that draft Article 15-A(1) and draft Article 15-A(2) incorporated into the Constitution, as substantive due process guarantees, provisions which were part of the Code of Criminal Procedure of 1898. This was on the whole 'sufficient against illegal or arbitrary arrests.'[16]

Additionally, by introducing draft Article 15-A and sanctifying in the Constitution what was already contained in the ordinary law of criminal procedure, Dr Ambedkar hoped that through this 'fundamental change'[17] the Constitution would impose limits on the powers of the legislature to make laws affecting the personal liberty of the people, and that it would be impossible for these guarantees to be reduced to a nullity by ordinary law making.[18] What this essentially meant was that no legislature could, for instance, pass a law declaring that the people had no right to a lawyer or had no right to be heard with regard to their arrest by a police officer.

Dr Ambedkar also noted that many 'enthusiasts of personal liberty'[19] felt that draft Article 15-A was not entirely sufficient in preserving personal liberty. But although draft Article 15-A could possibly contain many more due process rights and be broadened in terms of its scope and content, the enumeration of this right itself would operate as an appropriately satisfactory safeguard against 'illegal or arbitrary arrests.'[20]

That the voice of reason had prevailed was something that Dr Ambedkar himself acknowledged. The introduction of draft Article 15-A was an effort towards making amends, a compensation of sorts, and a step towards providing due process guarantees to those who wish to question their detention. And all of this was despite the fact that draft Article 15 had studiously avoided any mention of due process.[21] Ending his speech on a congratulatory note, Dr Ambedkar had this to say on the true purpose of introducing draft Article 15-A:

> I think, on the whole, those who are fighting for the protection of individual freedom ought to congratulate themselves that it has been found possible to introduce this clause which, although it may not satisfy those who hold absolute views in this matter, certainly saves a great deal which had been lost by the non-introduction of the words 'due process of law'.[22]

The Renewed Debate

The birth of draft Article 15-A was nothing short of an accident of history and an endeavour to remedy the slings and arrows of criticism due process had suffered. From Dr Ambedkar's speech itself, we can see that draft Article 15-A(1) and draft Article 15-A(2) offered only the most basic and rudimentary form of protection against arrests. Draft Article 15-A was not even close to the charter of due process rights contained in the Constitution of Japan.

With the introduction of draft Article 15-A, however, there was now a glimmer of hope of moving fundamental rights ever so closer towards a robust charter on due process, and a few members of the Constituent Assembly used the debates on draft Article 15-A to attempt to push through their conceptions of a broader due process guarantee.

Pandit Thakur Dass Bhargava moved numerous amendments in a bid to virtually recast draft Article 15-A, and introduce additional articles to incorporate in the Constitution a charter of rights and remedies against illegal and arbitrary arrests and detention. Through his amendments, Bhargava attempted to incorporate in the Constitution other due process rights such as the right to cross-examine a witness, freedom from torture and from unnecessary restraints and unreasonable searches.[23]

Bhargava began his speech by noting that draft Article 15-A was an admission that due process cannot be given a go by. For him, due process was needed 'cent per cent' given that India was 'full of autocratic ideas.'[24] He then attacked the act of deleting due process in the first place. Although Dr Ambedkar had now come to realize that abandoning due process had been imprudent, it had unfortunately been his ambivalence which resulted in due process being virtually jettisoned from the Constitution. The ultimate irony had been that in a bid to protect liberty itself, due process had been abandoned.[25]

Coming to draft Article 15, Bhargava considered it nothing less than a 'crown of our failures'[26] since the function of fundamental rights was to impose limits on state action. But here an unconscionable inversion had taken place with the Constitution simply handing over unbridled powers to the State to trample upon rights without checks or questions. With draft Article 15, the State was put on notice that to impose unquestioned restrictions on the right to life and personal liberty, only a law needs to be made.[27]

Responding to Dr Ambedkar's claim that draft Article 15-A was compensatory in nature, Bhargava argued that what was contained in it was so fundamental and basic to democracy that it ought to have been part of the Constitution in the first place itself. Setting the record straight that this new fundamental right should not be seen as a favour to Indians, he posited that draft Articles 15-A(1) and 15-A(2) were guarantees that ought not to be hard fought for, especially since they were guarantees which 'no civilized country, no civilized legislature, can have the heart to say that even these should not be recognized.'[28]

Apart from presenting detailed proposals for improving Article 15-A with the aim of ensuring that any person coming into the criminal justice system must have the protection of due process rights, Bhargava also argued that it was necessary for the Constitution to allow for the substantive review of laws.[29] He was a strong proponent of due process rights and for him it was essential that many more due process rights be recognized by the Constitution. Shaken to his core when due process was not approved by the Constituent Assembly,[30] he did not hold back when he noted that for him the presence of draft Article 15 along with draft Article 15-A was nothing less than a 'blot upon the Constitution.'[31]

Towards the end of his speech, Bhargava trenchantly criticized the way in which the Drafting Committee had functioned. He believed that the Drafting Committee had on numerous occasions failed in its responsibility of giving effect to what the Constituent Assembly had settled on. This was not a new objection since even members of the Drafting Committee such as KM Munshi had been highly critical of the way in which the Drafting Committee operated and its decision-making process.[32]

In fact, Bhargava went to the extent of demanding that Dr Ambedkar should have stepped down from the Drafting Committee once pressure was brought to bear in a bid to ensure that the Constitution does not enumerate due process rights.[33] Till the end, Bhargava presented numerous additions which ought to be made to draft Article 15-A, in the hope of ensuring that 'personal liberty may be secured to the individual in full measure.'[34]

When one reads the speech of Dr Ambedkar introducing draft Article 15-A, one wonders how could Dr Ambedkar have been satisfied with the wording of draft Article 15 when he was one of the earliest proponents of due process himself. As we saw in Chapter 1, Dr Ambedkar was the first person to emphasize the importance of a constitution needing to enumerate a due process guarantee which he had done when replying to Nehru's Objectives Resolution, on 17 December 1946.[35] Moreover, Dr Ambedkar had in his Memorandum and Draft Articles on the Rights of States and Minorities[36] enumerated a guarantee on due process.[37] For Dr Bakshi Tek Chand, Dr Ambedkar's change of heart had been one of the greatest mysteries.

Dr Bakshi Tek Chand termed draft Article 15-A as the 'most reactionary article that has been placed by the Drafting Committee.'[38] In his view, there was hardly a constitution to be found anywhere in the world, permitting extended periods of detention as a general matter, especially in times not marred by an emergency. And it was surprising that a Drafting Committee composed of legal scholars of great renown advanced such a fundamental right for the Constituent Assembly's consideration. What complicated matters further was that even the Constitution of Japan, the apparent source of inspiration for draft Article 15, did not have any provision which granted the State all pervasive powers in matters of detention.[39]

In that sense, India was second to none when it came to a constitution which in the name of fundamental rights instituted a system of long periods of detention in times of peace. Which is why Dr Bakshi Tek Chand thought that draft Article 15-A was not a fundamental right but a 'charter for denial of liberties'[40] since it would allow people to be detained, subject to the outer limit of the period of detention being fixed by Parliament.[41]

Dr Bakshi Tek Chand then turned his attention to draft Article 15. He argued that the incorporation of the due process guarantee was something which Dr Ambedkar had advocated for in his States and Minorities report and it was a guarantee which on the recommendation of the Advisory Committee, the Constituent Assembly voted to accept as a fundamental right. However, as he observed, when it came to the Drafting Committee, due process was rejected and draft Article 15 was recommended by it, on the supposition that the meaning of the phrase 'procedure established by law' which was taken from the Constitution of Japan, was brimming with certainty. Like many others before him, he argued that in modelling draft Article 15 on the Japanese Constitution, none of the other due process rights enumerated in that Constitution were replicated in the Drafting Committee's Draft Constitution.[42]

Moreover, the reversal suffered by due process was quite perplexing given that Dr Ambedkar, and the Advisory Committee, had advocated for a clause on due process inspired by the 14th Amendment to the American Constitution, which according to Dr Bakshi Tek Chand had been heralded as a right which had done the most to uphold liberty in the USA.[43]

Seeking to attack the manner in which draft Article 15 had been justified, Dr Bakshi Tek Chand referred to Articles 33–37 of the Japanese Constitution[44] to show that Article 31 of the Japanese Constitution ought not to be studied in isolation but along with these other articles, which, according to him, 'form one consistent, integrated whole and incorporate the pith and substance of the phrase "due process of law"'.[45]

Dr Bakshi Tek Chand's criticism, which had also been voiced earlier by several members, was that there was no good reason to not replicate in the Draft Constitution the other due process rights which were enumerated in the Constitution of Japan. In an effort to ensure that draft Article 15-A provided robust protection to persons who enter the criminal justice system, he recommended that the specific language from some of the other due process rights enumerated in the Constitution of Japan (such as Articles 32 and 35), must find mention in draft Article 15-A.[46]

Nevertheless, Dr Bakshi Tek Chand could not hide his disappointment for he felt that draft Article 15-A was woefully inadequate so far as providing guarantees for the preservation of a person's personal liberty was concerned. In reality, this new fundamental right was nothing more than a 'cloak for denying the liberty of the individual.'[47] For him, draft Article 15-A was really an act of fig–leafing a gaping hole in the Constitution left by the absence of due process, for draft Article 15-A was only 'intended to make a show that some sort of protection is given'.[48]

Dr Ambedkar and Alladi Krishnaswami Ayyar's Defence

When it came to Alladi Krishnaswami Ayyar, he began his speech by defending draft Article 15. With a sense of gratification, Ayyar noted that the Constituent Assembly had rightly voted against due process for if it had been incorporated as a fundamental right, laws of all kinds would be open to challenge, regardless of their hue, scope and purpose. With the admittance of due process, the Constitution would have allowed justices to judge the sanctity of laws according to their own individual leanings. The vote on draft Article 15, was preceded by a debate in which due process had been examined in some detail. This, according to him, was the end of the matter so far as draft Article 15 was concerned.[49] Almost immediately, Ayyar contradicted himself when speaking on the need for draft Article 15-A:

> At the same time on that occasion it was felt that there should be some guarantee for personal liberty; some essential rules of fair play and justice should be adopted. It is because of some division of opinion and fighting over immaterial points that we were not able to insert any provisions in respect of those matters on that occasion. [50]

Ayyar also reserved special praise for Dr Ambedkar because of whom draft Article 15-A was introduced in the Constituent Assembly:

> The Honourable Dr Ambedkar, who is as keen today on the problem of personal liberty as he has always been, has thought fit to bring forward this amendment and he thought that this article must find a place in the Constitution.[51]

These statements are extraordinary because they contain a clear admission that when draft Article 15 was included in the Draft Constitution, and draft Article 15-A was nowhere on the horizon, there simply was no enumerated fundamental right whatsoever in the Constitution which protected personal liberty. Further, according to Ayyar, on its own, draft Article 15 neither advanced the personal liberty right, nor did it guarantee that certain rights would be non-negotiable so far as an individual who came into contact with the criminal justice system was concerned. Ironically, Ayyar ended up confirming what many critics of draft Article 15 had cried hoarse over—it was not a fundamental right at all for by its wording, it was impossible to say with confidence that personal liberty was actually safe from harm's way.

Ayyar spoke of draft Article 15 in glorious terms and as being a right, which was perfectly suited for India. But with these statements of his, the sheen of draft Article 15 had been rubbed off. Ayyar had now himself admitted that it was the presence of draft Article 15 which in fact had influenced the Drafting Committee to draft a new fundamental right which would offer some form of protection for the right to personal liberty. Despite this admission, Ayyar proclaimed that draft Article 15-A had to be discussed on its own terms.[52] For Ayyar, draft Articles 15-A (1) and Article 15-A(2) wrote into the Constitution as rights, what was already enumerated in the Criminal Procedure Code. This was critical since unlike the Code, the guarantee of draft Article 15-A was not subject to routine legislative change. Ayyar attached critical importance to this aspect of draft Article 15-A.[53]

After presenting a detailed defence of draft Article 15-A, Ayyar ended his speech with a pointed riposte aimed at Dr Bakshi Tek Chand. Ayyar proclaimed that draft Article 15-A was so well layered and so detailed, that in fact no other constitution in the world enumerated such safeguards for personal liberty. He virtually dared Dr Bakshi Tek Chand to present any constitution, as an example, which travelled such a great distance for preserving personal liberty as did draft Article 15-A.[54]

The debates carried over to the next day, and on 16 September 1948, after other members had spoken, Dr Ambedkar once again addressed the Constituent Assembly on the need to incorporate draft Article 15-A as a fundamental right.[55] As he pointed out, the passage of draft Article 15 brought to light the reality that in that article the Drafting Committee had fallen short of providing 'sufficient attention to the safety and security of individual freedom.'[56]

Faced with that fact, Dr Ambedkar and others began devising a way of including some form of due process rights in the chapter on fundamental rights. For the Drafting Committee, the solution to this conundrum lay in the introduction of draft Article 15-A to 'restore the content of due procedure in its fundamentals without using the words "due process".'[57] However, despite this effort, many viewed draft Article 15-A as still insufficiently protecting personal liberty.[58]

Dr Ambedkar spoke at length on the different aspects of draft Article 15-A as well as on the many changes that had been suggested, even answering questions posed by different members. Eventually over thirty amendments were moved to amend draft Article 15-A which were put to vote, with some of them being adopted by the Constituent Assembly.[59]

On 16 September 1949, the Constituent Assembly voted to make draft Article 15-A a part of the Constitution.[60] Despite the pressure generated in the Constituent Assembly, draft Article 15 somehow managed to fend off all efforts at reform. And in the days leading up to the finalization of the Indian Constitution, it would remain impervious to the influence of due process.

Endnotes

1   B Shiva Rao, *Framing of India's Constitution*, vol. III, pp. 327–329.
2   See Id., pp. 406-409. Minutes of the Meeting of the Drafting Committee dated 19 January 1948.
3   FS Nariman, 'Due Process of Law: its origins and current manifestation in the USA and its relevance to Constitutional Law in India' *The Indian Advocate, Journal of the Bar Association of India* (1992): 2.
4   Id., pp. 2–3 (citing P Sitaramayya, *History of the Indian National Congress*, vol. 1, pp. 153–154).

5   Id., p. 3.
6   Id., p. 4.
7   B Shiva Rao, *A Study*, p. 238. Also see,Tripathi, 'Perspectives', p. 89.
8   B Shiva Rao, *A Study*, p. 238; Seervai, *Constitutional Law*, p. 971.
9   CAD, vol. XI, p. 1498.
10 Id., pp. 1498–1499.
    'That after Article 15, the following Article be inserted:—
    '15-A. (1) No person who is arrested shall be detained in custody without being informed, as soon as may be, of the grounds for such arrest nor shall he be denied the right to consult a legal practitioner of his choice.
    (2) Every person who is arrested and detained in custody shall be produced before the nearest magistrate within a period of twenty-four hours of such arrest excluding the time necessary for the journey from the place of arrest to the court of the magistrate and no such person shall be detained in custody beyond the said period without the authority of a magistrate.
    (3) Nothing in this Article shall apply—
    (a) to any person who for the time being is an enemy alien, or
    (b) to any person who is arrested under any law providing for preventive detention;
    Provided that nothing in sub-clause (b) of clause (3) of this Article shall permit the detention of a person for a longer period than three months unless—
    (a) an Advisory Board consisting of persons who are or have been or are qualified to be appointed as judges of a High Court has reported before the expiration of the said period of three months that there is in its opinion sufficient cause for such detention, or
    (b) such person is detained in accordance with the provisions of any law made by Parliament under clause (4) of this Article.
    (4) Parliament may by law prescribe the circumstances under which and the class or classes of cases in which a person who is arrested under any law providing for preventive detention may be detained for a period longer than three months and also the maximum period for which any such person may be so detained.'
11 For a history of preventive detention laws in India see *Austin, The Indian Constitution*, pp. 134–136.
12 CAD, vol. IX, p. 1499.
13 Ibid.
14 Ibid. (Emphasis added.)

15 Ibid. (Emphasis added.)

16 Ibid.

17 Ibid.

18 Draft Article 15-A(2) was along the lines of Section 61 of the Code of Criminal Procedure, 1898. Section 61 read as follows: 'No police-officer shall detain in custody a person arrested without warrant for a longer period than under all the circumstances of the case is reasonable, and such period shall not, in the absence of a special order of a Magistrate under section 167, exceed twenty-four hours exclusive of the time necessary for the journey from the place of arrest to the Magistrate's Court.' This is something that Pandit Thakur Dass Bhargava would also highlight in his speech. See CAD, vol. IX, p. 1504.

19 Id., p. 1499.

20 Id., p. 1499.

21 Id., p. 1500.

22 Ibid.

23 Id., pp. 1500–1502.

24 Id., p. 1503.

25 Ibid.

26 Ibid.

27 Ibid.

28 Ibid.

29 Id., p. 1507.

30 Id., p. 1503. ('I cannot describe the state of mind in which I felt myself when I could not succeed in getting this House to agree to the due process clause.')

31 Id., p. 1506.

32 Id., p. 1508.

33 Id., p. 1507. ('We must bring all the pressure on Dr Ambedkar, and tell him that these are the minimum rights which we want to secure to the people at large. I would have rather liked that Dr Ambedkar, instead of resisting the attempts of these people, should have, resigned from his post as a protest against the pressure which is being brought upon him by the powers so that these fundamental rights may not be put in.')

34 Id., p. 1509.

35 CAD, vol. I, p. 100.

36 B Shiva Rao, *Framing of India's Constitution*, vol. II, pp. 84–114.

37 Id., p. 86.

38 CAD, Vol IX, p. 1531.

39 Ibid.

40   Ibid.
41   Ibid.
42   Id., pp. 1531–1533.
43   Id., p. 1533.
44   Id., pp. 1533–1534.
45   Id., p. 1534.
46   Id., pp. 1535–1536.
47   Id., p. 1536.
48   Ibid.
49   Id., p. 1537.
50   Id., pp. 1537–1538.
51   Id., p. 1538.
52   Id., p. 1537.
53   Ibid.
54   Id., p. 1540.
55   Id., pp. 1558–1566.
56   Id., p. 1558.
57   Ibid.
58   Ibid.
59   Id., pp. 1567–1572.
60   Id., p. 1572.

6

The Winter of (Dis)Content

———•———

THE DEBATES ON THE DRAFT CONSTITUTION AND ITS CLAUSE-WISE discussion continued until October 1949. On 17 October 1949, the last item to be considered by the Constituent Assembly was the Preamble. Like other parts of the Constitution, the Preamble too bore the effect of Mahatma Gandhi's assassination—the inclusion of 'fraternity' in the Preamble by the Drafting Committee was settled on days after Gandhi's demise.[1]

After debating the Preamble, the Constituent Assembly voted to adopt it on the same day and make it a part of the Constitution.[2] The adoption of the Preamble signalled the conclusion of the second reading of the Draft Constitution. Dr Rajendra Prasad then invited the Drafting Committee to once again review the Draft Constitution along with the amendments that had been passed, and to also make whatever changes the Drafting Committee felt necessary.[3]

The Final Touch

The Drafting Committee took a little over two weeks to complete this task. On 3 November 1949, Dr Ambedkar submitted the revised draft of the Constitution to Dr Rajendra Prasad.[4]

In his letter which accompanied the newly revised Draft Constitution, Dr Ambedkar outlined the nature of the modifications made. Apart from making editorial changes and renumbering the articles, one of the major modifications made was that new articles were added, and other articles were revised to cure the drawbacks that the Drafting Committee felt they suffered from.[5]

This act of introducing new articles in the Draft Constitution at this late stage revealed that even after the second reading of the Constitution, the Drafting Committee still had the final say on what the newly revised Draft Constitution must look like. It had the full mandate to change any part of the Constitution, including adding new articles and amending existing ones. In the exercise of this power, the Drafting Committee introduced important new articles.

Article 34 pertaining to validation and indemnification of acts done when martial law has been declared was introduced;[6] Article 222 was introduced, authorizing the President of India to transfer judges from one High Court to another;[7] Article 365 was introduced which authorized the President of India to declare that a particular state government was unable to carry out its functions under the Constitution due to its failure to heed directions issued by the Union Government's Executive.[8]

The rationale behind the Drafting Committee's recommendation for introducing entirely new articles was to ensure that 'defects and omissions' in respect of the Constitution which had come to the

Drafting Committee's attention were immediately corrected.[9] But, these could not become a part of the final Constitution, unless the Constituent Assembly agreed to them.

Many other articles were also modified and amended, including draft Article 15 and draft Article 15-A. In the newly revised Draft Constitution, draft Article 15 underwent two changes. As we have seen, all along draft Article 15 had contained two distinct rights. The first part contained the right to life and personal liberty, and the second part contained the right to equality. In respect of draft Article 15, the Drafting Committee decided that it would be 'more appropriate' to divide it into two and make the equality right into a separate fundamental right.[10] Thus, the Drafting Committee converted the equality right into a new fundamental right which would now be enumerated in a new article, Article 14, with the heading 'Right to Equality.'[11] This was the first change.

The second change was that draft Article 15 with only the right to life and personal liberty was renumbered as Article 21, which is how it was to be known henceforth.[12] Moreover, draft Article 15-A was renumbered as Article 22 and certain modifications were made without disturbing the content of the right.[13]

It is here, at this stage, that the Drafting Committee ought to have recommended the due process guarantee as a fundamental right in Article 21—an opportunity which the Drafting Committee did not seize.

If the Drafting Committee had come to the realization that Article 21 was a very weak fundamental right, it is incomprehensible why the Drafting Committee did not bring back the due process guarantee. What is more, even during the debates on Article 22, opponents of due process like Alladi Krishnaswami

Ayyar had openly admitted that Article 21 had fallen short of fully safeguarding a person's liberty interest.

All of this goes to show that so far as Article 21 was concerned there was near universal consensus amongst the members of the Drafting Committee that it did not really protect personal liberty. Faced with this reality, it became the bounden duty of the Drafting Committee to bring back the due process guarantee. After all, the Drafting Committee virtually exercised plenary powers and could recommend the incorporation of any article which it considered necessary and important for the Constitution.

That the Drafting Committee had recommended new articles as well as made substantive changes to existing articles, demonstrated that the Drafting Committee was well within its right to recommend the due process guarantee for inclusion in the chapter on fundamental rights.

Further, since the recommendations of the Drafting Committee were subject to the vote of the Constituent Assembly, the recommendation of a due process guarantee would have meant that the Assembly would have had another opportunity to consider whether it was important to incorporate due process as a fundamental right. Given the passionate debates which had taken place over Article 21 (originally draft Article 15) and Article 22 (originally draft Article 15-A) it would not have been out of place to recommend a fundamental right on due process. Yet, at this penultimate stage, the Drafting Committee failed to seize the opportunity.

What makes it more intriguing is that when Article 22 had been introduced in the Constituent Assembly, Dr Ambedkar had noted that the absence of the due process guarantees from the Draft Constitution had come in for severe public condemnation. As we have previously seen, this had been one of the important reasons which convinced the Drafting Committee that certain substantive due process rights ought to be introduced.

When the public had made its disappointment so clearly known, it would not have been out of place for the Drafting Committee to re-introduce the due process guarantee, even at this late stage in October–November 1949. Had this been done, it would have demonstrated the Drafting Committee's utmost respect for public opinion on a matter affecting the life and liberty itself.

On 14 November 1949, Dr Ambedkar moved a resolution in the Constituent Assembly that stated that the 'amendments recommended by the Drafting Committee in the Draft Constitution of India be taken into consideration.'[14] After adopting the motion,[15] the Assembly took up the newly revised Draft Constitution for a clause-wise discussion. The debates carried on till 16 November 1948, since amendments had been moved yet again to amend a large number of articles.[16]

Interestingly, during these debates, Article 21 did not attract any attention and no amendment was moved to change its language. However, amendments were moved to alter the scope of Article 22, and through these amendments a new clause 4 and clause 7 were introduced in it. These amendments to Article 22 were approved by the Constituent Assembly on 16 November 1949.[17]

The probable reasons for Article 21 attracting such little attention at this stage are several. To begin with, given the fact that on all the previous occasions the Constituent Assembly had voted not to include a due process guarantee in the chapter on fundamental rights perhaps gave reason to believe that at this belated stage, the Assembly would not change its voting pattern. Numerous amendments had been moved when Article 21 had been debated, to incorporate a due process guarantee, but they all met with failure.

Moreover, the fact that Article 22 was present in the Constitution, may have given confidence to the Constituent Assembly that arbitrary arrests and detentions would no longer be a palpable threat. As we saw, during the debates on Article 21, the main fear that was voiced was that there was no fundamental right which made available basic rights in the criminal justice system.

It was the absence of such guarantees, that in part had led to the incorporation of Article 22. Now that the Constituent Assembly had before it a fundamental right which applied to cases of arrests and preventive detention, the Assembly may have felt there was no longer a pressing need, so to speak, to also incorporate a broader due process guarantee.

Further, the fact that the Constituent Assembly had confidence in Article 22 performing the salutary function of protecting persons from arrests without cause and giving them protections, such as prohibiting detention beyond twenty hours unless authorized by a court of law, is borne out by the fact that when Article 22 (originally draft Article 15-A) was introduced, Dr Ambedkar had assured the Assembly that Article 22 would act as a bulwark against prolonged and unjustified arrests. Now at least, there was perhaps some consolation so far as a right against arbitrary arrests and detentions was concerned.

Perhaps no amendments were moved to introduce the due process guarantee in Article 21 at this final stage also because the proponents of due process had become dejected with their repeated efforts yielding little success. From the days of the Drafting Committee discussing the Draft Constitution in 1948 till the debates on due process in the Constituent Assembly, several members such as KM Munshi, Pandit Thakur Dass Bhargava, Kazi Syed Karimuddin and ZH Lari had attempted to have the due process guarantee become a part of the chapter on fundamental rights but had failed in their attempts.

The Constitution had now been finalized, and perhaps members may simply have seen no point in yet again attempting to seek the incorporation of a due process guarantee when the possibility of failure stared them in the face. Despite this being the one final moment to make a last-ditch effort at resurrecting the due process guarantee, the gravity of this moment perhaps passed over the Constituent Assembly and a crucial opportunity to bring back the due process guarantee was lost.

Furthermore, even the Drafting Committee had not recommended a due process guarantee as a new fundamental right in the final version of the Draft Constitution, and so the occasion to discuss due process did not arise. With the deadline to give India a new Constitution looming large, the Constituent Assembly was keen to settle on the Constitution so that they could give their final vote of approval. With the Assembly mainly concerned with expeditiously approving the Constitution, introducing new fundamental rights at this final stage might have been viewed as an exercise in futility.

Article 21 and the Third Reading of the Constitution

On 16 November 1948, the President put to vote the numerous amendments that had been moved to amend a large number of articles. After debating and voting on all the amendments, the Constitution approached its final form.[18] On 17 November 1948, Dr Ambedkar moved to joyous jubilations the resolution: 'That the Constitution as settled by the Assembly be passed.'[19]

The Assembly would now begin the third reading of the Draft Constitution, which continued till 25 November 1949.[20]

The speeches made in the course of the third reading suggest a sharp division amongst the members on the general question of fundamental rights, and on the specific issue of the absence of a due process guarantee in the chapter on fundamental rights. Several members expressed their happiness at the fact that the Constitution would herald a new dawn for India.[21] Many others, however, expressed their disappointment with the Constitution, and particularly with the chapter containing the fundamental rights. They used the third reading of the Constitution as an opportunity to draw the attention of the Assembly to the problems which India, and indeed Indians, would face due to the absence of the due process guarantee.

The Critics of Article 21

For KT Shah, although the Drafting Committee had shown great zeal in drafting the Constitution, the document 'when judged as a piece of art in drafting' could not be considered 'as a gem of its kind.'[22] The chapter pertaining to fundamental rights held out a hollow assurance since almost all the fundamental rights were in some way subject to either restrictions or made conditional.[23]

In particular, the rights pertaining to 'personal freedom' were so narrowly worded that they could be suspended during an Emergency and that a person could be detained on false pretences, with the right being of no avail. For him, the right to personal freedom was really reduced to 'a right to remain under detention without trial, without any proper judicial proceedings for a period of three months.'[24] There was nothing 'more painful to read' and nothing 'more disappointing in this Constitution' than the chapter on fundamental rights.[25]

As HV Patskar saw it, the entire controversy pertaining to due process seemed to have served no useful purpose. Even though the chapter on fundamental rights was detailed, the right to personal liberty was left wanting. In an effort to avoid any reference to due process the Assembly settled on the language of Article 21 selecting the phrase 'procedure established by law', but then to undo the drawbacks of Article 21, Article 22 was introduced which really contained due process rights.[26]

However, Article 22 granted the lowest level of protection and would prove insufficient to safeguard persons against prolonged detention, since under it the Advisory Board was conferred with great powers to decide the length of preventive detention; a Board which was not a judicial body at all.[27] For Patskar, the only sliver of hope available now was that in time, Parliament would amend the Constitution, using the amending powers, and make appropriate amends.[28]

For Shibban Lal Saksena, Articles 21 and 22 was the 'darkest blot' on the Constitution since it had achieved the unimaginable: it permitted 'detention without trial.'[29] Saksena, pained by these two articles, proclaimed that 'liberty had been a casualty in our Constitution.'[30]

Articles 21 and 22 were also an enormous personal loss for Saksena and he could never come to truly accept these two articles. He himself had suffered detention under the British for over three decades and knew only too well the cruelties which were inflicted on those who were preventively detained.[31] 'I know the tortures which detention without trial means', Saksena told the Assembly, 'and I can never reconcile myself to it.'[32]

Further, in his view, what made it worse was the fact that under Articles 358 and 359, fundamental rights could be suspended during an Emergency and would be rendered unenforceable and non-justiciable. This, for Saksena was to make 'a mockery of Fundamental Rights.'[33] For him, Article 21 along with Article 22 were nothing less than a constitutional travesty and they signalled the retreat of liberty rights so far as the Constitution was concerned.[34]

Kazi Syed Karimuddin was certain that so long as due process was absent from the Constitution, fundamental rights would be insufficiently realized. In the absence of due process, there was no fundamental right which could keep a check on the 'invasion of the Fundamental Rights by the Legislature.'[35]

As he put his point illustratively, the absence of a due process guarantee would help to validate a law which allowed for punishment by execution even though the law was highly unjust. Although he was acutely aware that the Constitution was being debated and settled amidst a period of great churning and turmoil, he expressed a fervent hope that as soon as India entered a period of peace, due process would find its way back into the Constitution. Otherwise, Karimuddin predicted, the only result would be 'chaos and anarchy.'[36]

When Pandit Thakur Dass Bhargava addressed the Constituent Assembly, he seemed somewhat satisfied with Article 21 and Article 22 since he believed that these Articles conferred 'sufficient rights' but noted that it was an undeniable fact that it was quite possible to provide for several more rights in the Constitution.[37]

The Defenders of Article 21

Alladi Krishnaswami Ayyar's speech in support of Dr Ambedkar's motion makes for interesting reading, for it presented a masterly defence of the Constitution. After surveying various parts of the Constitution, Ayyar turned his attention to Articles 21 and 22.

Ayyar proclaimed that the real function of Article 22 was to 'secure against any abuse' of Article 21, but he made an astonishing statement. Ayyar admitted that Article 22 had to necessarily follow Article 21 or else 'indefinite detention' would be a reality since all that Article 21 required was a law which laid out a procedure for detention, a scenario which was avoided by incorporating Article 22.[38] It is astonishing because here was an admission that Article 21 in itself had no force and meant nothing in the face of State action which marched towards eclipsing the basic liberties of the people.

For Ram Chandra Gupta, Article 21 was indeed broadly worded but the fears over Article 21 being insufficient were misplaced, and it was presumptuous to assume that the State will abuse its powers, for it was highly unlikely that laws would either be passed or implemented in a 'wanton or irresponsible manner.'[39] Even otherwise for Gupta, the breadth of Article 21 would act as a cautionary mechanism since governments would use their powers to truncate the right in times of emergencies alone.[40]

Article 21 had proven to be, for Frank Anthony, a cause for some concern, since the State could abuse the right to personal liberty by simply making laws which would upset all canons of justice. As Anthony put it:

> I am afraid, that in this form article 21, if the Executive and the Government of the day choose to, can be *abused and made a handle for totalitarian oppression*. The Executive can make it a handle for superseding [the] rule of law they can make it a handle for *depriving citizens of the elementary principles of natural justice*, and of jurisprudence.[41]

As a lawyer by training, Anthony was convinced that the spectre of this fundamental right being easily abused would haunt the new republic. Intriguingly, despite his serious misgivings about Article 21, Anthony proclaimed that he had decided not to oppose its incorporation because India was transitioning into a constitutional democracy under difficult and trying times, during which the government must have the greatest flexibility in dealing with any eventualities. For Anthony, during these troubled times there was no option but to accept a truncated right on personal liberty. Having said that, Anthony then expressed only a hope that Article 21 would not be abused by future governments.[42]

We are thus able to see that even those who spoke in favour of Article 21 were not entirely sure whether it would operate as a proper safeguard against State action infringing personal liberty. It was this uncertainty which led, for instance, Frank Anthony to proclaim that all they could do now was to 'sincerely hope'[43] that the State would not abuse Article 21, even though it could do so unchecked, without as much as a question being raised against the motives for restricting the right to life and personal liberty.

On 25 November 1949, Dr Ambedkar addressed the Constituent Assembly on the final version of the Constitution.[44] Dr Ambedkar was careful not to comment on the merits of the Constitution, focusing rather on its general features and thanking all the members who played an instrumental role in the shaping of the Constitution.

In his speech, a special mention was made of BN Rau who, according to Dr Ambedkar, deserved a fair share of the credit for the Constitution since it was his Draft Constitution which set things in motion for the Drafting Committee. Dr Ambedkar also profusely thanked SN Mukherjee, who was the Chief Draftsman of the Constitution. Dr Ambedkar's tribute paid to them both was met with cheers in the Constituent Assembly.[45]

Dr Ambedkar was aware that the Constitution was not the end of the journey, but the beginning. He was at pains to, therefore, emphasize that regardless of its structure and language, a constitution was only as good or as bad as the people who were charged with working it. As Dr Ambedkar put it:

> I shall not therefore enter into the merits of the Constitution. Because I feel, however good a Constitution may be, it is sure to turn out bad because those who are called to work it, happen to be a bad lot. However bad a Constitution may be, it may turn out to be good if those who are called to work it, happen to be a good lot. The working of a Constitution does not depend wholly upon the nature of the Constitution.[46]

Towards the end of his speech, Dr Ambedkar was filled with hope and expectation, and he concluded by expressing the hope that the general populace would rise to the occasion of making the Constitution a document which resulted in India's progress.[47] Since Dr Ambedkar had decided not to discuss the contents of the Constitution, Dr Ambedkar made no comment on Article 21 or on the absence of the Constitution containing a due process guarantee.

Dr Ambedkar's speech marked the conclusion of the third reading of the Constitution, and now all that was left was for the Constituent Assembly to give its seal of approval to the Indian Constitution. On 26 November 1949, the President of the Constituent Assembly after speaking at length on the features of the Constitution,[48] put Dr Ambedkar's motion of 17 November 1949, to vote. Amidst rousing cheers, the Assembly voted to adopt Dr Ambedkar's motion, thus giving to free India her new Constitution.[49]

The Constituent Assembly would meet for the final time, on 24 January 1950, in its capacity as a constituent body, for the members to affix their signatures to the Constitution.[50]

Coming to Life

Owing to its historical significance, the Constituent Assembly chose 26 January 1950 as the day on which the Constitution would come to life. During the freedom struggle the nationalist movement had demanded that India be granted *'Purna Swaraj'* (complete independence) by 26 January 1930.[51] From then onwards, 26 January had been referred to as 'Independence Day' and annually, people across India would take the 'independence pledge'. The day had attained a special meaning in the public imagination, and it was considered 'fitting that the new republic should come into being on that day'.[52] Undoubtedly, the Constituent Assembly had performed a remarkable and unprecedented exercise in constitutional making, overcoming numerous obstacles before it finally gave to free India her Constitution.[53]

Formally though, the Constituent Assembly had adopted Article 21 without a clause on due process. In adopting the 'colourless expression'[54] 'procedure established by law', the Assembly disavowed enumerating a clause on due process, even though Article 22 was introduced to afford a semblance of due process protection in cases of arrests and preventive detention. However, even Article 22 had been viewed as providing insufficient protections.[55]

All then that Article 21 stood for was to proclaim to free India that the State can deprive a person of their life or personal liberty in whatever manner it likes, so long as a law was enacted for that purpose. In doing so, the State could neither be held accountable nor responsible, and least of all answerable, for the egregiousness and irrationality of the process which inhered in the law. The catch-all defence available to the State against any such charge was a succinctly complete one: that a law was in place.[56]

Article 21 essentially reversed the function of fundamental rights. Rather than operating as a mechanism to impose boundaries which confine the State's law-making powers, here was a fundamental right which pushed the frontiers of inviting the State to enact laws to run roughshod over the right to life and personal liberty.[57] The fact that Article 21 neither granted substantive due process nor procedural due process rights would go on to become a serious bone of contention when the Supreme Court of India would begin interpreting fundamental rights guaranteed by Part III of the Constitution.[58]

At any rate, in the winter of 1950, the Constituent Assembly gave to free India its foundational document whose overarching influence would doubtless shape the nation's destiny. In large measure, the winter season had been a central fixture in the making of Article 21, and indeed the Constitution itself.

It was in the winter of 1946, that the newly elected Constituent Assembly first met to begin its deliberations on a new Constitution, and it was in that winter that Nehru introduced the Objectives Resolution in the Assembly.

It was in the winter of 1949, that the Assembly voted to approve the final Constitution, and it was in the winter of 1950, that the Assembly formally adopted the Indian Constitution. But winter was also the season of dread and discontent.

It was in the winter of 1948, that the Drafting Committee decided to eject due process from the Draft Constitution, and bring in its stead the text of Article 21. So, too, in the winter of 1948 did the Constituent Assembly vigorously debate Article 21 (then draft Article 15) and in that winter, adopt it without a clause on due process.

That even otherwise, New Delhi was a place to be dreaded in the time of winter was something which K Hanumanthaiya, the member from Mysore, was at pains to highlight when beseeching the Constituent Assembly that the nation's capital must be shifted to a state with hospitable climes.[59]

It is perhaps only by happenstance, a coincidence, that the cold and vacuous right to life and personal liberty was drafted, debated, voted on and then finally approved by the Constituent Assembly in the grey of winter. In 1950 then, the only hope that the people of India could perhaps have for Article 21 was to remember and recall Dr Ambedkar's talisman: that hopefully, the people charged with working the Constitution would be respectful of due process rights, regardless of its absence from the text of the Constitution.

Endnotes

1   Rajmohan Gandhi, 'The Answer is Fraternity', *The Indian Express*, 22 October 2020 (available at https://indianexpress.com/article/opinion/columns/india-constitution-preamble-fraternity-fundamental-rights-6824790/).
2   CAD, vol. X, p. 456.
3   CAD, vol. X, p. 457.
4   B Shiva Rao, *Framing of India's Constitution*, vol. IV, pp. 745–932.
5   Id., p. 746.
6   Id., pp. 747, 761.
7   Id., pp. 748, 826.
8   Id., pp. 748, 884–885.
9   Id., p. 746.

10   Id., p. 747.

11   Ibid. Article 14 reads as follows: 'The State shall not deny to any person equality before the law or the equal protection of the laws within the territory of India.' See B Shiva Rao, *Framing of India's Constitution*, vol. IV, p. 754.

12   Id., p. 747. Also see, B Shiva Rao, *A Study*, p. 246.

13   B Shiva Rao, vol. IV, p. 747. HM Seervai is greatly critical of the exercise of renumbering Articles 21 and 22 in this particular manner. See Seervai, *Constitutional Law*, pp. 971–973.

14   CAD, vol. XI, pp. 462–464.

15   Id., p. 465.

16   Id., pp. 465–606.

17   See B Shiva Rao, *A Study*, pp. 246–248. Also see, CAD, vol. XI, p. 600.

18   CAD, vol. XI, pp. 584–606.

19   Id., p. 607.

20   Id., pp. 607–981.

21   See speech of VI Muniswamy Pillay. Id., pp. 608–610.

22   Id., p. 619

23   Id., p. 620.

24   Ibid.

25   Ibid.

26   Id., p. 673

27   Id., pp. 673–674.

28   Id., p. 674.

29   Id., p. 705.

30   Ibid.

31   Id., pp. 705–706.

32   Id., p. 706.

33   Ibid.

34   Id., p. 705.

35   Id., p. 725.

36   Ibid.

37   Id., p. 686.

38   Id., p. 838. ('In the chapter on Fundamental Rights, there is one other matter which requires more than a passing notice. Clause (4) of article 22 has been animadverted upon as if it were a charter to the Executive to detain a person for three months. There is no such thing. The whole of article 22 is designed to secure against any abuse of the provisions of article 21 which says in general terms that "No person shall be deprived of his life or personal liberty except according to procedure

established by law". If article 21 stood by itself, it may authorise an indefinite detention if only it conforms to the procedure established by law. Article 22 has been put in to prevent any such indefinite detention. The Constituent Assembly which was quite alive to the dangers confronting the new State could not rule out detention altogether.')

39   Id., p. 921.

40   Ibid.

41   Id., p. 942.

42   Ibid.

43   Ibid.

44   Id., pp. 972–981.

45   Id., p. 974.

46   Id., p. 975.

47   Id., pp. 980–981.

48   Id., pp. 984–995.

49   Id., p. 995.

50   CAD, vol XII, pp. 6–7.

51   Bipin Chandra, 'The Gathering Storm, 1927–1929', in *India's Struggle for Independence: 1857–1947*, ed. Bipin Chandra, Mridula Mukherjee, Aditya Mukherjee, KN Pannikar, Sucheta Mahajan (India: Penguin Books, 1989), p. 268.

52   Mridula Mukherjee, 'The Evolution of the Constitution and Main Provisions', in *India after Independence: 1947–2000*, ed. Bipin Chandra, Mridula Mukherjee, Aditya Mukherjee (India: Penguin Books, 2000), p. 31.

53   Pratap Bhanu Mehta, 'State and Democracy in India', *Polish Sociological Review*, No. 178 (2012): p. 205.

54   *Puttaswamy*, para 477 (per RF Nariman, J.). ('The phrase "due process" was distinctly avoided by the Framers of the Constitution and replaced by the colourless expression "procedure established by law."')

55   Anthony Lester, 'The Overseas Trade in the American Bill of Rights', *Columbia Law Review*, vol. 88 (1988): p. 544.

56   Generally, see Fali S Nariman, 'Fifty Years of Human Rights Protection in India—The Record of 50 Years of Constitutional Practice', *NLSIR Special Issue* (2013): pp. 15–16 [hereinafter Nariman, 'Fifty Years']; Rehan Abeyratne, 'Socioeconomic Rights in the Indian Constitution: Toward A Broader Conception of Legitimacy', *Brooklyn Journal of International Law*, vol. 39 (2014): p. 30.

57   Seervai, *Constitutional Law*, pp. 972–973.

58   This is discussed in Chapter 8.

59   CAD, vol. VII, p. 340. ('Here in Delhi excepting for two months either we have to sweat or shiver and in this extremity of climates, it is almost impossible to do any hard work. The capital of a country, it is reasonable to expect, should be in the centre of the country and we can locate our capital in the C.P. or somewhere near about.')

7

The Dissonant Constitution

———◆———

THE ADOPTION OF THE CONSTITUTION MARKED A MILESTONE FOR THE Indian Republic. But one could not wish away the fact that on due process, stark dissonance permeated the chapter on fundamental rights.

Unanswered Questions

The introduction of Article 22 (originally draft Article 15-A) in the Constituent Assembly had been hailed by Dr Ambedkar and Alladi Krishnaswami Ayyar as a moment of victory for due process rights. But the reasons for introducing Article 22, despite being well-intentioned raised more questions than it answered.

In the first place, due process had not been recommended by the Drafting Committee for a variety of reasons. After Article 21 (originally draft Article 15) had been approved, it was realized that nothing in the Constitution adequately protected personal liberty. But, the absence of the due process guarantee in Article

21 occasioned the introduction of Article 22 to guarantee certain substantive due process rights to persons coming into contact with the criminal justice system. If, in September 1949, due process was suddenly considered important enough for a brand-new article to be introduced in its respect, then what became of the justification for avoiding the recommendation of the due process guarantee in the first place?

After all, less than a year before Article 22 was introduced in the Constituent Assembly, Dr Ambedkar and Ayyar had been committed to avoiding any reference to due process with the latter being quite adamant about it. But in September 1949, both of them had had a change of heart and spoke in support of Article 22, which in their view brought back due process guarantees into the Constitution.

Moreover, the introduction of this new fundamental right itself begot a larger question: if Article 22 was considered necessary, what then did Article 21 protect people from? The short answer was: nothing. Indeed, the fact that Article 22 was introduced itself constituted an admission that Article 21 provide no protection at all against arbitrary arrests and detentions, and for that matter, did not extend any kind of protection to the individual whatsoever.

There was another problem with Article 22. By Dr Ambedkar's own admission, its first two clauses were replicas of the rights contained in the Criminal Procedure Code of 1898. As we saw, early in the debates in September 1949, it was admitted that these clauses—making available the right to counsel of choice, and the right of not being detained beyond twenty-four hours without a valid court order—had been bodily lifted from the 1898 Criminal Code, a law which had been formulated by an oppressive colonial power for a nation held captive.

This Code predated the Constitution by more than fifty years, and it seemed hollow to champion the cause of due process by putting into the Constitution what was contained in a colonial era statute. At any rate, even without Article 22, these rights would have been available to all persons as legal rights.[1]

There was no substantial intellectual advance made by the Drafting Committee so far as Article 22 was concerned and there was nothing revolutionary about this article for it provided only the most minimal levels of protection. Had Article 21 performed some tangible function, there would have been no need for Article 22. In the ultimate analysis, nothing but the sheer emptiness of Article 21 had necessitated Article 22.

What exacerbated the paradox was that if Article 22 was introduced as a measure of incorporating substantive due process guarantees in the realm of the criminal justice system, then nothing prevented the Drafting Committee from recommending the version of the due process guarantee voted on by the Constituent Assembly on 30 April 1947, as a new fundamental right in the Constitution.[2] The only possible reason for giving short shrift to due process was because the Drafting Committee had an aversion for *too much* due process being part of the Constitution, even though it had finally acknowledged that the new Constitution could not altogether avoid incorporating substantive due process guarantees.

Between 30 April 1947, when the Constituent Assembly voted on the due process guarantee, and 16 September 1949, when the initial version of Article 22 was approved by the Assembly, due process had gone from acceptance, to abandonment, to partial acceptance. Unfortunately, all this happened without the Assembly properly looking into why a broader due process guarantee could not also be incorporated into the chapter on fundamental rights.

That the Drafting Committee could, in the middle of the debates on the Draft Constitution, introduce a brand new fundamental right, as had been done in the case of Article 22 only goes to show that the introduction of a new fundamental right which encompassed broader forms of due process protections— one which applied to all aspects of human life and not just to rights pertaining to the criminal justice system—while the Draft Constitution was still being debated, was not beyond the realm of possibility. Whether it was the Drafting Committee's obduracy or the pressure of having to quickly finalize the Constitution, none of this was done, and the only compromise agreed upon was Article 22.

Due Process and the Dissonance in Article 22

Article 22 created another note of dissonance in the Constitution. The latter part of Article 22 contained a series of clauses which authorized preventive detention. Under preventive detention a person can be detained not because they are convicted by a court of law but because they might do something.[3] For preventive detention, suspicion and apprehension is tantamount to *de facto* guilt.

In the Constituent Assembly, tempers ran high when the Drafting Committee threw its support behind Article 22 containing provisions which enabled a regime of preventive detention.[4] The Assembly finally came round and in the initial version of Article 22, which the Assembly voted upon in September 1949, a certain balance was struck between preventive detention and the liberty interest of individuals. The balance came in the form of constituting Advisory Boards (which would be composed of men and women who were learned in the law and who were either serving as High Court judges, or had been judges, or were eligible for being appointed as one) which had the mandate of reviewing the cases of preventive detention.[5]

However, when the Constitution came to life, the last clause of Article 22—Article 22(7)—contained a provision which upended the delicate balance that Article 22 had attempted to strike between liberty and preventive detention. And the balance was now tilted against due process.[6]

Under the scheme of Article 22(7)(a), Parliament could enact laws for preventive detention and stipulate that the Advisory Board was not to exercise any judicial oversight at all [Article 22(7)(a)]; that such parliamentary legislation had to stipulate the maximum period of preventive detention [Article 22(7)(b)]; and, that by law, Parliament could decide on the procedure that the Advisory Board must follow when reviewing cases of preventive detention [Article 22(7)(c)].

From the perspective of due process this was a stunning about face. The Constitution would now actually allow for preventive detention without any judicial, regulatory or administrative oversight.

The motivating purpose for introducing Article 22, in the first place, had been to introduce a semblance of due process guarantees in the Constitution when it came to the criminal justice system. But Article 22(7) created a constitutionally sanctified no man's land: once a person was caught in the snare of a law of the kind mentioned in Article 22(7)(a), there would be no hope whatsoever for fundamental rights of any kind. Detention would last for as long as the law wished.[7]

Article 21 and the International Dissonance

The adoption of Article 21, without a due process guarantee, was deeply unsettling and paradoxical in terms of India's international obligations as well. Two years and a day after the Constituent Assembly had met for the first time, the General Assembly of the United Nations, on 10 December 1948, gave to the world the Universal Declaration of Human Rights.[8]

The Second World War had left the world broken and divided, and it was realized that for any progress to take place, nations must be united. This idea lay behind the formation of the United Nations. The fact that India's Independence coincided with the setting up of the UN meant that it became an institution 'closely intertwined with India's hopes itself and the future of humanity.'[9]

The Declaration was an endeavour to distil into a charter those rights which were fundamental, basic and ought to be guaranteed to all human beings unconditionally. In the Declaration, we find that several articles spoke directly about the importance of preserving, protecting and promoting the liberty interest of individuals. To that end the Declaration enumerates a right to life, liberty and security of persons (Article 3); freedom from slavery (Article 4); freedom from torture (Article 5); freedom from arbitrary arrests (Article 9); the freedom of being tried by a neutral court which decides in an impartial manner (Article 10); and the right to privacy and security (Article 12).

What makes the Declaration all the more important is that India had an outsized role to play in its crafting and preparation. Hansa Mehta, a member of the Constituent Assembly who was also a member of the Advisory Committee and of the Fundamental Rights Sub-Committee was India's representative at the UN's Human Rights Commission, which was in charge of drafting the

Declaration.[10] So great was her contribution in the Commission that in 2018, the Secretary General of the United Nations, Antonio Guterres, paid homage to Mehta as one of the key members who played an influential role in the drafting of the Declaration and who was responsible for ensuring that the Declaration applied to all human beings rather than only to men.[11]

Given India's outsized role in the crafting of the Declaration, it seems all the more incongruent that none of the above-mentioned important rights pertaining to individual liberty found mention in the text of India's Constitution. By 1948, the world had come to realize the fundamental value in ensuring that a person's liberty needs to be protected in order for society to progress and survive. But surprisingly the Constituent Assembly did not draw any lessons from it.

This dissonance becomes more curious given that Mehta steadfastly believed that the high principles enshrined in the Declaration must find mention in the Indian Constitution. To that end, Mehta had in 1949 sounded an important note of caution—that India's future Constitution ought to be a document that measures up to the proclamation of rights contained in the Declaration. Mehta had correctly pointed out that even though the Declaration may not yet be a binding legal document which could be enforced by the judicial system, it would be in the fitness of things if the Constituent Assembly endeavoured to give independent India a charter of rights which closely reflected those contained in the Declaration.[12]

Mehta, however, was not the only one who commended to the Constituent Assembly the importance of following the universal rights contained in the Declaration. When the Assembly was debating Article 22 (then draft Article 15-A) in September 1949, Dr Bakshi Tek Chand had pointed out that a contemporaneous international development of enormous importance was taking place at the United Nations, giving the world 'the Charter of Human Rights.'[13] He was quick to recognize the solemnity of the Declaration and referred to a series of rights contained in it to impress upon the Constituent Assembly that the Declaration really contained the 'substance of Fundamental Human Rights for civilized nations.'[14]

That, however, was not to be. Without the Indian Constitution ultimately reflecting the rights which the Declaration gave to the world, as fundamental rights in the Constitution, India had in 1950 unfortunately abandoned its core obligation of respecting this great international charter of freedoms which it had worked so hard to promote and for which, to this day, India is remembered favourably across the world.

The Dissonant Victory of Due Process

As originally conceived, the Constituent Assembly had decided that due process protection ought to apply only to a person's life and liberty, and not to property rights. In taking this decision, the Assembly had knowingly departed from the American version of the due process guarantee, which provided due process protection for property rights too.

As we saw in Chapter 1, in the Advisory Committee, it had been quite openly discussed that in free India, the states would embark on a massive land reform project to essentially dismantle the *zamindari* system of land tenure. If those who stood to lose their landholdings, the argument went, had the advantage of the due process guarantee, then there was no real possibility of achieving any form of either land reform or agrarian reform. So, it was decided, on the suggestion of KM Pannikar and C

Rajagopalachari, and on the strength of the powerful arguments made by Govind Ballabh Pant and several others, that it was better to keep property rights out of the ambit of the due process guarantee.[15]

However, through the years a strange dissonance crept in which was cemented in the final Constitution. In 1950, so far as a person's life and personal liberty interest were concerned, the Constitution, in Article 21, did not speak about due process protection at all. But, for property rights, the Constitution contained not one but two forms of due process protection.

The first layer of due process protection was in the form of Article 19(1)(f).

Article 19(1) (originally draft Article 13) contained the charter of civil liberty rights [from Article 19(1)(a) to Article 19(1)(g)] such as the freedom of speech and expression, freedom of movement throughout India, the freedom of association and the freedom to choose one's work. Under Article 19(1)(f), all citizens had the fundamental right to 'acquire, hold and dispose of property.' This was the fundamental right to property clause.

For each of the fundamental rights enumerated in Article 19(1), there was a corresponding clause which enumerated the grounds on which the particular right could be restricted. Article 19(1)(f) was qualified by Article 19(5) which allowed the State to impose reasonable restrictions in the public interest.

The presence of the phrase 'reasonable restrictions' in Article 19(5) introduced due process protection for property rights.[16] Under the rubric of the 'reasonable restrictions' standard of review, courts were free to investigate the rationale, justification and merits of laws. Courts were invested with the power to rigorously probe the feasibility of laws and question their very wisdom. Incidentally, for the other fundamental rights mentioned in Article 19(1), except for the fundamental right to free speech and expression [Article 19(1)(a)], the corresponding clause enumerating the grounds for restrictions contained the 'reasonable restrictions' standard.

As the constitutional law scholar and Professor of Law at the Faculty of Law, University of Delhi, PK Tripathi tells us, although due process was not present anywhere in the text of Article 19, the Constituent Assembly by approving the reasonable restrictions standard 'basically stuck to the core of "due process".'[17] How was this possible? The answer, it appears, lies in unravelling the problem of characterization.

Writing in 1988, PK Tripathi propounded the idea that by introducing the reasonable restrictions standard in Article 19, the Constituent Assembly essentially incorporated into the Constitution, the concept that the freedoms in Article 19 'should be secure against arbitrary deprivation or encroachment ... through the operation of judicial review on the broad ground of reasonability or propriety of all government action.'[18]

This characterization of the reasonable restrictions standard of review was nothing else but substantive due process review by another name. Which is why Tripathi convincingly argues that: '[c]onsequently when the Constitution of India provided for the various freedoms in clause (1) of Article 19 and laid down the judicially supervised limits of permissible restraints ... it *provided for due process* as well as police powers.'[19]

The fact that Article 19 introduced due process review was recognized by scholars early on. Writing in 1957, Charles Henry Alexandrowicz, a scholar of the Indian Constitution who was a Barrister of Law at Lincoln's Inn and Professor of International and Constitutional Law at the University of Madras, noted that when the judicial branch engages in an inquiry to discover whether a restriction is reasonable, that inquiry is akin to due process review.[20] And because the powers of review under Article 19 were nothing but the powers available under the due process guarantee, the judicial branch in deciding whether a restriction is reasonable could 'go into both the substantive and procedural aspects of the law under consideration.'[21]

Both Tripathi and Alexandrowicz had uncovered an important truth about the true meaning of what reasonable restrictions meant: that it, in reality, called for due process review. Applying this to Article 19, the result was that the fundamental right to property was cloaked with due process protection.

The second layer of due process protection for property rights came in the form of Article 31, which principally guaranteed to all persons that they could not be deprived of their property unless a law to that effect had been enacted, which provided compensation for the property taken by the State.

In the Constituent Assembly, when Article 31 was being finalized, there seemed to be some uncertainty over whether laws made under it would hold up in courts. But KM Munshi and Nehru were of the view that once a law fixed the quantum of compensation, courts would most likely not interfere, with Munshi suggesting that courts would only intervene if the quantum of compensation could not also be sustained under the fundamental right to property.[22]

In a surprising turn of events the Constitution had enacted a role reversal. Strong due process protection was made available for property rights, and none were available for protecting and preserving life and personal liberty. Given that India wanted to embark on a robust land reform project, it seemed rather odd that property rights would receive due process protection in the Constitution. This was not only an analytical error but a design flaw, and soon after the Constitution came to life, the chickens came home to roost.

Within the first year of the new republic, those who had had their property taken by the State began to mount legal challenges in the High Courts and met with some success, with one of the cases reaching the Supreme Court.[23] In fact, the Patna High Court had invalidated the law in question as not being saved by Article 31 because it violated Article 19(1)(f) and Article 19(5).[24]

This made the Constituent Assembly, which between 1950 and 1952 functioned as India's Provisional Parliament, a worried lot. And so, in 1951, the Provisional Parliament passed the First Amendment to the Constitution which introduced new articles in Part III of the Constitution, to neutralize the threat which these judicial decisions apparently presented.[25]

This much was clear from the Preamble to the First Amendment which enunciated in no uncertain terms that Article 31 had led to 'agrarian reform measures' being bogged down with 'dilatory litigation, as a result of which the implementation of these important measures, affecting large number of people, has been held up.' With the aim of 'fully securing the constitutional validity of zamindari abolition laws', the First Amendment introduced new articles to achieve this goal.[26]

Section 4 of the First Amendment introduced Article 31A and Section 5 introduced Article 31B. Indeed, even the Supreme Court had realized that the First Amendment had been passed by the Provisional Parliament pre-emptively and with a 'view to put an end to the litigation of zamindars' which was pending consideration before it.[27]

Article 31A aimed at completely shielding any law which either directly or incidentally affected property rights.[28] Under the scheme of Article 31A, the constitutionality of laws which led to the acquisition of estates or the acquisition of rights in them, or a law which effected an extinguishment or modification of rights in estates could never be called into question, and no court could entertain a complaint that such laws violated any of the Fundamental Rights enumerated in Part III. Essentially Article 31A created a fortification around the laws which it spoke of, from *all* Fundamental Rights.

The introduction of Article 31B was accompanied by a companion schedule, the Ninth Schedule.[29] Under the scheme of Article 31B, *any law* of *any kind*, and not just those which pertained to property rights, when placed in the Ninth Schedule would forever be immune from being challenged in a court of law even if it violated the rights enumerated in Part III of the Constitution. Further, if a law placed in the Ninth Schedule had been previously invalidated by any court, then placing such a law in the Ninth Schedule was sufficient to bring it back to life without doing anything else, such as amending the law which led to the violation of fundamental rights. Article 31B was put to use immediately, for the First Amendment inserted thirteen laws related to land reform in the Ninth Schedule.[30]

Nonetheless, these initial amendments to the Constitution far from calming the mood of the country, emboldened people to challenge them and for the next two decades, contentious battles would be waged in the Supreme Court on the power of Parliament to amend the Constitution.[31] The battle culminated in 1973, when a thirteen-judge bench of the Supreme Court, the largest bench ever constituted, declared by a majority of seven to six, in the famous case of *Kesavananda Bharti* that Parliament could amend the Constitution so long as the basic structure of the Constitution remained intact.[32]

Then close on the heels of the First Amendment came the Fourth Amendment to the Constitution in 1955, which was aimed at countering the effect of specific judicial decisions which had been handed down in the preceding years.[33]

The Fourth Amendment introduced stipulations in Article 31 to ensure that the adequacy of compensation paid under a law pertaining to the taking of property by the State could not be called into question in a court of law. This change was introduced to overturn a 1954 decision of the Supreme Court in which it had been declared that under Article 31, full compensation was to be paid to the person who lost their property, so that they are made whole again.[34]

The Fourth Amendment also recast Article 31A substantially but made an important change: the laws which Article 31A spoke of were now only saved when a challenge was mounted either on a complaint that it violated Article 14 (the fundamental right to equality), Article 19 or Article 31.[35] Article 31A had to specifically exclude Article 19 otherwise challenges could be raised under Article 19(1)(f) and Article 19(5) against laws which Article 31A endeavoured to sustain.

The Fourth Amendment was also used as an opportunity by Parliament to add seven other laws in the Ninth Schedule. But this time some laws unrelated to property rights, such as certain amendments made to the Insurance Act of 1938, were placed in the Ninth Schedule.[36]

With the First and the Fourth Amendment to the Constitution putting legislative measures affecting property rights beyond question, property rights no longer enjoyed strong protection, for through these amendments 'so far as property was concerned, due process was dead.'[37]

The reign of due process protection for property rights finally came to an end in 1978. In that year, Parliament passed the Forty-Fourth Amendment to the Constitution.[38] Amongst other things, through the Forty-Fourth Amendment, Article 31 and Article 19(1)(f) were deleted and would no longer find mention in the text of the Constitution.[39] But for preserving some form of protection for property rights, the Forty-Fourth Amendment introduced a new Article 300A, which completely watered down constitutional protection for property rights.[40] With Article 300A, property rights would no longer enjoy any due process protection, being now reduced to the status of ordinary constitutional rights.

It will forever remain a matter of supreme irony that the Constituent Assembly which had initially sought to provide due process protection for a person's life and liberty and not for their property interest, ended up elevating property rights to the status of due process rights, leaving life and individual liberty by the wayside. And even though Parliament eventually saw to it that property rights were taken out of the framework of due process, neither the First Amendment nor any other constitutional amendment which followed it, ever attempted to introduce the due process guarantee in the text of Article 21.

Endnotes

1   Under Article 372(1) and Article 366(10) of the Constitution, all laws enacted in pre-independent India would remain in force, even after the Constitution came into existence. Which is why the Code of Criminal Procedure of 1898 remained operational in post-independent India until it was replaced by a new Code of Criminal Procedure in 1973.
2   See Chapter 1.
3   Generally see Alexandrowicz, *Constitutional Developments*, p. 25.
4   See speech of RK Sidhwa, CAD, vol. XI, p. 1527; speech of Dr Bakshi Tek Chand, CAD, vol. XI, p. 1530.

5   See Article 22(4).

6   Article 22(7) reads as follows:
'(7) Parliament may be law prescribe—
(a) the circumstances under which, and the class or classes of cases in which, a person may be detained for a period longer than three months under any law providing for preventive detention without obtaining the opinion of an Advisory Board in accordance with the provisions of sub-clause (a) of clause (4);
(b) the maximum period for which any person may in any class or classes of cases be detained under any law providing for such detention; and
(c) the procedure to be followed by an Advisory Board in an inquiry under sub-clause (a) of clause (4).'

7   See Austin, *The Indian Constitution*, pp. 140–143.

8   See Universal Declaration of Human Rights (available at https://www.un.org/en/universal-declaration-human-rights/).

9   Manu Bhagvan, 'A New Hope: India, the United Nations and the Making of the Universal Declaration of Human Rights', *Modern South Asian Studies*, vol. 44 (2010): p. 312 [hereinafter Bhagvan, 'A New Hope'].

10 Id., pp. 324–335.

11 PTI, 'UN Chief honours India reformer Hansa Mehta's role in shaping Universal Declaration of Human Rights', *The Economic Times*, 7 December 2018 (available at https://economictimes.indiatimes.com/news/politics-and-nation/un-chief-honours-indian-reformer-hansa-mehtas-role-in-shaping-universal-declaration-of-human-rights/articleshow/66983960.cms?from=mdr).

12 Bhagvan, *A New Hope*, pp. 333–334.

13 CAD, vol. IX, p. 1536.

14 Ibid.

15 See Chapter 1.

16 See Tripathi, 'Perspectives', pp. 91–92.

17 Id., pp. 89–90.

18 Id., p. 90.

19 Ibid. (Emphasis added.)

20 Alexandrowicz, *Constitutional Developments*, p. 46.

21 Id., p. 55.

22 Granville Austin, *Working a Democratic Constitution: The Indian Experience* (New Delhi: Oxford University Press,1999), pp. 76–77 [hereinafter Austin, *Democratic Constitution*].

23 *State of Bihar v. Kameshwar Singh*, 1952 SCR 889 (SCC Online version).
24 Austin, *Democratic Constitution*, pp. 78–79.
25 For an analysis of how the First Amendment was crafted and the debates which took place, see Austin, *Democratic Constitution*, pp. 78–92.
26 The Constitution (First Amendment) Act, 1951 (available at http://legislative.gov.in/constitution-first-amendment-act-1951#:~:text=The%2010th%20May%2C%201951.&text=%5B18th%20June%2C1951.%5D,amend%20the%20Constitution%20of%20India). The First Amendment also introduced far-reaching changes to other parts of the Constitution, including in respect of several fundamental rights such as Article 15.
27 *Kameshwar Singh*, para 32.
28 '4. Insertion of new article 31A.-
After article 31 of the Constitution, the following article shall be inserted, and shall be deemed always to have been inserted, namely: -
31A. Saving of laws providing for acquisition of estates, etc.-
Notwithstanding anything in the foregoing provisions of this Part, no law providing for the acquisition by the State of any estate or of any rights therein or for the extinguishment or modification of any such rights shall be deemed to be void on the ground that it is inconsistent with, or takes away or abridges any of the rights conferred by, any provisions of this Part:
Provided that where such law is a law made by the Legislature of a State, the provisions of this article shall not apply thereto unless such law, having been reserved for the consideration of the President, has received his assent.
In this article,-
the expression "estate" shall, in relation to any local area, have the same meaning as that expression or its local equivalent has in the existing law relating to land tenures in force in that area, and shall also include any jagir, inam or muafi or other similar grant;
(b) the expression "rights", in relation to an estate, shall include any rights vesting in a proprietor, sub-proprietor, under-proprietor, tenure-holder or other intermediary and any rights or privileges in respect of land revenue.'
29 '5. Insertion of new article 31B.-
After article 31A of the Constitution as inserted by section 4, the following article shall be inserted, namely:-
31 B. Validation of certain Acts and Regulations.-
Without prejudice to the generality of the provisions contained in article 31A, none of the Acts and Regulations specified in the Ninth

Schedule nor any of the provisions thereof shall be deemed to be void, or ever to have become void, on the ground that such Act, Regulation or provision is inconsistent with, or takes away or abridges any of the rights conferred by, any provisions of this Part, and notwithstanding any judgment, decree or order of any court or tribunal to the contrary, each of the said Acts and Regulations shall, subject to the power of any competent Legislature to repeal or amend it, continue in force.'

30   See Section 14 of the First Amendment.

31   These battles were waged in a trio of cases in the Supreme Court. They were *Sankari Prasad v. Union of India*, 1952 SCR 89; *Sajjan Singh v. State of Rajasthan*, 1965 (1) SCR 933; *IC Golak Nath v. State of Punjab*, 1967 (2) SCR 762.

32   *Kesavananda Bharti v. State of Kerala*, (1973) 4 SCC 225. In 2007, a nine-judge bench of the Supreme Court neutralized the effect of Article 31B and the Ninth Schedule, by declaring that any amendment made to the Constitution on or after 24 April 1973, by which a new law was made a part of the Ninth Schedule would be open to constitutional scrutiny. The date of 24 April 1973 was chosen because that was the day on which the decision in *Kesavananda Bharti* was announced. See *IR Coelho v. State of Tamil Nadu*, (2007) 2 SCC 1.

33   See Austin, *Democratic Constitution*, pp. 101–110.

34   Charles Henry Alexandrowicz-Alexander, 'American Influence on Constitutional Interpretation in India', *The American Journal of Comparative Law*, vol. 5 (1956): pp. 101–104 [hereinafter Alexandrowicz-Alexander, 'Constitutional Interpretation'].

35   See The Constitution (Fourth Amendment) Act, 1955 (available at http://legislative.gov.in/constitution-fourth-amendment-act-1955#:~:text=%22(2)%20No%20property%20shall,the%20manner%20in%20which%2C%20the).

36   See Section 5 of the Fourth Amendment.

37   Austin, *The Indian Constitution*, p. 128 (internal citation omitted).

38   See The Constitution (Forty-Fourth Amendment) Act, 1978 published in the Gazette of India (available at http://www.egazette.nic.in/WriteReadData/1979/E-1080-1979-0018-47011.pdf).

39   The Forty-Fourth Amendment also made other amendments such as deleting reference to Article 19(1)(f) in Article 19(5) and deleting reference to Article 19 from Article 31A(1).

40   Article 300A: No person shall be deprived of his property save by authority of law.

8

Article 21 and the Chimera of Original Intent

———◆———

WHEN A CONSTITUENT BODY VOTES ON A CONSTITUTION, THE WORDS and phrases used in the founding document are assumed to be the result of careful choices and deliberations. For that reason, it is often believed that, in order to be respectful of the efforts that were made by such a constituent body, the constitution must be conceived in a manner consistent with which the framers intended it to be. How then do we understand Article 21? Is there at all the possibility of ascribing some form of original intention or original meaning to Article 21?

When reading Article 21 it may be plausible to take the view that this article was worded with great care and caution and, therefore, through the language and structure of Article 21, the Constituent Assembly intended that the due process guarantee would not be a part of the fundamental right to life and personal liberty. However, given the fraught history of Article 21, and the twists and turns which the due process guarantee underwent from December 1946 to January 1950, it is not possible to ascribe to Article 21 any particular original intention or original meaning.

Original Meaning: A Typology

Theories about interpreting a constitution in terms of its original intent were developed in the context of the American Constitution. In an influential article 'The Misconceived Quest for the Original Understanding',[1] the legal scholar Paul Brest proposed that original understanding of a Constitution—originalism—meant attaching 'binding authority to the text of the Constitution or the intention of its adopters.'[2] And although many articles in the Constitution may have a clear meaning, other articles are seemingly 'open-textured.'[3] Brest presented the numerous difficulties which arose when viewing the Constitution from the lens of originalism, but for the present purpose two important critiques are worth noting.

To begin with, Brest argued that it is quite difficult to ascertain with confidence what each member of the constituent body took an article in the Constitution to mean. Without fully knowing the mental make-up of each member of the constituent body, it is difficult to decide what kind of original meaning is to be attributed to the Constitution.[4] Moreover, an article in the Constitution may only embody a principle, thus presenting a roadmap where future developments are to inform the meaning of the Constitution.[5]

These and other considerations led Brest to observe that the interpretative exercise in determining the original meaning of the Constitution is not an easy task, for the 'originalist constitutional historian may be questing after a chimera.'[6]

When it comes to deciphering the original meaning of a constitution a variety of methods can be applied. Jack N Rakove sets out a three-part model to understand the original meaning of a constitution.[7]

The first is the 'Original Meaning' model where the interpretative exercise undertaken is strictly confined to examining the text of the constitution and analysing the 'literal wording—the language—of its many provisions.'[8]

The second is the 'Original Intention' model in which the exercise of constitutional interpretation endeavours to discover the meaning of a constitutional provision as understood by the founders of the Constitution. Here, attention is paid to the 'purpose and forethought' which informs the actions of those charged with drafting the Constitution.[9]

The third is the 'Original Understanding' model, which shifts the attention of what the Constitution means not in the view of the constituent body, but what it means in the view of the people who are to be governed by it, since one of the modes of bringing a constitution into existence is to have it ratified by the general populace.[10]

Nevertheless, we must also remember that constitutions are a reflection of their time and their implementation can, in fact, render a constitution unworkable. In his magisterial work *The Framers' Coup*, the renowned scholar Michael J Klarman offers several examples to show that even though the Framers of the American Constitution worded certain articles with a particular and specific meaning in mind, over which there was broad consensus and not much controversy, those articles were relevant only to the time at which they were ratified.[11]

Article 21: There Is No Original Intent

One view on Article 21 is that when determining its original intent, it is difficult to interpret this article as affording due process protection primarily because the Drafting Committee had taken a conscious decision to use the phrase 'procedure established by law.' In this view, due process cannot be read into Article 21 because the Drafting Committee had after careful deliberation, intended that the due process guarantee ought not to be a part of the fundamental right to life and personal liberty. This view gained easy acceptance in the jurisprudence surrounding Article 21, for the most notable proponent of this viewpoint was the Supreme Court of India.[12]

On 19 May 1950, the Supreme Court handed its decision in *AK Gopalan v. State of Madras*.[13] *Gopalan* was the first ever case in which the Supreme Court had the opportunity to interpret the meaning of Article 21.[14] *Gopalan* was heard by a Constitution Bench comprising the first Chief Justice of India, Harilal Kania and Justices Fazl Ali, Patanjali Sastri, Meher Chand Mahajan, BK Mukherjea and SR Das.[15] One of the questions which arose was whether it was possible to interpret Article 21 as securing due process guarantees.

Three of the justices held that it was not possible to interpret Article 21 as extending any form of due process protection, given that the Drafting Committee had decided not to make any reference to due process in the Draft Constitution.

In Chief Justice Kania's view, it was impermissible to read Article 21 as containing any due process guarantee, and to even venture to make such an argument would be 'misleading.'[16] Chief Justice Kania engaged in a strict textualist construction of Article 21 to observe that from its plain words, it was impossible to read into it any due process guarantee. Even otherwise the original intent of Article 21 did not allow for due process to be read into it given the fact that the Drafting Committee had, after careful deliberation, decided not to recommend a due process guarantee in the Draft Constitution.[17]

Here we can see that Chief Justice Kania was laying the foundation for the idea that the meaning of Article 21 was to be somewhat brought into accord with what the Drafting Committee had intended it to mean.[18]

Chief Justice Kania's observations on the Drafting Committee's approach to the fundamental right to life and personal liberty resonated with Justice Patanjali Sastri. In his separate judgment, Justice Sastri held that given the ups and downs the due process guarantee went through in the USA, the Drafting Committee had wanted to avoid such a scenario in India, which is what led it to delete the due process guarantee and replace it with what was now Article 21.[19]

For Justice Sastri, in light of the importance of this particular decision of the Drafting Committee, the Supreme Court had to remain respectful of the intent behind the wording of Article 21 and it could not be interpreted to extend either substantive or procedural due process protection.[20] Here too, it was considered proper to use the Drafting Committee's intent in deleting the due process guarantee, as informing the meaning of Article 21.

The premium placed on the recommendations of the Drafting Committee was reiterated by Justice BK Mukherjea. In his separate judgment, he expressed confidence in the fact that in interpreting the fundamental rights enumerated in Part III of the Constitution, the recommendations contained in the Drafting Committee's Report provided an important guiding light.[21]

Relying almost exclusively on it, Justice Mukherjea held that when compared with the Constituent Assembly debates, the Drafting Committee's Report was entitled to a 'higher value'[22] and the deliberate deletion of the due process guarantee by the Drafting Committee very clearly meant that Article 21 could not be interpreted as providing due process protection to any person.[23] For Justice Mukherjea, since this was the Drafting Committee's clear intent behind Article 21, the Supreme Court had to be respectful of it.[24] Essentially for Justice Mukherjea, it would have been completely out of order to read into Article 21 the due process guarantee in the face of the Drafting Committee's aversion to it.

What is interesting to note is that Justice Mukherjea clearly placed the decision of the Drafting Committee on a higher pedestal but used the phrase 'framers of the Indian Constitution' in several places when holding that the framers had taken a conscious decision to not incorporate a due process guarantee in the Constitution.[25] This is a cause for some confusion for it is unclear who Justice Mukherjea treats as the framers of Article 21—the Drafting Committee or the Constituent Assembly as a whole, or both.

Justice Fazl Ali, in his judgment, observed that the plain text of Article 21 made clear that the due process guarantee was not encompassed within it.[26] However, for Justice Fazl Ali, this did not mean the unavailability of ordinary procedural safeguards, and here he struck a discordant note.

Unlike the other justices who held that Article 21 did not provide any sort of safeguards when it came to a fair hearing, Justice Fazl Ali observed that despite the phrase 'procedure established by law' being used in Article 21, any person who was proceeded against under a law was entitled to a notice being issued, to a hearing, to be judged by persons who were neutral and to otherwise be proceeded against in accordance with the procedure contained in the law.[27] Justice Fazl Ali's dissent is widely regarded as one of the greatest dissenting judgments in the history of India.[28]

Surprisingly, the justices did not treat the debates which had taken place over Article 21 in the Constituent Assembly with the same level of importance as the Report of the Drafting Committee. For instance, Justice Sastri reasoned that the speeches presented the individual viewpoint of the speaker and represented 'inarticulate mental processes' as far as the voting pattern in the Constituent Assembly was concerned from which it was difficult to 'assume that the minds of all legislators were in accord.'[29] Similarly, Justice Mukherjea reasoned that the debates which took place in the Constituent Assembly were of 'doubtful value'[30] and that it was best if such 'extrinsic evidence is left out.'[31]

This meant that the Supreme Court essentially disregarded the fact that within the Constituent Assembly, Article 21 had not received universal support and that a large section of the Assembly repeatedly voiced their unhappiness with the language of Article 21.[32] To this day, the Supreme Court is generally unwilling to use the debates which took place in the Constituent Assembly, as a reliable basis for informing the meaning of the Constitution.[33]

A few years after *Gopalan*, the Supreme Court explained why the *Gopalan* Court had placed high importance on the views of the Drafting Committee when interpreting Article 21, rather than on the debates which occurred in the Constituent Assembly.

In *Aswini Kumar Ghose v. Arabinda Ghose*,[34] Justice SR Das as part of a Constitution Bench noted that in *Gopalan* the Drafting Committee was viewed as an 'agent' of the Constituent Assembly. Since the Drafting Committee's recommendations on due process were accepted by the Assembly, the Drafting Committee's Report was treated as 'historical material throwing some light on the question of construction of Article 21.'[35]

Gopalan is an old case but the fact remains that the originalist interpretation which the justices engaged in still retains an enduring appeal. In contemporary discussions of Article 21, *Gopalan's* originalist formulation of the right to life and personal liberty has found approval amongst leading scholars of the Indian Constitution, including HM Seervai.[36]

Since *Gopalan* treated the Drafting Committee's report as an important reason to rule that Article 21's original intent was to exclude due process protections, it raises questions regarding the sanctity of the Drafting Committee's conduct. *Gopalan* will have us believe that the Drafting Committee had conducted its affairs with attention to detail and in a united fashion. However, as the facts of history show, the conduct of the Drafting Committee was quite to the contrary.

A Few Speak for Many

When on 4 November 1948, Dr Ambedkar introduced the resolution in the Constituent Assembly placing the Draft Constitution for consideration,[37] a long debate took place on the motion. During those debates, numerous members drew attention to the fragmented and haphazard way in which the Drafting Committee had discharged its duties. For many, the way in which the Drafting Committee itself had functioned had left much to be desired. At this stage of the deliberations, the right to life and personal liberty had been enumerated in draft Article 15 of the Draft Constitution.

Early on in the debates, on 5 November 1948, TT Krishnamachari rose to address the Constituent Assembly and immediately raised the issue of the unstructured and unsystematic functioning of the Drafting Committee, of which he himself was a member. For Krishnamachari, it was astounding that when the nation's founding document was to be drafted, the Drafting Committee charged with that particular task was unable to pay close attention to the enormity of the responsibility cast upon it. For him, it was disquieting that for various reasons ranging from ill-health to some members being away on matters of state, to vacancies in the Drafting Committee remaining unfulfilled, several members did not fully participate in proceedings, resulting in Dr Ambedkar having to single-handedly shoulder the task of settling the Draft Constitution.[38]

According to Krishnamachari, the absence and absenteeism of members from the Drafting Committee was one of the main reasons why the Draft Constitution did not receive the care and consideration that it deserved and that ultimately it reflected the views of only a few members.[39] He also pointed out that there were parts of the Constitution which warranted, but did not receive, 'expert attention that was necessary'. For him, if other members of the Drafting Committee such as Gopalaswami Ayyangar and KM Munshi had participated in full, then perhaps the Constitution would have received the care and attention to detail that it truly deserved.[40]

Krishnamachari's grievances about the manner in which the Drafting Committee functioned raised pertinent questions but he was not alone in thinking that the Drafting Committee could have functioned more cohesively, or for that matter worked in a much more structured manner. Krishanmachari's speech stirred a hornet's nest and taking a cue from him, several members questioned the manner in which the Drafting Committee had functioned.

Following Krishnamachari, Biswanath Das in a long speech launched a scathing attack at the manner in which the Drafting Committee had gone about preparing the Draft Constitution. For Das, the primary problem with the Drafting Committee was that it had transgressed the powers conferred on it. In Das' view, the Drafting Committee had operated as if it were itself the

Constituent Assembly, for it had 'made certain changes for which they had no authority.'[41]

As Das pointed out, the Drafting Committee had suggested changes in the Draft Constitution that had not been authorized by the Constituent Assembly, and even introduced certain articles in the Draft Constitution on matters which had not yet been discussed by the Constituent Assembly.[42] What exacerbated this was the fact that when the Draft Constitution was eventually circulated for comments and feedback, members hardly had sufficient time to examine the document and present their ideas on it. Due to this, Das lamented that the assistance received by the Drafting Committee had been 'very small and inadequate'.[43] For Das, these actions of the Drafting Committee were a cause of considerable discomfiture.

Das then moved on to highlight that the internal affairs of the Drafting Committee had not been in order. Several members of the Drafting Committee had not fully participated in its proceedings and more troublingly, many members did not apply themselves fully to the decisions which had to be taken by the Drafting Committee.[44]

Echoing the thoughts of Krishnamachari, Das pointed that the unstructured working of the Drafting Committee really meant that the Draft Constitution was not the result of a sedulous process of drafting but reflected the views of a few. It was unfortunate, Das told the Assembly, that the Draft Constitution did not receive the benefit of 'more minds, more thought, and more discussion.'[45]

Several others also expressed serious misgivings they had over the conduct of the Drafting Committee. For Arun Chandra Guha, the tragedy was that in preparing the Draft Constitution, the Drafting Committee had exceeded its jurisdiction for it did not reflect 'the main principles laid down by the Constituent

Assembly.'[46] Another member, T Prakasam, was shocked to learn from Krishnamachari's speech that, the entire burden in the Drafting Committee had fallen on Dr Ambedkar since almost all the other members were not fully available to discharge the task of preparing the Draft Constitution.[47] What pained Prakasam was the fact that the hopes and dreams of those who had fought the 'battle of freedom' was not fully reflected in the Draft Constitution.[48]

When it came to K Santhanam, the conduct of the Drafting Committee would come in for strong reprobation. For him, the Drafting Committee had 'illegitimately converted themselves into a Constitution Committee.' This, Santhanam argued, had led the Drafting Committee to believe that it had the ill-conceived right of recommending articles which were contrary to what the Constituent Assembly had previously voted upon, even openly disregarding recommendations made by committees which had been specifically constituted by the Assembly.[49]

Echoing these feelings, RR Diwakar pointed out that the Constituent Assembly must be fully aware that the Drafting Committee far exceeded its limited mandate of embodying as articles in the Draft Constitution, matters on which the Assembly had already taken decisions. As for how it had treated these past decisions, Diwakar was of the view that the Drafting Committee had 'reviewed the decisions, it has revised some of the decisions and possibly recast a number of them.'[50]

However, for some Drafting Committee members, the avalanche of criticism directed against the Drafting Committee was unfounded. When Alladi Krishnaswami Ayyar addressed the Constituent Assembly on 8 November 1948, he decided to meet Krishnamachari's criticism of the Drafting Committee head on and set the record straight, for he perhaps felt that Krishnamachri's speech contained a veiled attack on his role.

Speaking as to the extent of his participation, Ayyar frankly admitted that until the time the Drafting Committee had published the initial version of the Draft Constitution, he had ensured that he was present for most of the meetings, and when he was not able to attend them, he submitted detailed memoranda on different aspects and articles for the Drafting Committee's consideration.

However, he did admit that after the Draft Constitution had been published, his participation in the Drafting Committee reduced owing to his weakening health and that he played almost no role in the revision of the Draft Constitution after its publication.[51] As Ayyar put it, he could 'claim no credit for the suggestions as to the modifications of the draft.'[52] This revelation in fact confirmed Krishnamachari's concerns that the Drafting Committee never had the benefit of sustained attention being paid by all the members of the Drafting Committee to the task of preparing the Draft Constitution.

Other members of the Drafting Committee such as N Madhava Rao and Syed Muhammad Saadulla endeavoured to allay concerns that the Drafting Committee had exceeded its mandate when preparing the Draft Constitution.

According to N Madhava Rao, the Draft Constitution was akin to a 'basic working paper'[53] which provided a template for the Constituent Assembly, just as did the recommendations made by the other committees constituted by the Assembly.[54] What this meant was that nothing in the Draft Constitution was final, for the Constituent Assembly would take the ultimate decision of what must be contained in the Constitution.

For Saadulla, the Drafting Committee had maintained complete fidelity to its responsibilities and wherever the Draft Constitution contained articles which were not in accordance with the Constituent Assembly's previous decisions on that aspect, the Drafting Committee had adequately explained the reasons for introducing them. This was done so that the Assembly may have the benefit of considering an alternative viewpoint on such articles in the Draft Constitution.[55]

It is also worth pointing out that during these debates in November 1948, many members criticized the Drafting Committee for its mistreatment of the due process guarantee and how the Drafting Committee's version of the fundamental right to life and liberty was unsupported by the Constituent Assembly's previous decision on it.

The fact that the Drafting Committee had deleted the due process guarantee and replaced it with the phrase 'procedure established by law' in Article 21 (originally draft Article 15) only came to light when the Draft Constitution was submitted for the first time on 21 February 1948 by Dr Ambedkar to the President of the Assembly.

As we have also seen, nowhere in the minutes of the meetings of the Drafting Committee which are available today was there any concrete discussion to delete the due process guarantee. In fact, all along the Drafting Committee had seemingly decided to retain an article on due process, as formulated in Clause 16 of BN Rau's Draft Constitution. This much is clear from the minutes of the Drafting Committee's meetings of 31 October 1947 and 19 January 1948. The disappearance of the due process guarantee had seemingly occurred without major deliberation or debates.[56]

In fact, only from the initial version of the Draft Constitution do we know the proffered reason for using the phrase 'procedure established by law': to introduce specificity of meaning. What we however, do not know, is the mental make-up of all the members of the Drafting Committee so far as the introduction of this phrase was concerned.

When Dr Ambedkar's motion of 4 November 1948, was being debated, several members trained their guns specifically at the language of the right to life and personal liberty being subject to procedure established by law, which at that time was draft Article 15.

RK Sidhwa criticized the chapter on fundamental rights mainly on the ground that it did not reflect the resolutions and previous decisions passed unanimously by the Constituent Assembly and that the Drafting Committee had not sufficiently respected them. For him, even though the resolutions were in the nature of recommendations, they should have been accorded a high degree of deference for the Assembly had passed those resolutions after careful deliberation. Deviating from them, according to Sidhwa, was a case of the Drafting Committee having 'exceeded their rights in making even those recommendations'.[57]

To make his point even clearer, Sidhwa pointed out that the fundamental right to life and personal liberty was so drastically different from the due process guarantee the Constituent Assembly had voted on as a fundamental right in the summer of 1947 that it was nothing short of a 'revolutionary change'.[58] For him, even the version of the due process guarantee that had been voted on by the Assembly on 30 April 1947, had been considered by many as not travelling sufficient distance to fully protect individuals. But now, by further making life and liberty contingent on legally established procedures alone, the 'very nomenclature of the Fundamental Rights would be ridiculed.'[59]

When ZH Lari spoke on Dr Ambedkar's motion, he singled out draft Article 15 as a glaring instance of Fundamental Rights being wholly inadequate to protect individuals. He was speaking in the background of several developments which betrayed the idea of the people having full freedoms.[60]

Lari, like Sidhwa before him, pointed out that the decision to replace the due process guarantee with draft Article 15 was an unwarranted and indefensible repudiation of the decision that the Constituent Assembly had previously taken to accept due process as part of Fundamental Rights. For him, draft Article 15 'absolutely nullifies the intention of those who wanted this article to appear in the Constitution'.[61] Through draft Article 15, Lari observed, the Drafting Committee had succeeded in handing to the State the unquestionable power of simply enacting a law to deprive a person of their life and personal liberty.[62]

At any rate, by 1949, it had also become clear that draft Article 15 was one of the low points when it came to the crafting of Fundamental Rights. This was succinctly pointed out by none other than Dr Ambedkar when he introduced draft Article 15-A (which became Article 22 in the final Constitution) in the Constituent Assembly on 15 September 1949.

At that time, he had remarked that the right to life and personal liberty had the dubious reputation of being an article which a majority of the Constituent Assembly were dissatisfied with; an article which the general public had condemned as being unworthy of a fundamental right, and that even as the Chairman of the Drafting Committee, he viewed this important right as wanting in some respects.[63] As we have seen, it was the combination of these reasons which led to the passage of Article 22.[64]

Treading Cautiously

We can now begin to see why we must remain tentative before relying on the Drafting Committee's decisions to decipher what it intended for Article 21 to mean. After all, to say that the Drafting Committee *intended* that Article 21 must have only one particular meaning would be to assume that a concord had been reached amongst the members of the Drafting Committee, and that they all acted together and projected their shared belief on what Article 21 ought to mean in perpetuity. It would also have to be assumed that in framing Article 21, the Drafting Committee, without division in opinion, was in agreement and that there was common consensus that the Constitution must contain an article with only a precise and specific meaning attached to it. The Drafting Committee's original intent could then only be attached to Article 21 because its incorporation was not opposed by members of the constituent body.

Furthermore, we would also have to assume that public opinion was solidly in favour of the fundamental right to life and personal liberty as cast by the Drafting Committee and that the formulation of this fundamental right was accepted across the board. Put simply, we can attempt to divine some form of original intent from Article 21 only if we operate on the plane of assumptions.

The way in which the Drafting Committee functioned left a lot to be desired. It is an unfortunate reality that in preparing the draft of the nation's founding document, not all the members were able to provide their input, and the Drafting Committee did not receive sustained and close attention from its members.

Article 21 had been drafted with little discussion and without much attention being paid to the problems that would arise if the Constitution did not enumerate a due process guarantee. Even within the Drafting Committee, KM Munshi kept expressing his opposition to the fact that the Drafting Committee had not enumerated a due process guarantee and his opposition was voiced both within the Drafting Committee and during the debates which took place in the Constituent Assembly.[65]

The reality is that Article 21 was not prepared in a manner in which *all* the members of Drafting Committee participated. At many crucial junctures, and at any rate at the time in which the Draft Constitution was being revised prior to its introduction in the Constituent Assembly in 1948, the input of many members of the Drafting Committee was not obtained. In respect of Article 21, we are also not exactly certain as to the nature of discussions which led to the decision to delete the due process guarantee.

Added to all of this is the fact that even public opinion leaned heavily against the exclusion of the due process guarantee from the Draft Constitution and that even otherwise, in the due course of time, the Drafting Committee or at least some of its members, had come to realize the doubtful authenticity of Article 21 leading them to make amends for it.

All this casts a shadow of doubt on whether Article 21 could truly have represented the intent of the Drafting Committee as a whole. Seen in this light and given this history of the Drafting Committee's deliberations generally, and on Article 21 specifically, it is in fact fully possible to say that there is no original intention of the Drafting Committee which can be attributed to Article 21.

Endnotes

1   Paul Brest, 'The Misconceived Quest for the Original Understanding', *Boston University Law Review*, vol. 60 (1980): 204. According to information available on HeinOnline, an online repository of scholarly works, this article has been cited by over 1,200 other articles.

2   Id., p. 204.

3   Id., p. 205.

4   Id., p. 214.

5   Id., pp. 216–217.

6   Id., p. 222.
7   Jack N Rakove, *Original Meanings: Politics and Ideas in the Making of the Constitution* (New York: Alfred A Knopf, 1996).
8   Id., p. 7.
9   Ibid.
10   Ibid.
11   Michael J Klarman, *The Framers' Coup: The Making of the United States Constitution* (New York: Oxford University Press, 2016), p. 630.
12   See Nariman, 'Fifty Years', p. 15. Also see, Chandrachud, *Due Process of Law*, pp. 66–71 (examining the importance of an originalist interpretation of the Indian Constitution).
13   1950 SCR 88 (SCC Online version).
14   *Gopalan* also involved the interpretation of Article 22 of the Constitution and the relationship between Article 19 and Article 21. However, an exhaustive analysis of this case is beyond the scope of this book.
15   Incidentally, apart from Justice Fazl Ali, all the other justices would go on to serve as Chief Justice of India.
16   *Gopalan*, para 17.
17   Ibid.
18   It is important to note that Chief Justice Kania prefaced these observations by observing that he himself believed that reliance on the Drafting Committee's Report was not essential since Article 21 could be interpreted on its own terms.
19   Id., paras 124–125.
20   Id., para 125.
21   Id., para 202.
22   Id., para 220.
23   Id., para 221.
24   Id., para 222.
25   Id., paras 221, 222.
26   Id., paras 71, 72. Justice Fazl Ali noted that although recourse to the Constituent Assembly debates was unnecessary, the debates did reveal that the Assembly had deliberately not made reference to 'without due process of law.' Id., para 72.
27   Id., paras 78, 85. In so holding, Justice Fazl Ali was in a minority of one since the other justices were of the view that such safeguards could not be read into Article 21.
28   See Rohinton F Nariman, *Discordant Notes: The Voice of Dissent in the Court of Last Resort*, vol. 1 (Gurugram: Penguin Random House India, 2021), pp. 231–241.

29   Id., para 126.
30   Id., para 218.
31   Id., para 219.
32   This aspect has also been discussed in Chapters 4, 5 and 6.
33   See, for instance, *Shivraj Singh Chouhan v. Speaker, Madhya Pradesh Legislative Assembly*, 2020 SCC Online SC 363, para 60.
34   1953 SCR 1 (SCC Online version).
35   Id., para 91.
36   Seervai, *Constitutional Law*, p. 980. Also see, Burt Neuborne, 'The Supreme Court of India', *International Journal of Constitutional Law*, vol. 1 (2003): p. 479, note 21 [hereinafter Neuborne, 'Supreme Court']. The originalist formulation of Article 21 in *Gopalan* has been critiqued not because it was erroneous, but because it was unnecessary given the plain text of Article 21. See Alexandrowicz-Alexander, 'Constitutional Interpretation', pp. 100–101.
37   CAD, vol. VII, pp. 31–44.
38   Id., p. 231.
39   Ibid. ('The House is perhaps aware that of the seven members nominated by you, one had resigned from the House and was replaced. One died and was not replaced. One was away in America and his place was not filled up and another person was engaged in State affairs, and there was a void to that extent. One or two people were far away from Delhi and perhaps reasons of health did not permit them to attend. So it happened ultimately that the burden of drafting this Constitution fell on Dr Ambedkar and I have no doubt that we are grateful to him for having achieved this task in a manner which is undoubtedly commendable. But my point really is that the attention that was due to a matter like this has not been given to it by the Committee as a whole.'
40   Id., p. 232.
41   Id., p. 237.
42   Ibid.
43   Ibid.
44   Id., p. 238.
45   Ibid.
46   Id., p. 255.
47   Id., p. 257.
48   Ibid.
49   Id., p. 262.
50   Id., p. 291.
51   Id., p. 334.

52 Ibid.
53 Id., pp. 387.
54 Id., pp. 386–387.
55 Id., p. 390.
56 See Chapter 3.
57 CAD, vol. VII, p. 266.
58 Ibid.
59 Ibid.
60 Id., p. 298. ('I would like to point out in this connection the various Security Acts which have been passed by the various legislatures, particularly the Safety Act in one province which even excluded the right to move the High Courts under section 491 of the Criminal Procedure Code. 'The second admission that he made is: 'Constitutional morality is not a natural sentiment. It has to be cultivated. We must realise that our people have yet to learn it.')
61 Ibid.
62 Id., pp. 298–299.
63 See CAD, vol. IX, p. 1499.
64 See Chapter 4.
65 This has been discussed in Chapter 3.

Epilogue
Life, Liberty and Due Process
The Past's Future

———•———

A principle to be vital must be of wider application than the mischief that gave it birth. Constitutions are not ephemeral documents, designed to meet passing occasions. The future is their care, and therefore, in their application, our contemplation cannot be only of what has been but of what may be.[1]

Justice William J. Brennan, Jr
Associate Justice, US Supreme
Court (1956–1990)

The Case for an Open-textured Reading: Due Process and Article 21

DOUBTLESS, THE JURISPRUDENTIAL FORMULATION IN *GOPALAN* ON the meaning of Article 21 was profound. For nearly three decades, the Supreme Court toed the line drawn by it and treated Article 21 as an immutable right which was incapable of any other meaning. By a mix of taking Article 21 at its face value combined with an originalist interpretation, the *Gopalan* Court kept due process guarantees out of the Constitution. Once, however, *Gopalan's* originalist formulation of Article 21 has been unpacked, it remains to be seen whether the only way to read Article 21 is in a strictly textual manner.

To be sure, the *Gopalan* Court's refusal to read Article 21 as affording due process protections was based on the idea that it *would not* read into the article such rights and guarantees, for they did not find mention in the article's text. But that does not mean that Article 21 *cannot* be so read.

In this regard, what must be accounted for is the fact that despite its plain language, some of the phrases and words in Article 21 such as 'personal liberty', 'procedure' and 'law' are open-textured and could have different meanings and conceptions, and in fact could be interpreted to incorporate due process rights. Indeed, Article 21 must be treated as an open-textured fundamental right, whose meaning cannot be circumscribed by how the Drafting Committee treated the fundamental right to life and personal liberty.

An open-textured provision conveys the idea that despite using the clearest language, legal provisions may still be haunted by the problem of indeterminacy because we cannot always anticipate future facts and developments.[2] And because of it, laws with the clearest of words used in them, can in the face of an unanticipated development be subject to multiple and varied interpretations.[3]

Insistence on laws having a fixed meaning regardless of other considerations would mean that in the pursuit of obtaining specificity of meaning, laws are rendered inflexible, and incapable of countenancing and resolving dilemmas which future developments bring with them. To consider a law open-textured would allow future developments to be harmonized with existent laws.[4] Furthermore, to consider laws as being open-textured also indicates that in certain scenarios, it would be judicial authorities which can properly reconcile opposing considerations, and thus, guide and influence the direction of growth of the law.[5]

By the late 1970s, the winds of change began to blow. The Supreme Court started to view Article 21 not as an inflexible fundamental right, which was fixed in time. The Supreme Court started to recognize that despite its plain words, requirements which mirrored due process guarantees had to be read into Article 21. Dynamism would be something which would be infused into the fundamental right to life and liberty, which became possible primarily because the body of juristic thought from the 1970s viewed Article 21 as open-textured.[6]

If one were to mark the date on which Article 21 was transformed forevermore, it would be on the eve of India's twenty-eighth year as a Republic—25 January 1978.[7] On that day, a Constitution Bench comprising seven justices of the Supreme Court announced its verdict in *Maneka Gandhi v. Union of India*.[8]

Maneka Gandhi involved a question of whether a person's passport could be impounded by the authorities, absent a proper hearing. In a decided move to depart from *Gopalan's* narrow formulation, Justice Bhagwati in his plurality opinion[9] viewed the words and phrases in Article 21 as open-textured and as encompassing due process guarantees. Thus, for the Supreme Court now, personal liberty did not simply mean freedom from restraints, or freedom in the sense of being bodily free as *Gopalan* had understood it to mean. Rather it was a phrase of the 'widest amplitude' which applied to 'a variety of rights which go on to constitute personal liberty'.[10] For all purposes, 'personal liberty' was treated as 'liberty' with the word 'personal' no longer performing any weighty role.

When it came to the meaning of the phrase 'procedure established by law' the old view enunciated in *Gopalan,* that this phrase did not extend any due process rights and only meant a validly enacted law, was discarded. Now, the Supreme Court would view the same phrase in an entirely different light for it was interpreted to mean not just an enacted law but a law which was 'not arbitrary, fanciful or oppressive; otherwise, it would be no procedure at all and the requirement of Article 21 would not be satisfied.'[11]

What this essentially meant was that the courts would examine the substance of the measure in question to see whether it was something that could measure up to a permissive constitutional standard. In sum, the new understanding of Article 21 was that 'personal liberty' was a vast repository of rights and when this fundamental right was affected by any law, courts would seriously interrogate and probe the purpose, rationale and legitimacy of the law.

In arriving at this fundamentally transformed understanding of Article 21, the Supreme Court used an important development which occurred in the early part of the 1970s, as a stepping stone.

Starting with the 1970 decision of an eleven-judge bench in *RC Cooper v. Union of India*[12] the Supreme Court made it clear that it was difficult to view the different fundamental rights enumerated in Part III of the Constitution as operating in separate spheres and to the exclusion of one another. Later decisions built on this idea and came to hold that Article 14 (right to equality), Article 19 (which enumerates the civil liberty rights), and Article 21 were fundamental rights which had to be read together, and in a holistic manner. As Justice Bhagwati himself recognized, this would have a profound impact on the way in which Article 21 was to be now understood.[13]

With *Cooper* having signalled that the constitutional sluice gates ought to be opened, fundamental rights enumerated in Part III of the Constitution were now able to wash over each other.[14] What this meant for Article 21 was that the due process requirements present in Article 19, in the form of the reasonable restrictions standard of review could now also be applied to Article 21.[15]

The walls which separated fundamental rights for nearly two decades were collapsed to now build a unifying bridge between them. The synergy which the interrelationship of fundamental rights brought with it introduced in the Constitution a new dimension by which due process requirements were understood and indeed applied to preserve life and personal liberty. And through it, the due process standard of review present in Article 19 would now enlighten Article 21.[16]

Justice Krishna Iyer, one of the greatest Supreme Court judges, was also a part of this Constitution Bench, and in his separate opinion he observed that 'procedure established by law' could not possibly only mean a validly enacted law. It really meant that the content of the law had to conform to certain standards of constitutionally acceptable principles. For Justice Krishna Iyer, laws aimed at 'regulating, restricting or even rejecting a fundamental right falling within Article 21 has to be *fair, not foolish*, carefully designed to *effectuate, not to subvert, the substantive right itself.*[17]

As he put it in a stirring illustration, even if validly enacted, a law really could not pass constitutional muster if, for instance, it stipulated that a 'passport is [to be] granted or refused by taking lots, ordeal of fire or by other strange or mystical methods.'[18] For Justice Krishna Iyer, the authority of the law no longer obtained only from its proper mode of enactment, but rather from its moral content and its core, which in the ultimate analysis had to be consistent with constitutional standards.[19] Unmistakably, the Supreme Court was speaking the language of due process.

For the Supreme Court in *Maneka Gandhi*, what had complicated matters was that the *Gopalan* Court's holding had really created a fundamental contradiction in the Indian Constitution: was the survival of Article 21 to forevermore depend entirely on how it was treated by a law, or should it be a fundamental right which operated as a shield against oppressive laws and contested forms of state action?[20] The resolution of this contradiction lay at the heart of *Maneka Gandhi* and the path which the Supreme Court ultimately adopted was to place Article 21 on a pedestal which was higher than and above the law-making powers of the State.[21]

Interestingly, by holding that it is the law which must measure up to the high standards of constitutional order stipulated by Article 21, and that the growth and development of this fundamental right could not be dictated by the ordinary law-making powers of the State, the Supreme Court ended up channelling the advice BN Rau had given on how liberty rights ought to be enumerated in a constitution.

As we saw in Chapter 2, writing in 1946, BN Rau was convinced that for the personal liberty right to be truly meaningful it had to operate as a shield against oppressive state action. For Rau, a personal liberty right would be but an effete creature in the Constitution if for its very implementation it depended only on State action, or more troublingly, its scope was to be defined only by ordinary laws. It is then a matter of great historical meaning that the note of caution which Rau had sounded in 1946, came to be heeded by the Supreme Court in 1978.

Although strong as was *Maneka Gandhi's* commitment of reading due process into Article 21, the Supreme Court did not really use those very words when refashioning Article 21. Nevertheless, whatever doubts remained about that were put to rest by Justice Krishna Iyer. As part of another Constitution Bench in *Sunil Batra's* case, Justice Krishna Iyer noted in his judgment, which was announced a few months after *Maneka Gandhi*, that although the Indian Constitution did not enumerate a due process guarantee, after the decision in *Maneka Gandhi*, due process guarantees were for all intents and purposes recognized by the Constitution.[22]

The Triumph of Due Process

Today, for all purposes, requirements that mirror the due process guarantee lie within the scope of Article 21, which both preserves and extends procedural and substantive due process rights.[23] *Maneka Gandhi* made it possible for the Indian Constitution to be understood as a document which 'embraced a broad purposive approach' and that Article 21 is a right where the 'implied substantive component to the term "liberty" … provides broad protection against unreasonable and arbitrary curtailment.'[24]

The application of due process from the 1980s, till the present raises some interesting insights in the way India has treated and understood due process. One notable aspect is that when a law is reviewed for violating Article 21, rather than invalidating it, courts have attempted to harmonize the law with Article 21, in the process ensuring that the law continues on the statute books but does not offend the fundamental right to life and personal liberty. This is something that Justice Krishna Iyer himself did in the 1980s.

When faced with a law which allowed courts to imprison a person who was unable to pay their debts payable under the judgment of a court, Justice Iyer viewed the law as grossly offending Article 21. However, rather than invalidating the law, Justice Iyer saved the law by reducing its scope of operation and held that only those who wilfully disobeyed a court's judgment ordering for payment of monies could be imprisoned.[25]

The practice of 'reading down' a law so that it does not offend Article 21 but remains in operation is an acceptable middle path between the options of either invalidating the entire law or leaving it in place without any caveats whatsoever. To be sure, when faced with a law which violates due process and cannot be balanced in any way, the Supreme Court has not shied away from striking such laws down.[26] The balancing approach exemplified by Justice Krishna Iyer, however, demonstrates that Article 21 can be used to temper the effect of legislations.

Another notable and well-known aspect is that armed with Article 21 encompassing due process, the Supreme Court has used the fundamental right to life and personal liberty to incorporate into it an exceptionally large number of rights which apply to all aspects of human life such as civil rights, socio-economic rights, environmental rights, education rights, health rights, dignitarian rights, and housing and shelter rights, to name a few.[27] Indeed, the range of rights which can still be recognized under it is unending.[28]

In recognizing these new and unenumerated rights, the Supreme Court has used Article 21 to achieve impressive socially ameliorative goals and advance social welfare and public progress.[29] In fact, in some decisions, the Supreme Court has even used the goals and principles enumerated in the chapter on Directive Principles of State Policy, which are otherwise unenforceable[30] as informing the meaning of Article 21.[31]

It is also worth noting that in recent years when the Indian Supreme Court declared that Article 21 provides that persons have a fundamental right to privacy, and that Article 21 does not permit the criminalization of homosexuality, decisions of the US Supreme Court which had used due process to develop the selfsame ideas and rights proved to be of enormous persuasive value.

Nonetheless these decisions of the Indian Supreme Court were informed by the need for a broad outlook to effect deep social change, for the implementation of the Constitution would be fundamentally meaningful only if persons were given the whole range of rights which are essential to truly enjoy the protections which the Constitution seeks to offer.

Taken together, this particular direction in which Article 21 has developed is interesting, when seen in the background of the debates which occurred in the Constituent Assembly. As we have seen, in the years when the due process guarantee was being debated between 1946 and 1950, opponents of due process had voiced the fear that the American experiment with due process in the first half of the twentieth century offered a cautionary tale. If due process was incorporated in the Indian Constitution, then in all likelihood and just like in America, social welfare and public progress would be set at naught.

Essentially, they feared that with due process, India would undoubtedly witness its very own '*Lochner* era'. But in the vast array of cases in which unenumerated rights have been read into Article 21, the motivating purpose for the Supreme Court to do so has been to advance social progress and public welfare, rather than stalling public good. In fact, the Indian Supreme Court has through its unique application of due process rights and Article 21 heralded a 'Counter *Lochner* era', for a renewed understanding of Article 21 has been used incrementally to promote and not stall, what is appropriate for public good.[32]

However, the greatest benefit that a transformed understanding of Article 21 has had is in the realm of the criminal justice system.[33] As we saw in the previous chapters, during the debates on Article 21 in the Constituent Assembly, the mainstay of the criticism against the exclusion of the due process guarantee had been that those who are subjected to the processes of criminal justice will find themselves entirely without protection.

Fittingly then, when the Supreme Court did recognize that Article 21 encompasses due process guarantees, it was applied to reform the criminal justice system in India. For instance, in the wake of *Maneka Gandhi*, the Supreme Court in 1989 held that public executions constitute an egregious violation of Article 21 and that since no law could ever allow it, the Supreme Court went ahead and issued a blanket injunction order restraining all Indian states from making any regulation which even remotely allowed public executions.[34] If Article 21 was set in stone and fixed in time, then perhaps public executions would have been an unwholesome reality in India.

Since the 1980s, the march of Article 21 has been towards not only ensuring that persons who find themselves in the criminal justice system are entitled to due process rights but to also ensure that such persons are not subjected to dehumanizing treatment within the justice system. In that spirit, a range of rights such as the right to a speedy trial, the right against solitary confinement in prisons, the right to obtain legal aid and assistance, the right against handcuffing and the right against custodial violence, which despite not being enumerated in the Constitution, flow from Article 21.[35]

In the contemporary statement of due process, the Indian Supreme Court recognizes that a person's due process rights under Article 21 are violated when in a trial they are victims of prosecutorial misconduct;[36] when a convict on death row is made to wait interminably for a decision on their petition seeking executive clemency;[37] and when persons are forcefully subjected to narco-analysis and lie detector tests in a bid to elicit information regarding matters under investigation.[38] And in 2020, the Supreme Court made it emphatically and clarion clear once and for all that the right to legal representation is *'part of the due process clause'* which flows from Article 21.[39]

Despite the march of the law, some doubts still seem to persist over whether Article 21 speaks of due process, particularly substantive due process,[40] even though it has now been asserted overwhelmingly by the Supreme Court that both substantive and procedural due process rights inhere in Article 21 because the 'wheel has turned full circle'.[41] The fact that a transformed understanding of Article 21 enables the discovery of unenumerated rights such as the fundamental right to privacy, apart from enabling the substantive review of laws which allows courts to ask searching questions when laws deleteriously affect a person's life and personal liberty and strike them down, as was done by the Supreme Court when it decriminalized homosexuality, is possible only because due process is now very much part of Indian jurisprudence.

Semantics must not cloud the fact, and indeed our judgment, about the central importance of due process, and the fact that it has now been accepted as a part of Article 21. The sooner we recognize this the better it will be for the cause of constitutional justice, given that it is in the nature of Article 21 to resolve emerging and vitally important questions concerning the liberty and freedom of individuals. And since the Indian Constitution does not enumerate a detailed list of rights which apply to all aspects of human life, the open-textured reading of Article 21 as incorporating the due process guarantee becomes the vehicle by which new rights are to be realized for the people.

It is due process which has made Article 21 a robust fundamental right and which has today enabled the triumph of individual freedom. If we can exercise individual autonomy as free agents in India, it is largely because of what Article 21 has come to mean, and we are fortunate for it. From a promising start in 1946–1947, the slings and arrows of outrageous fortune had something entirely else in store for due process.

By the time the Indian Constitution came to life in 1950, the due process guarantee was absent from the Constitution's text. Nevertheless, from the ashes of its unsavoury rejection by the Drafting Committee, due process against all odds found its way into the Indian Constitution.

It had to.

Endnotes

1   Brennan, 'Individual Rights', p. 495.
2   HLA Hart, *The Concept of Law* (New York: Oxford University Press, 2nd edition, 1996), p. 128.
3   Id., p. 129.
4   Id., p. 129–130.
5   Id., p. 135.
6   Baxi, 'Social Action Litigation', pp. 108–111, 115.
7   See Basu, *Commentary on the Constitution*, p. 3108.
8   (1978) 1 SCC 248.
9   Id., paras 1–46. Justice Bhagwati's opinion was joined by Justices NL Untwalia and S Murtaza Fazal Ali.
10   Id., para 5.

11   Id., para 7.
12   (1970) 1 SCC 248.
13   *Maneka Gandhi*, paras 5–6.
14   See Rohinton F Nariman, *Discordant Notes: The Voice of Dissent in the Court of Last Resort*, vol. 2 (Gurugram: Penguin Random House India, 2021), p. 15.
15   *Maneka Gandhi*, paras 5–6.
16   Generally, see Sripati, 'Fifty Years', pp. 438–439.
17   *Maneka Gandhi*, para 82. (Emphasis added.)
18   Ibid. (Emphasis added.)
19   Id., paras 81–82, 84–85.
20   In fact, in *Gopalan*, Chief Justice Kania in his judgment acknowledged that one of the arguments that had been made was that the principles of natural justice must be read into Article 21. Otherwise, there was really no need for Article 21 to even be present in the Constitution if all it meant was that the state could make a law to whittle down the right. Chief Justice Kania, however, rejected this argument. See *Gopalan*, paras 16–19. In the Supreme Court, AK Gopalan was represented by the legendary counsel MK Nambiar.
21   Nariman, 'Fifty Years', p. 17.
22   *Sunil Batra v. Delhi Admn*, (1978) 4 SCC 494, para 52. ('True, our Constitution has no "due process" clause or the VIII Amendment; but, in this branch of law, after *Cooper* [*RC Cooper* v. *Union of India*, (1970) 1 SCC 248: (1970) 3 SCR 531] and *Manika Gandhi* (sic) [*Maneka Gandhi* v. *Union of India*, (1978) 1 SCC 248] the consequence is the same. For what is punitively outrageous, scandalizingly unusual or cruel and rehabilitatively counter-productive, is unarguably unreasonable and arbitrary and is shot down by Articles 14 and 19 and if inflicted with procedural unfairness, falls foul of Article 21.')
23   See *Rajesh Kumar v. State*, (2011) 13 SCC 706, para 63. ('Therefore, "law" as interpreted under Article 21 by this Court is more than mere "lex". It implies a due process, both procedurally and substantively.')
24   Neuborne, 'Supreme Court', p. 480.
25   *Jolly George Varghese v. The Bank of Cochin*, (1980) 2 SCC 360.
26   See *Nikesh Tarachand Shah v. Union of India*, (2018) 11 SCC 1.
27   Basu, *Commentary on the Constitution*, pp. 3116–3138.
28   See *NALSA v. Union of India*, (2014) 5 SCC 438, para 80 (holding that Article 21 encompasses the right to determine one's gender identity).
29   See *Neuborne, Supreme Court*, pp. 500–501.

30 Article 37: The provisions contained in this Part shall not be enforceable by any court, but the principles therein laid down are nevertheless fundamental in the governance of the country and it shall be the duty of the State to apply these principles in making laws.

31 See PP Craig and SL Deshpande, 'Rights, Autonomy and Process: Public Interest Litigation in India', *Oxford Journal of Legal Studies*, vol. 9 (1989): 356 Also see, Chandrachud, *Due Process of Law*, p. 73. An interesting theory that has been put forth is that much of the Supreme Court's activity in the sphere of Public Interest Litigation was motivated by an institutional desire to reclaim its position of importance in the aftermath of the 1975 Emergency. See Baxi, 'Social Action Litigation', p. 113.

32 A similar point is made in Chandrachud, 'Due Process', p. 793.

33 Baxi, 'Social Action Litigation', pp. 115–116. Upendra Baxi credits Justice Krishan Iyer's judicial statesmanship in the realm of criminal justice as being a guiding force which resulted in the humane treatment of 'prisoners and detainees.' See Id., p. 115.

34 *Attorney-General for India v. Lachma Devi*, (1989) Supp (1) SCC 264.

35 See *Unni Krishnan v. State of AP*, (1993) 1 SCC 645, paras 29–30.

36 *Varkey Joesph v. State of Kerala*, 1993 Supp (3) SCC 745.

37 *V Sriharan v. Union of India*, (2014) 4 SCC 242.

38 *Selvi v. State of Karnataka*, (2010) 7 SCC 263 [hereinafter *Selvi*].

39 *Subedar v. State of Uttar Pradesh*, 2020 SCC Online SC 1084, para 8 (Emphasis added.)

40 See *Puttaswamy*, paras 273, 296.

41 *Mohd Arif*, para 28 (per RF Nariman, J.). Also see, *Selvi*, para 88. ('... Hence, we must examine the "right against self-incrimination" in respect of its relationship with the multiple dimensions of "personal liberty" under Article 21, which include guarantees such as the "right to fair trial" and "substantive due process."')

Acknowledgements

———◆———

Without Nina, none of this would have been possible. Since the time I first met her at the Campus Law Centre during our LLB days, she has been a powerhouse of love, encouragement, unfailing support, and an unflappable sounding board. This book is as much hers as it is mine.

This book owes its origins to a dinner-table conversation. I had initially thought of writing a short piece on the history of Article 21, and a passing comment by my parents, Padma and Chittaranjan Alva one evening, that I should think of writing a book on it (now that I had the time because of the pandemic and because my 'short piece' had crossed 40 pages) is what spurred me to take this project on. That apart, they painstakingly proofread and then re-read drafts of this book. My sister, Manisha Alva, was always at hand whenever I needed to discuss any of my ideas. To them I owe an irredeemable debt.

Words of constant encouragement from my parents-in-law, Sanaya and Rohinton Nariman, and sister-in-law, Khursheed

Nariman, went a long way in ensuring that I wrote this book in the first place. I owe a special thanks to my father-in-law whose comments and advice proved invaluable. His tremendous insights made me see things in an entirely different light. A special thank you to my grandfather-in-law, Fali Nariman, for our many engaging conversations, in which he drew on his wealth of experience to give me a nuanced perspective of the Constitution.

I have been fortunate to have a large and loving family, whose support and friendship over the years has remained unyielding. The Alvas, particularly my aunt Margaret Alva who is really like my second grandmother, the Raos, especially my aunt and uncle, Samita and MY Rao, and the Hatangadis, have all had a significant hand in making this and everything else, possible. I am thankful to my grand-uncle, Bhaskar Rau, who happily shared some of the original photos that he had of BN Rau and his immediate family, which I was able to use in this book. This book would never have seen the light of day if not for Anuja Chauhan. She not only put me in touch with HarperCollins, but also gave me much-needed advice on what to do with my manuscript.

There are those who would have been delighted to hold this book in their hands but left us all too soon. My grandparents, Malti and MB Rao, who raised me from the day I was born and who were a fountain of love and support. My grandmother, particularly, would have been excited beyond words just at the thought of leafing through this book. So, too, my uncle, Niranjan Alva, whose affection, wit, and love for joy I miss every day. This book was also written during a time of suffering. We lost Nina's grandmother, Bapsi Nariman. She would have been over the moon to see yet another author in the family (she is the most prolific—an author of eleven cookbooks!).

I owe a special thanks to my professor and mentor from the Campus Law Centre, Dr Kamala Sankaran, whose insights proved enormously beneficial for this book. Her spell-binding lectures on Constitutional Law, which I attended during my LLB, are what spurred my interest in the subject, and in a large measure, this book owes its origins to those lectures.

Many dear friends gave me a huge share of their time to look over the book, and even, as one of them remarked, powered through to 'endure the enduring teachings' of this book. Thank you Omprasad, Arun Sarkar, Aditi Gopalakrishnan, Faiz Tajuddin and Shiv Swaminathan.

Finally, the entire team at HarperCollins, including Ananth Padmanabhan, Krishan Chopra, Siddhesh Inamdar, Anuja Naorem, Pooja Sanyal, Saurav Das and Gavin Morris, deserve a special thanks for taking great care to ensure that this book went ahead as planned.

Index

Abell, George, 49–50
Ahmed, Naziruddin, 137
Alexandrowicz, Charles Henry,
  235–236
Ali, Fazl, 247, 249
Ambedkar, B.R., xviii, 3–5, 7,
  23–25, 27–28, 35, 50, 97, 101,
  105, 122–124, 172, 191, 226;
  addressed to Constituent
  Assembly on final version of
  draft Constitution, 218–220;
  debate on draft Article 15,
  173–177, 191–195; (renewed,
  195–200); draft Article
  15, defence of, 200–203;
  introduced resolution on Draft
  Constitution for consideration
  and debate, 251–258;
  submitted Draft Constitution
  to Constituent Assembly
  President, 101–104; submitted
  Memorandum and Draft

Articles on the Rights of States
  and Minorities, 17; submitted
  revised draft Constitution to
  Dr Prasad, 208–213
Anthony, Frank, 3, 217–218
Atlee, Clement, 12
Austin, Granville, 104–105,
  108–109, 167–168
Ayyangar, N. Gopalaswami, 3, 50,
  105, 252
Ayyar, Alladi Krishnaswami, 3,
  13–14, 17, 21–23, 33, 35, 50–52,
  76, 99, 104–111, 128, 152–153,
  226, 254–255; address to
  Constituent Assembly on due
  process guarantee, 162–173;
  defence of draft Article 15,
  200–203; on draft Article 21,
  209–210, 216–217; scepticism
  of judicial branch, 167
Azad, Maulana Abul Kalam, 18

Baig Sahib Bahadur, Mahboob Ali,
137, 141, 148–150, 190–191
Bakeshop Act 1895, 8
Barman, Upendranath, 121, 136
Bhargava, Pandit Thakur Dass,
142–145, 176, 190–191,
196–198, 213, 216
Black Law (Act XIV of 1908), 143
Bose, Subhas Chandra, 54
Brennan, William J. Jr, 265
Brest, Paul, 245

Cabinet Mission, 12–13, 58
Chand, Bakshi Tek, 25, 198–200,
202, 232–233
Chandra, Bipin, 109
*Commentary on the Constitution of
India* (D D Basu), 5
Constituent Assembly, xv–xix,
xxi, 1, 3, 5, 12, 36, 49–50, 68,
96, 174–175, 229, 231; adopted
Article 21 without clause on
due process, 220–221; adopted
Constitution on 26 January
1950, 220; vote for accept due
process guarantee, xvii
Constitution of India, 276; adopted
in 26 January 1950, xiv; Article
21, 244–245; (international
disagreement on, 231–233;
original intention of, 246–251);
Article 22, disagreement in,
229–230; and due process
guarantee (*see also* Due
process guarantee in Draft
Constitution); unanswered
question on Article 22, 226–229

Das, Biswanath, 252–253
Das, S.R., 247

Day, William, 8
Defence of India Act, 156
democracy, 110, 154, 157, 160,
163, 196, 218; opportunity to
Governments, 159; process
of continuous engagement
between state and the people,
155; strengthened by due
process guarantee existence,
159; weakened by due process
guarantee, 155
Desai, Bhulabhai, 54
Directive Principles of State Policy,
18, 28, 81, 83, 85, 95, 272
Diwakar, RR, 254
Draft Constitution, 50–51,
55, 94, 96; Chief Justice
Kania's observations on,
248; clause-wise debates and
discussion on, 135–136, 207,
251–258; (Article 15, proposed
amendments in, 136–138;
debates of 6 December 1948
on Articles, 138–152; Munshi-
Ayyar debate on Article 15,
152–173); Article 21 and 22,
213–214; (criticism of, 214–
216; defenders of, 216–220);
introduced in Constituent
Assembly, 120–124; layers of
protection, 56–57; phrase(s):
(procedure established by law,
xvii, 150, 171, 247, 249; save
in accordance with law, 150);
submission of revised draft by
Dr Ambedkar, 208–213; third
reading of, 213–214
Drafting Committee of
Constitution, xviii–xx, 50–52,
76, 85, 94, 109; and adoption

of Preamble, 207; agreed
with due process guarantee,
98; cautious about draft
Article 21, 258–260; clause-
wise discussion and debate,
95–96, 107–108, 135–136;
(agreed on Clause 16 (due
process), 110–111); decision
to delete due process from
Article 21, xxi; Japanese and
Irish Constitution influence
on, 114–120; use of phrase
personal liberty in, 58, 78, 85,
96, 98–100, 111–114, 170
due process guarantee in Draft
Constitution, 143, 146, 148,
229–230; and American
Constitution, 7–12; and Article
21, 265–276; atonement and
partial rebirth of, 191–195;
conceptions of: (intermediate,
190; minimalist, 189–190;
synergistic model, 190–191);
Constituent Assembly decision
on, 233–240; defined, 5;
delinking property from, 25–
32; guarantee as a fundamental
right, 32–37; importance
of, xiv–xvi; and originalism
paradox, xx–xxii; procedural,
6; and prolonged detention,
23–25; reaches an inflection
point, 187–189; substantive,
6–7; twists and turns of, xvii–xx

*Famous Judges, Lawyers and Cases
of Bombay* (P. B. Vacha), 155
Field, Stephen, 10
Framers' Coup, The (Michael J.
Klarman), 246

fundamental rights, xi, xiii, xv–xxi,
4–5, 13–15, 17, 20, 35–36, 58,
64–66, 68, 80, 96–97, 118, 127–
128, 138–139, 141–142, 144–
146, 151–153, 156, 162–163,
168–169, 173, 234; conditions
for effective guarantee of, 16;
define contours of rights, 59;
and due process guarantee,
119–120, 176–177; on personal
liberty, 67; to privacy, xii

Germany, Constitution of 1919:
Article 115, 59; Article 153, 59
Great Depression of 1929, 10
Guha, Arun Chandra, 253
Gupta, Ram Chandra, 217

Hanumanthaiya, K., 222
Harlan, John Marshall, 8
Holmes, Oliver Wendell Jr, 9
Hussain, Tajamul, 51

Indian Independence Act, 1947, 50
Indian National Army (INA), 54
Indian National Congress, 188
Iyer, Krishna, 269, 271

Japanese Constitution, 108,
114–120
Jayakar, M.R., 3–4
judicial review, 147–148
justiciability of rights, 16

Kania, Harilal, 247–248
Karimuddin, Kazi Syed, 136,
138–139, 190, 213, 216
Khaitan, D.P., 3, 50, 76, 95–96,
105–106
Kher, B.G., 50–52

Kripalani, J.B., 20
Krishnamachari, T.T., 135, 251–255

Lari, Z.H., 137, 190, 213; on draft Article 15, 257–258; on due process guarantee, 170–171, 173; on elected legislatures, 171; on Japanese Constitution, 172–173
Lincoln, Abraham, 11

MacArthur, General Douglas, 117
Magna Carta, 5, 59, 146, 151
Mahajan, Meher Chand, 247
Mahatma Gandhi: assassination on 30 January 1948, 108–110, 207
Mehta, Hansa, 231–232
Mitter, B.L., 50, 94
Mookherjee, Syama Prasad, 3
Mukherjea, B.K., 247–250
Mukherjee, S.N., 218–219
Munshi, K.M., 13–18, 24, 27, 31–32, 35, 50, 76, 96, 100, 104–105, 122, 152–153, 164, 167–168, 191, 213, 236, 252; on draft Article 15, 162; model of democracy, 154; opposition for not enumerated due process guarantee, 259–260; proponent of due process rights, 153–162
Muslim League, 3

Nariman, F.S., 188
Nariman, R.F., 156
Nehru, Jawaharlal, 1–2, 53–54, 198, 236; Tryst with Destiny speech, 50
New Deal era, 10, 21

Objectives Resolution of Constituent Assembly, 198; Advisory Committee, 29; constitution of, 12–13; Dr Ambedkar concerns over, 3–5; Dr Jayakar moved amendment on postponement of, 3; Fundamental Rights Sub-Committee deliberations on due process guarantee, 13–21, 33–34, 69–71, 73, 231; introduced by Jawaharlal Nehru, 1–2; paragraph 5 of, 2
Original Intention model, 246
original meaning of constitution, 245–246
Original Understanding model, 246

Pannikar, K.M., 25–27, 233
Pant, Govind Ballabh, 12, 23, 25, 109, 234
partition of India, 109
Patel, Sardar Vallabhbhai, 13, 21–23, 25, 27, 36, 106; introduced resolution in Constituent Assembly, 30; speech on Clause 22 debate, 36–37; submitted Interim Report on the Subject of Fundamental Rights, 28–31, 35
Patskar, H.V., 152, 190, 215
Petition of Grievances of 1610, 5–6
Petition of Rights of 1628, 6
Prakasam, T., 54
Prasad, Brajeshwar, 136
Prasad, Rajendra, xix, 1, 3, 95, 104, 120, 207–208
Preamble, 207, 237
Privy Council, 2

Purna Swaraj, 220

Radhakrishnan, S., 3
Rajagopalachari, C., 22–25, 27, 36,
     233–234
Rakove, Jack N., 245–246
Rao, N. Madhava, 97, 101, 105–
     106, 122, 255
Rao, S.V. Krishnamurthy, 136–137,
     176
Rau, Benegal Narsing, xviii,
     107, 218; appointment
     as Constituent Assembly
     constitutional advisor, 49–52;
     career of, 52–55; discussion
     on due process clause between
     Justice Felix Frankfurter, 76–
     85; Draft Constitution, 65, 102,
     104, 111, 114–116, 147, 187;
     (drafted Clause 16, 161–162,
     256; save in accordance with
     law, 150; use of phrase personal
     liberty in, 58, 66–67, 72–76,
     78, 85, 96, 98, 103); early
     conception of due process,
     58–68; on fundamental rights,
     74, 83; Irish Constitution
     of 1937, analysis of, 66–67,
     108, 115, 149–150; note of
     (8 April 1947), 68–72; on
     personal liberty right, 270;
     submitted Draft Constitution
     for comments, 94–95; task to
     reshape due process guarantee,
     55–58; use of word liberty in
     due process clause, 72–76;
     warning on weak fundamental
     right on right to life and
     personal liberty, 120
reading down practice, 272

Roosevelt, Franklin D, 10–11

Saadulla, Saiyid Mohammad, 50,
     105, 109–110, 255–256
Saksena, Shibban Lal, 215
Santhanam, K., 254
Sapru, Tej Bahadur, 54
Sastri, Patanjali, 247–248, 250
Seervai, H.M., 112
Setalvad, M.C.: *War and Civil
     Liberties,* 156
Seth, Damodar Swarup, 136
Shah, Chimanlal Chakkubhai,
     146–150, 190–191
Shah, K.T., 16–17, 35, 123; attempt
     to incorporate due process,
     124–128; on draft Constitution,
     214
Sharma, Krishna Chandra,
     151–152, 190
Sidhwa, R.K., 257
Sinha, Satyanarayan, 50
Sitaramayya, B. Pattabhi, 120
Supreme Court of India:
     Constitution Bench decision
     on Article 21 in 2017, xi–
     xiv, xx–xxi; criminalize
     homosexuality (Section 377
     of IPC), xiii–xiv; decision/
     judgment: (*AK Gopalan v.
     State of Madras,* 247, 250–251,
     265, 267–268; *Aswini Kumar
     Ghose v. Arabinda Ghose,*
     250; *Kesavananda Bharti,*
     238; *Maneka Gandhi v. Union
     of India,* 267, 270–271, 274;
     RC Cooper v Union of India,
     268–269; Sabrimala temple,
     156; *Sunil Batra v. Delhi Admn,*
     271); use of Article 21, 272–273

Tripathi, P.K., 235–236

UN General Assembly, 54
Universal Declaration of Human
    Rights 1948, 231–233
UN's Human Rights Commission,
    231–232
US Civil War 1868, 6
US Constitution, xv, 20, 245–246;
    5th Amendment of, 6, 60,
    151; 14th Amendment of,
    6–7, 9, 11, 14, 33, 35, 60, 74,
    97–99, 115, 168; system of
    interpretation, 8

US Supreme Court, 14, 164, 273;
    due process clause, 60; *Lochner
    v. State of New York,* 8–9, 61,
    63; *Meyer v. State of Nebraska,*
    63; *Mineresville School Dist v.
    Gobitis,* 65; *Pierce v. Society
    of Sisters,* 63; strength of nine
    justices, 10–11; *West Virginia
    State Board of Education v.
    Barnette,* 65

White, Edward, 8

zamindari system of land tenure,
    26, 233

About the Author

———◆———

ROHAN J. ALVA is a counsel practising in the Supreme Court of India and the High Court of Delhi. He graduated with an LLM from Harvard Law School, where he focused on constitutional law, and which he read for on numerous scholarships including as a Tata Scholar. He holds a BA in history from Loyola College, University of Madras, and an LLB from Campus Law Centre, University of Delhi, where he was editor of the *Delhi Law Review*. His second book, *A Constitution to Keep: Sedition and Free Speech in Modern India*, is out in February 2023.

30 Years *of*
HarperCollins *Publishers* India

At HarperCollins, we believe in telling the best stories and finding the widest possible readership for our books in every format possible. We started publishing 30 years ago; a great deal has changed since then, but what has remained constant is the passion with which our authors write their books, the love with which readers receive them, and the sheer joy and excitement that we as publishers feel in being a part of the publishing process.

Over the years, we've had the pleasure of publishing some of the finest writing from the subcontinent and around the world, and some of the biggest bestsellers in India's publishing history. Our books and authors have won a phenomenal range of awards, and we ourselves have been named Publisher of the Year the greatest number of times. But nothing has meant more to us than the fact that millions of people have read the books we published, and somewhere, a book of ours might have made a difference.

As we step into our fourth decade, we go back to that one word – a word which has been a driving force for us all these years.

Read.

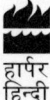